Lord Leverhulme's Ghosts

Lord Leverhulme's Ghosts

Colonial Exploitation in the Congo

JULES MARCHAL

Translated by Martin Thom
Introduced by Adam Hochschild

VERSO

London • New York

This edition published by Verso 2008
Copyright © Verso 2008
Translation © Martin Thom 2008
Introduction © Adam Hochschild 2008
First published as *Travail forcé pour l'huile de palme de Lord Leverhulme: L'histoire du Congo 1910–1945, tome 3* by Editions Paula Bellings 2001
Copyright © Editions Paula Bellings 2001

1 3 5 7 9 10 8 6 4 2

Verso
UK: 6 Meard Street, London W1F 0EG
USA: 180 Varick Street, New York, NY 10014-4606
www.versobooks.com

Verso is the imprint of New Left Books

ISBN-13: 978-1-84467-239-4

British Library Cataloguing in Publication Data
A catalogue record for this book is available from the British Library

Library of Congress Cataloging-in-Publication Data
A catalog record for this book is available from the Library of Congress

Typeset in Bembo by Hewer Text UK Ltd, Edinburgh
Printed in the USA by Maple Vail

Contents

INTRODUCTION[*]

Adam Hochschild

The territory that Jules Marchal writes about in this book has had one of the most violent and unhappy histories of any on the African continent. Parts of that history have become better known in recent years, but not the chapter of it that he tells here, involving the raw materials that fed the factories of the great Lever Brothers soap empire. As with so much of the history of central Africa, it is a story of atrocities hidden from view, of white men in Africa portraying themselves to the world as philanthropists, of human suffering that lay behind a product millions of Europeans and Americans used daily, and, above all, a story of forced labour.

To set Marchal's account in context, it is first worth carefully reviewing the long chain of events, over several centuries, that preceded the period about which he writes.

The country that is today the Democratic Republic of Congo largely consists of the great swathe of central Africa drained by the Congo River. The river is the world's second biggest; only the Amazon carries more water. It descends over more than 200 miles of enormous intermittent rapids before pouring into the Atlantic Ocean, and, until late in the nineteenth century, these rapids blocked the efforts of European explorers to get their boats on to the upper reaches of the river and the tributaries they presumed must flow into it.

The rapids did not, however, prevent exploitation of the region's people by outsiders. Portuguese mariners first landed near the great river's mouth in 1482; missionaries, soldiers and adventurers soon followed, and by several decades later thousands of Africans were being shipped every year as slaves from this area to the New World. The land that surrounded the river's mouth and extended some distance inland and to the south, the kingdom of

---

[*] Adapted, in part, from the *Oxford Encyclopedia of Human Rights* (forthcoming) and *King Leopold's Ghost*, Boston 1998.

Kongo, was controlled by a ruler known as the ManiKongo. In 1506, a ManiKongo named Nzinga Mbemba took the throne. He learned Portuguese and took on the name of Affonso. During the nearly 40 years of his rule, he saw his kingdom decimated by the slave trade. An eloquent set of letters from Affonso to successive kings of Portugal are the first known documents written by a black African in a European language. "Each day", Affonso wrote in desperation to King João III of Portugal in 1526, "the traders are kidnapping our people—children of this country, sons of our nobles and vassals, even people of our own family . . . Our land is entirely depopulated."

Affonso's pleas were in vain. For several centuries the Atlantic slave trade continued to victimise both the people of his kingdom and Africans living for hundreds of miles into the interior. All told, several million Africans were taken from the region around the river's mouth and its hinterland, chiefly to work on the plantations of Brazil.

Similarly, over an even longer period of time, Arab and Afro-Arab slave traders had been ravaging the east coast of Africa, buying slaves as far inland as the eastern side of the Congo River basin, and shipping them to the Arab and Islamic world. Slave ship captains and traders could buy slaves so easily on both coasts because most people in Africa south of the Sahara Desert lived in slave societies. The ethnic groups of the Congo River basin were no exception; Affonso himself, for example, owned slaves. In some ways indigenous African slavery was less brutal than slavery in the Americas: slaves were more status objects than a source of labour; they could often intermarry with free people and could frequently earn their freedom after several generations. But in other ways, African slavery was harsh: slaves were sometimes killed in human sacrifice rituals—many might be slain when an important chief died, for example, to give his soul company on its journey to the next world. When a treaty was made between two rival tribes or groups, a slave might have his bones broken and be left to die painfully in a remote spot, as a symbol of what might happen to anyone who broke the treaty. People could become slaves in Africa as a punishment for a crime, or as payment for a family debt, or, most commonly, by being captured as prisoners of war. The widespread heritage of indigenous slavery would eventually mean that when the Congo became notorious as the site of forced labour systems run by King Leopold II of Belgium and his successors, and by private companies like the one described in this volume, there were local chiefs willing to collaborate in supplying these labourers.

Soon after the Atlantic slave trade finally came to an end in the middle of the nineteenth century, the major part of Europe's conquest and colonisation of Africa began. The Scramble for Africa, as it is often called, was one of the greatest land grabs in history—and one of the swiftest. In 1870, roughly four fifths of sub-Saharan Africa was governed by local chiefs, kings or other indigenous rulers. A mere 40 years later, in 1910, nearly all of this vast expanse of territory had become colonies or protectorates controlled by European countries or, as in South Africa, by white settlers. The bloodiest single phase of Africa's colonisation was centred on the territory known, from the river that flowed through it, as the Congo.

Besides the river's huge rapids, heat and tropical diseases had long kept the Congo's interior a mystery to Europeans. The big step forward for them—although arguably a step backward for Africans—came between 1874 and 1877, when the British explorer-journalist Henry Morton Stanley (1841–1904) made an epic journey across Africa from east to west. Stanley's travels made him a great celebrity. He was also a brutal taskmaster, quick to flog his porters or to lay waste any African villages that threatened to impede his progress, and, at all times, to shoot first and ask questions later. These traits were visible in the best-selling books he wrote about his journeys, but biographers and historians did not begin to focus on them until some three quarters of a century after his death, in a world that had left outright colonialism behind.

Despite the dead bodies he left in his wake, Stanley's crossing of Africa was a rare and difficult feat for a European at the time. He also became the first man to map most of the course of the Congo River. For much of his journey he floated down it, noting with great awe that its many tributaries potentially constituted, in the age of steamboats, a built-in transportation network of thousands of miles for whoever could take control of the region.

There has been a surprisingly consistent pattern in the Congo over the centuries. Outsiders want some commodity the territory possesses. They extract the commodity, causing the deaths of thousands or millions of people in the process. They justify their seizure by portraying themselves as generous-hearted. A few brave souls blow the whistle and portray the exploitation that is going on. The world sometimes briefly pays attention. Then the cycle begins again with a new commodity. All this is happening today, incidentally: more than four million Congolese have died in war-related violence since 1997, while local warlords and multinational corporations extract billions of dollars' worth of gold, uranium, timber, diamonds, coltan and other minerals.

The first such commodity to be extracted was human beings, and Europeans happily justified the slave trade by saying that they were introducing Africans to civilisation, the dignity of labour, and Christianity: those taken to Brazil from the Congo were often quickly baptised first.

Affonso was the first whistle-blower, but the world did not pay him much attention. This book concerns a later wave of exploitation that began in 1911, orchestrated by William Lever of Britain, later Lord Leverhulme. At home he had a reputation as an enlightened employer, because of the relatively good working and living conditions of his labourers. But overseas, he was all business, looking for a place where he could acquire palm oil for his soap more cheaply than in the British colonies in West Africa, where it could only be bought from local Africans at market prices. He settled on the Congo. There were pitifully few whistle-blowers to draw the world's attention to the resulting exploitation, and this book is the first up-close, comprehensive look at how Lever's Congo operations worked and at the human suffering they inflicted.

Between the end of the South Atlantic slave trade in the mid-nineteenth century and the beginning of Lever's operations some 60 or 70 years later came the most painful chapter of all in Congo history. It merits going into in some detail, because it so ruthlessly established the pattern of state confiscation of land and imposition of forced labour that made Lever's Congo empire possible—and which drew him to the territory in the first place.

Henry Morton Stanley had hoped that the Congo's colonial master would be Britain, but the British were coping with various rebellions and crises elsewhere in their empire and had little interest in adding to it the Congo, with its troublesome rapids, heat, malaria and sleeping sickness. Someone who did lust after this territory, however, was King Leopold II of Belgium. Leopold (1835–1909) had taken his country's throne in 1865. An imposing, bearded, august man of great charm, ruthlessness and greed, he was openly frustrated at heading such a small country, and, moreover, at doing so at a time in history when western European monarchs were rapidly losing power to elected parliaments. He had long wanted a colony where he could rule supreme, and in Stanley he saw someone who could help secure it for him. The Belgian government at the time did not want colonies, which seemed an extravagance for a small nation with no navy and no merchant fleet. To Leopold, the Belgian cabinet's lack of desire for colonies posed no problem; if they weren't interested, he would acquire one of his own.

Leopold courted and flattered Stanley, and before long persuaded the explorer to return to the Congo as the king's agent. Although Stanley is conventionally remembered as the man who had years earlier found the missing explorer David Livingstone, by far his greatest impact on history came from the five years he spent staking out the Congo for Leopold. From 1879 to 1884 he set up riverbank outposts, built a road around the rapids, and, using small steamboats that exhausted African porters had carried up the road in pieces, travelled up and down the river network. Alternately passing out gifts and displaying the power of his men's repeating rifles, Stanley forced or bamboozled hundreds of African chiefs into signing away their land to King Leopold II. Virtually all were illiterate and had little or no idea of what they were agreeing to.

Stanley returned to Europe with these treaties in 1884. Meanwhile, Leopold had already begun an ultimately successful campaign to persuade first the United States, and then the nations of Europe, to recognise his claim. With a great mastery of public relations, he presented himself as a philanthropist earnestly striving to abolish the Arab slave trade which still flourished in East Africa. Making a profit, he implied, was the farthest thing from his mind. Leopold made further progress towards his goal at a diplomatic conference in Berlin in 1884–85 at which the European powers began the process of dividing the spoils in Africa. By the spring of 1885 most major nations had recognised his claim to the Congo. He then proclaimed its existence as the greatly misnamed *État Indépendant du Congo*, or, as it was known in English, the Congo Free State. He took the title of King-Sovereign, sometimes in future years referring to himself as the Congo's "proprietor". His was the world's only major colony owned by one man.

Over the following two decades, Leopold asserted his control of the vast territory. Its inhabitants were armed only with spears or antiquated muskets left over from slave-trading days, while the king put together a 19,000-man private army. With black soldiers under European officers, the army was equipped with repeating rifles, machine guns, Krupp cannon, and steam-boats for fast transport on the river network. Army posts sprang up along the riverbanks.

The royal conquest met frequent resistance. In the far south, for example, a chief named Mulume Niama led warriors of the Sanga people in a rebellion that killed one of the king's officers. Congo State troops pursued them, trapping Mulume Niama and his soldiers in a large cave. They refused to surrender, and when Leopold's troops finally entered the cave three months later, they found 178 bodies. Nzansu, a chief in the region near the great Congo River rapids, led rebels who killed a hated colonial official and pillaged several State posts, although they carefully spared the homes of nearby Swedish missionaries with whom they had good relations. Nzansu's men fought on sporadically for five years more, and no record of his fate exists.

The regime also faced resistance from within its own army, whose resentful African conscripts sometimes joined forces with the rebel groups they were supposed to be suppressing. The largest mutiny involved 3,000 troops and an equal number of auxiliaries and porters, and continued for three years. "The rebels displayed a courage worthy of a better cause," acknowledged the army's official history—which, remarkably, devoted fully one quarter of its pages to the various campaigns against mutineers from the army's own ranks.

In the early years, what Leopold and the agents he sent to Africa sought most avariciously was ivory. Because it was durable and could be carved into a variety of shapes, ivory served some of the uses of plastic today, but with the added cachet of its exotic origin. It was used to make jewellery, piano keys, small statuary and even, in a faint echo of its original use to the elephant, false teeth. Like illegal drugs in a later era, ivory had high value and low bulk: thousands of false teeth could be made from a single tusk.

From the very beginning of Leopold's colony, the foundation of its economy, as in most of colonial Africa, was forced labour—something that would continue well after the king's death, into the era of Lord Leverhulme's palm-oil enterprise that Jules Marchal writes about in this book. The black soldiers of Leopold's private army were conscripts, often sent to posts hundreds of miles away from their villages so that they could not easily desert and go home. The porters who carried the ivory tusks out of the interior and carried back everything from ammunition to bottles of wine for the European ivory agents were forced labourers. So were the workers who built a railway around the impassable river rapids. The woodcutters who travelled with each steam-boat to gather fuel for its boilers—up to several dozen men for a larger boat—were forced labourers. Convoys of sullen men in chains, force-marched from remote villages to wherever colonial officials needed them, were part of business as usual in central Africa. "The conquest of the earth," the character Marlow says in Joseph Conrad's *Heart of Darkness*, based on six months Conrad spent in the Congo in 1890, "which mostly means the taking it away from those who have a different complexion or slightly flatter noses than ourselves, is not a pretty thing when you look into it too much."

In Europe and North America few did much looking. Most people continued to think of Leopold as the philanthropic king who was fighting the evil Arab slave traders. Very little information on the true nature of the Congo Free State, especially the way it was founded upon forced labour, reached the outside world. This was a pattern that also would be repeated in the later period of the Lever Brothers' empire described in these pages: brutal exploitation in the Congo itself, and much talk in Europe about uplift and civilisation that Europeans were bringing to the benighted natives.

The first person to fully expose King Leopold II's regime was a remark-able American visitor, George Washington Williams. Williams, like Conrad, spent some six months in the Congo in 1890, and in early August of that year their steamboats probably crossed paths in Stanley Pool, a bulge in the Congo River at what was then the small post of Leopoldville.

Williams was an American Civil War veteran, a historian and journalist, a Baptist minister, a lawyer, and the first black member of the Ohio state legislature. As a journalist, he had interviewed King Leopold II in Brussels, and, like almost everyone, was charmed by the apparently modest and altruistic monarch. But when, on a trip around Africa, Williams reached the Congo, he was appalled to find what he called "the Siberia of the African Continent". He took extensive notes and was virtually the only early visitor to interview Africans about their white colonisers. From Stanley Falls, a thousand miles up the river, Williams wrote one of the great documents of human rights reporting, *An Open Letter to His Serene Majesty Leopold II, King of the Belgians and Sovereign of the Independent State of Congo*. It was the first comprehensive eyewitness indictment of the regime and its forced labour system. Published in many American and European newspapers, it caused Leopold considerable embarrassment. The uproar would doubtless have been prolonged had Williams lived to write the book he was planning on the Congo, but, sadly, he died of tuberculosis on his way home from Africa, at the age of 41. This first brave critic of the Congo regime also fired off several other letters from Africa, and in one of them, to the American Secretary of State, he used a phrase not commonly heard again until the Nuremberg trials more than half a century later. Leopold, Williams declared, was guilty of "crimes against humanity".

Ivory remained valuable, but in the early 1890s a much larger source of Congo wealth suddenly loomed. A few years before, the industrialised world had seen the invention of the inflatable bicycle tyre, followed by that of the automobile. In addition, the network of telephone and telegraph wires starting to span the globe needed rubber insulation, and thousands of types of industrial machinery needed rubber belts or other parts. An international rubber boom began. In tropical territory everywhere, planters rushed to set up rubber plantations. But new rubber trees can require as much as 15 years to reach the point when they can be tapped. This created a time window during which vast amounts of money could be made by whoever had land where rubber grew wild. No one owned more such land than King Leopold II, for the equatorial African rain forest, rich in wild rubber vines, covered roughly half of his Congo Free State.

These spongy vines were hundreds of feet long; one might twine upwards around a palm or other tree to a hundred feet or more above the ground, where it could get some sunlight, then wind and branch its way through the limbs of half a dozen more trees. The vines were scattered quite widely and sparsely through the forest. Even with a forced labour system in place, how could villagers be compelled to disperse for miles to gather the sap that these vines produced? Leopold's officials quickly devised a harshly effective system. The army would send a detachment of soldiers into a village and seize the women as hostages. To secure their wives' release, the men of each village would then have to go into the forest to begin the painstaking job of tapping the wild rubber vines and collecting the slow, milky drip of sap. They were given a monthly quota to fulfil, and, as rubber prices soared in Europe, the quotas rose as well. All the rubber vines near each village were soon drained dry, which meant that men sometimes had to walk for days to reach fresh vines. Eventually, men could be gone as long as several weeks out of each month, in the urgent scramble to reach their quota and get their wives briefly released. Discipline was pitiless: villagers who failed to gather enough rubber, like reluctant military conscripts or disobedient porters before them, fell victim to the notorious *chicotte*, a whip made of sun-dried hippopotamus hide with razor-sharp edges. A hundred lashes of the *chicotte*—a common punishment—could be fatal. Colonial officials earned bonuses that were based on how much rubber was collected in the area each controlled, a system that rewarded ruthless, devastating plunder.

The forced labour system for gathering rubber was at the core of a tremendous death toll in the Congo during and immediately after Leopold's rule. Many of the male forced labourers were in effect worked to death. Large numbers of women hostages—frequently raped by the regime's soldiers during their captivity—starved. And, with the women chained up in compounds and much of the male population off in the forest desperately trying to meet their monthly rubber quota, the birth rate plummeted. Few able-bodied adults were left in the villages to harvest food, hunt, or fish. Famine spread. Local uprisings against the regime erupted more frequently. They continued to do so over some two decades, and occasionally recurred later as well; tens of thousands more people died as the army suppressed them. A large but unknown number of additional men, women and children fled the forced labour regime, but they had nowhere to go except to more remote parts of the rain forest, where there was little food or shelter. Years later, travellers would come upon their bones.

The greatest toll of all came as soldiers, caravans of porters, and refugees from the rubber terror all moved back and forth across the country, bringing new diseases to people with no resistance to them. Many illnesses, particularly sleeping sickness, became far more lethal for people weakened by trauma and hunger. As the experience of those in Nazi and Soviet concentration camps would show decades later, in a regime of terror, it does not always require firing squads or gas chambers to cause the death of millions.

Unlike many other human rights catastrophes in history, what happened in Leopold's Congo was seen by outside witnesses—some of them with cameras. These were the missionaries.

To curry diplomatic favour, Leopold had allowed several hundred Protestant missionaries into the territory—British, American and Swedish. Most made no protest, but some were outraged at the forced labour system. In articles in church magazines and in speeches in the United States and Europe on visits home, they described what they had seen: Africans whipped to death, rivers full of corpses, and—a detail that quickly seared itself into the world's imagination—piles of severed hands. For the white officers of Leopold's army often demanded of their black conscripts a dead rebel's hand in return for each bullet issued to the soldier, as proof that it had been used as ordered and not wasted in hunting, or worse yet, saved for use in a mutiny. If a soldier had fired at someone and missed, he would sometimes cut the hand off a living person, so as not to have to brave his officer's wrath. Missionaries photographed a number of people without hands, some of them children. One American missionary saw a soldier slice off someone's hand "while the poor heart beat strongly enough to shoot the blood from the cut arteries".

Around 1900, Leopold's most formidable enemy surfaced in Europe, and suddenly the concerned missionaries had someone who could carry their stories to a far wider audience. A British shipping company had the monopoly on all cargo traffic between the Congo and Belgium, and every few weeks it sent to the Belgian port of Antwerp a burly, mustachioed junior official, Edmund Dene Morel. There he would supervise the unloading of a ship arriving from Africa and its loading for the voyage back. Morel, in his mid-twenties at the time, noticed that when his company's ships steamed in from the Congo, they were filled to the hatch covers with enormously valuable cargoes of rubber and ivory. But when the ships turned around and headed to Africa, they carried no merchandise in exchange. Nothing was being sent to the Congo to pay for the goods flowing to Europe. Instead, the ships carried soldiers and large quantities of firearms and ammunition. Standing on the dock at Antwerp, Morel realised that before his shocked eyes lay irrefutable proof that a forced labour system was in operation 4,000 miles away. "I was giddy and appalled at the cumulative significance of my discoveries", he wrote later. "It must be bad enough to stumble upon a murder. I had stumbled upon a secret society of murderers with a King for a croniman." This young shipping clerk's stunning moment of realisation gave rise to the first great international human rights movement of the twentieth century.

Morel went to the head of the steamship company to protest. The man tried to promote him to another job in another country. When that didn't work, his boss tried to pay Morel some money to stay quiet. That didn't work either. Morel soon quit his job and in short order turned himself into the greatest

British investigative journalist of his time. He was filled, he wrote, with "determination to do my best to expose and destroy what I then knew to be a legalised infamy . . . accompanied by unimaginable barbarities and responsible for a vast destruction of human life". For a dozen years, from 1901 to 1913, working sometimes 14 to 16 hours a day, he devoted his formidable energy and eloquence to putting the story of forced labour in King Leopold's Congo on the world's front pages. In Britain, where returned missionaries had already begun to find large audiences for their slide shows of Congo atrocities, Morel founded the Congo Reform Association. Affiliated groups quickly sprang up in the United States and other countries.

After Morel orchestrated a protest resolution by the House of Commons in 1903, the British government, in response, asked its representative in the Congo to investigate his charges. The British consul, a black-bearded Irishman named Roger Casement, who later in life was to die on the gallows as an Irish patriot, took the assignment seriously. Renting a missionary steamboat, he spent more than three months travelling in the interior. He produced an excoriating, detailed report, complete with sworn testimony, which was in many ways a model for the reports that began to be produced more than 50 years later by Amnesty International and other human rights organisations. In the first decade of the twentieth century, the efforts of Morel, Casement, key missionaries and their supporters succeeded in making the forced labour system of King Leopold's Congo the most widely publicised human rights scandal of its time. The king was condemned in the press, poets thundered against him, and cartoonists throughout Europe portrayed him surrounded by human skulls and severed hands.

Leopold himself never went to the Congo. Something of a hypochondriac, he always worried about germs. And perhaps he had good reason to do so, for Europeans had not yet found ways of combating all the major tropical diseases. Leopold knew—and kept secret—statistics which showed that before 1900, about one third of all white men who went to the Congo ended up succumbing to disease and dying there. The king chose to stay in Europe, where he spent his Congo profits on grand buildings and public monuments in Belgium, a huge array of clothes for his teenaged mistress, and an expanding array of properties on the French Riviera.

As a result of the international agitation over the atrocities, Leopold was finally pressured into relinquishing his private ownership of the Congo, reluctantly transferring it to the Belgian State in 1908—while making Belgium pay him for so doing. He died the following year, having made a profit from the territory conservatively estimated as equal to more than $1.1 billion in the American dollars of a century later.

★   ★   ★

Although the human rights violations in Leopold's Congo were egregious and the avaricious king an easy villain to target, in a sense, the protest movement's focus on that territory alone was unfair. For the king's system of exploitation became a model for surrounding colonies which also had rain forests rich in wild rubber—Portuguese-controlled Angola, the Cameroons under the Germans, and the French Congo, part of French Equatorial Africa, across the river from Leopold's Congo. Seeing what profits Leopold was reaping from forced labour, officials in the other colonies soon adopted exactly the same system—including women hostages, male forced labour and the *chicotte*—with equally high death rates. Forced labour of one kind or another was widely used in most parts of the continent until several decades into the twentieth century, although seldom with such fatal consequences as during the rubber boom in central Africa. This book describes the forced labour that, unknown to almost all Europeans, lay behind the production of something that millions of them used every day, soap.

After 1908, in the newly christened Belgian Congo, men were forced to continue gathering rubber, for its price remained high. Eventually, just before the First World War, the price fell as rubber plantations elsewhere in the world began producing. The Congo's wild rubber vines were also largely tapped out. But the war brought new hardships: large numbers of Africans were conscripted as porters, carrying supplies for Belgian military campaigns against Germany's African colonies. In 1916, according to statistics kept by Belgian officials, one district of the eastern Congo with a population of 83,518 adult men supplied more than three million man-days of porterage. 1359 of these porters were worked to death or died of disease.

Starting in the early 1920s, however, the system became considerably less draconian, mainly because colonial officials realised that otherwise they would soon have no labour force left. "We run the risk of someday seeing our native population collapse and disappear", declared the permanent committee of the National Colonial Congress of Belgium in 1924, "so that we will find ourselves confronted with a kind of desert". Between 1880, when Leopold started to assume control of the Congo and the 1920s, when the forced labour system became less severe, what happened could not, by strict definition, be called genocide, for there was no deliberate attempt to wipe out all members of one particular ethnic group. But the slashing of the territory's population—through the combination of forced labour and the consequent disease, famine and diminished birthrate, plus the suppression of rebellions—indisputably occurred on a genocidal scale.

In estimating population losses without the benefit of complete census data, demographers are more confident speaking of percentages than absolute numbers. Using a wide variety of local and church sources, Jan Vansina, professor emeritus of history and anthropology at the University of Wisconsin and the leading ethnographer of Congo basin peoples, calculates that the Congo's population dropped by some 50% during this period, an estimate with which a number of other modern scholars concur. Interestingly, a long-time high colonial official, Major Charles C. Liebrechts, made the same estimate in 1920. Shocked by local census statistics that showed less than one child per woman, the official *Commission Instituée pour la Protection des Indigènes* (Commission for the Protection of the Natives) made a similar reckoning in 1919. Its report that year to the Belgian king warned that the situation had reached "the point of threatening even the existence of certain Congolese peoples" and could completely depopulate the entire region. R.P. Van Wing, a Belgian Jesuit missionary who had long worked in the region, estimated that one subgroup of the Bakongo people had seen 80% of their number disappear.

More precise statistics do not exist, for census data before 1920 is scanty and only local. Furthermore, just before the Congo State was transferred out of his hands in 1908, King Leopold II ordered its archives burned. But numerous surviving records from the rubber-bearing land in the adjoining French Congo, which closely followed the model of the Leopoldian forced labour system, suggest a population loss there also of around 50%. If the estimates from varied sources of a 50% toll in King Leopold's Congo are correct, how many people does this mean? In the early 1920s the first territory-wide census, when adjusted for undercounting, placed the number of the colony's inhabitants at approximately ten million. If that figure is accurate and if it represents 50% of what the population had been in 1880, this would suggest a loss of some ten million people.

In the 1920s, in what was now the Belgian Congo, colonial officials began constructing the rudiments of a public health system and what eventually became one of the continent's best networks of primary schools. Colonialism's defenders often point to these, plus the wide network of roads and railways, as examples of the great positive benefits white rule brought to Africa. The clinics and schools were indeed built in the Congo, as elsewhere, but because Belgian industrialists and mine owners wanted a healthy workforce with enough education to be trained. And the roads and railways were built almost entirely to carry African raw materials to the ports where they could be shipped to Europe.

Although the death toll began dropping dramatically in the 1920s, Congolese had few legal rights, no vote, and, when it came to politics, little free speech. Along with the forced labour system, these were violations of human rights common throughout colonial Africa. In 1921, for example,

Congo authorities became deeply alarmed at the large following attracted by a religious prophet, Simon Kimbangu, who was said to heal the sick and make the blind see. His preaching was not overtly political, but thousands of workers left their jobs to follow him. He was swiftly arrested and kept in prison until his death, 30 years later.

Gradually taking on less murderous form, forced labour remained a crucial part of the Belgian Congo's economy. The enforcement mechanism of taking women or chiefs as hostages was gradually replaced by that of taxes—and the threat of severe punishment for Congolese who did not pay them. Throughout sub-Saharan Africa, European colonists and settlers used head taxes or hut taxes to force people away from subsistence agriculture and into mines, factories and other parts of the colonial economy that required labour.

The decades immediately after the First World War saw the growth of Belgian Congo production of new commodities, one of the most important being the palm-oil industry described in this volume, in which Lever Brothers played such an important role. But the *chicotte* remained a key tool of control, now often in the hands of private corporations. At the gold mines of Moto, on the Uele River, records show that 26,579 lashes were administered to miners in the first half of 1920 alone. When the key railway line around the great Congo River rapids was widened and rebuilt between 1923 and 1932, the regime mobilised 68,000 forced labourers and members of their families, of whom 7,700 died. (This was colonial business as usual: a competing railway built at the same time in French Equatorial Africa cost 20,000 lives.) To Africans throughout the Congo conscripted to work on these and other works of the white men's corporations, the business bankruptcies and slow-downs caused by the Great Depression brought, paradoxically, life-saving relief.

The coming of the Second World War, in which the Congo's treasure house of natural resources was a key source of supply for the Allies, saw the legal maximum for forced labour increased to 120 days per man per year. The penalty for evasion was six months in prison. Workers laboured at everything from the railways to rubber plantations to the heavily guarded uranium mine of Shinkolobwe, which produced more than 80% of the uranium used in the Hiroshima and Nagasaki bombs.

I first met Jules Marchal in 1995. Fascinated by the way the enormous death toll of King Leopold's Congo—the most notorious human rights scandal in the world during the first decade of the twentieth century—had been forgotten, I was writing a history of that period, and was about to make a research trip to Belgium. When I interviewed the distinguished anthropologist and historian Jan Vansina, he told me, "There's someone you should look up when you go. He has found out things about Congo history that no one else has."

And so I went to see Marchal, taking the train from Brussels to the station nearest the small village, Hoepertingen, where he and his wife Paula lived, in a rambling farmhouse surrounded by meadows, a few farm animals and a cherry orchard. Marchal had an extraordinary story to tell. He had lived in the Congo for many years, working first under the Belgian colonial administration, then for the newly independent regime. Then he had spent more than two decades in the Belgian diplomatic service, serving mostly in Africa. He was now retired.

Like most Belgians, Marchal had grown up learning nothing about the violence and enormous death toll that were part of the Congo's colonisation. In the early 1970s, he was serving as Belgian ambassador to a group of three Anglophone countries in West Africa: Ghana, Liberia and Sierra Leone. He came across a story in a Liberian newspaper that referred, in passing, to ten million deaths in King Leopold's Congo.

"I was startled", Marchal told me. "I wrote to the foreign minister in Brussels. I said, 'I have to write a letter to the editor correcting this story, this strange slander on our country. But I don't know the history of that period. Could you please have someone send me some information?' I waited. But I never got an answer. And that's when my curiosity began."

Marchal's curiosity turned to anger when he found, to his surprise, that despite his status as a Belgian ambassador, he was denied access to certain key records from the colonial era in the Belgian foreign ministry's own archives. For the next 15 years, still serving in the Belgian foreign service, he devoted all his spare time to Congo history. After reaching retirement age in 1989, he worked at it full time. Between then and his death in 2003, he published seven meticulously documented books on the subject. Four volumes— which he wrote first in his native Dutch, then translated and expanded in French—covered the Leopold period, with a thoroughness unmatched by any scholar before him. Three more books, written in French, covered the forced labour system in the Congo from 1910 to 1945. One was about mining,* one about railway construction, and the one translated and abridged in this volume about palm oil. Sadly, Marchal's death from cancer prevented him from completing a final book he had planned, about Congolese forced labour during the Second World War.

---

* Translated into English as *Forced Labour in the Gold and Copper Mines: A History of Congo Under Belgian Rule 1910–1945, Volume 1*, Popenguine, Senegal 2003.

Of all the former colonial powers in Europe, Belgium has made the least progress towards acknowledging the full truth of its colonial past. There are several reasons for this. One is that it is a small country, long uncomfortably divided between speakers of Dutch and French; one of the few things the two halves of the country have in common is the myth that their ancestors were benevolent, enlightened colonial rulers. Various institutions have perpetuated that myth, particularly the Royal Museum for Central Africa at Tervuren, on the outskirts of Brussels, and the large multilingual array of books published by the Royal Academy of Overseas Sciences (formerly the Royal Academy of Colonial Sciences). Another factor is that the small number of Africa scholars at Belgium's universities have until recently been—compared with their colleagues in Britain, France and the United States—an unusually conservative group. And, finally, there is not a population of former colonial subjects and their descendants in Belgium large enough to force a change in the way the country looks at its history, in the way that a critical mass of Britons of African and Caribbean origin have dramatically changed the way British history is taught today, compared with a generation or two ago.

Marchal's focus on forced labour deeply annoyed many of his fellow Belgians. Although his books are valued by Africa scholars in other countries, they were seldom reviewed in Belgium itself. Only in the last few years of his life did his work begin to get some recognition. He was right, I believe, to concentrate on forced labour as he did. For it was an essential part of colonialism, not just in the Congo, but in almost all of Africa. Surprisingly few writers deal with it. His contribution is an essential one. No other scholar, looking at any other part of Africa, has studied colonial forced labour as thoroughly as Marchal has in the Congo. A storyteller or a popular writer for a mass audience he is not, but as a researcher who knew how to find what was hidden in government and corporate documents he is unmatched. Marchal's 40 years in government service taught him how to uncover documents that writers of laudatory biographies and cheerful corporate histories have long ignored. This particular book is an implicit response to such volumes about Lord Leverhulme and the corporate empire he and his brother founded—books like the biography of Leverhulme by W.P. Jolly, whose upbeat chapter on the Congo is largely based on Leverhulme's diaries of the two trips he made there. Like so many white men engaged in the Congo, Leverhulme considered himself and his works there wise and enlightened. It is quite a different story that Marchal tells in these pages.

The first great phase of Congo colonialism, in King Leopold's time, revolved around rubber and ivory. The information on the palm-oil industry Marchal has gathered here belongs to the second phase of the country's exploitation as a colony, when these commodities were eclipsed by others such as palm oil, gold, tin, uranium, copper. But as a historian Marchal was struck by the continuities: the various forms of violence and coercion which continued to underlie the entire colonial economy.

The data Jules Marchal lays out in this book involves only one industry, in only certain parts of only one colony. But the picture it constructs is one that applies to the forced labour systems that pervaded so much of colonial Africa. Behind so many of the products that Europeans enjoyed using during the colonial period—ivory, rubber, cotton clothing, gold rings, copper wire and, in the case of the industry covered by this book, cakes of soap—lay stories of African men torn from their families, of whippings, murderous suppression of rebellions, dangerous working conditions, low wages and early death. Colonial Africa's full history is only beginning to be told, and it is books such as this that provide the raw material for such telling.

LIST OF ABBREVIATIONS

BCK:	Compagnie du chemin de fer du Bas–Congo au Katanga
CCB:	Compagnie du Congo Belge
CK:	Compagnie du Kasai
Comanco:	La commerciale anversoise du Congo
Forminière:	Société internationale forestière et minière du Congo
FP:	Force publique
HCB:	Huileries du Congo Belge
HPK:	Huileries et Plantations du Kwango
Huilever:	Compagnies réunies des Huileries du Congo Belge et Savonneries Lever Frères
Offitra:	Office du travail de Kinshasa
OP:	Orientale province
SAB:	Société anonyme belge pour le commerce du Haut-Congo
SEDEC:	Société d'enterprises commerciales du Congo Belge
SIEFAC:	Société industrielle d'exploitations forestières au Congo
Unatra:	Union nationale des transports fluviaux

Note to Readers

This English-language edition is an abridgement of the original French text.

1

The Early Years (1911–1922)

A magnate, purportedly a philanthropist,
launches himself upon the Congo

At the beginning of 1911, William Lever, the soap magnate from Port Sunlight in the suburbs of Liverpool, set foot in the Congo in order to secure raw material for his industry. This raw material, the oil of fruit taken from natural palm groves, was to be found in abundance in British West Africa, where it was freely sold by Africans to Europeans. Lever, however, was bent on gain, and therefore wished to circumvent this trade, and to obtain palm groves from the British government in the form of a concession. Because the latter decided that it could not expropriate collective property, Lever looked to achieve his goal in one of the other colonies in Africa. He settled on the Belgian Congo, where the government regarded all land, save that occupied or cultivated by Africans, as state property.

We have it on the authority of a then ailing Alfred Jones, the celebrated consul for the Congo in Liverpool, that Lever first made contact with Jules Renkin, the Belgian Colonial Minister, towards the end of 1909. With Max Horn of Antwerp, Renkin's emissary, acting as an intermediary, Lever obtained on behalf of his company, Lever Brothers, through a Convention signed on 21st February 1911, the option to purchase 750,000 hectares of natural palm groves at a knock-down price. He was free to choose them within five "circles" measuring sixty kilometres in radius, around Bumba and Barumbu on the river Congo, Lusanga on the river Kwilu, Basongo on the river Kasai, and Ingende on the river Ruki.[1]

These localities had been chosen by the Belgian Henri Dekeyser, in 1910, while on a mission to the Congo undertaken on Lever's behalf.[2] Dekeyser had embarked upon his colonial career in 1892, in Bumba, and had served from 1896 to 1898 in Basoko (opposite Barumbu) as district commissioner. These facts explain why the above names headed the list of "circles". In

Barumbu there had been a coffee plantation, established by the Belgian State, since 1896. As for the Basongo and Ingende circles, they had been added to the list in order to allow for a wider choice in types of land occupied by palm groves.

Dekeyser was not unknown in England. In September 1896, the British press had made much of his role as the commandant of soldiers who, in Bumba region, had cut off the feet of a chief's daughter, in order to seize the heavy brass anklets she was wearing.[3] At the end of March 1904 his name had again featured prominently in the same press, as principal plaintiff in a libel trial in London against the author and publisher of *The Curse of Central Africa*. In this book, Guy Burrows had accused Dekeyser of committing atrocities in Basoko district. The defendants had failed to produce any witnesses to corroborate their accusations; the judge therefore found in Dekeyser's favour, and awarded him substantial damages.[4]

Dekeyser had resigned from the service of the Congo Free State five years earlier, but in March 1911 he returned to the country, now called the Belgian Congo,[5] in the company of Lichfield Henry Moseley, a former employee of the Bank of Nigeria who was reputed to be an expert in West African affairs.[6] Their aim was to pave the way for the Huileries du Congo Belge (HCB), a company set up by Lever, in accordance with the terms of the Convention with Renkin, in order to exploit the palm groves. They chose the berths required for the river fleet of the recently founded company, namely, a strip of about 100 metres on the banks of the river Matadi, a one-hectare plot at Kinshasa, and a number of sites for the storage of logs to be burnt in the steamers, along the banks of the Congo, the Kwilu and the Kasai.[7] Dekeyser and Moseley noted that Lusanga circle, the nearest one to Kinshasa, contained the most dense palm groves.

Lever invested whatever capital was needed to equip his Congolese project with modern machinery. A thousand tons of such machinery were dispatched from Liverpool to Matadi in the summer of 1911, for the equipping of a factory at Lusanga, now renamed Leverville, and situated at the confluence of the Kwilu and Kwange rivers. The transportation of this heavy freight on the small railway line between Matadi and Kinshasa, which could carry only thirty tons a day, was effected with the utmost difficulty.[8] Nonetheless, the factory at Lusanga was ready that same year, and the first consignment of oil that had been pressed there arrived in Antwerp in March 1912. The following month the first tablet of soap made of Congolese palm oil was placed in an ivory casket, and solemnly presented to Albert I, King of the Belgians.

In November 1912, at the age of 61, Lever set out once again for the Congo, together with his wife and a number of company agents. He was determined to make a success of the HCB, and visited each of the five circles in an HCB steamer. He decided to set up a factory immediately at Ebonda, which was near to Bumba, another at Lukutu, twenty kilometres east of Barumbu, and a third in Lusanga circle, at Tango, not far from Bulungu. Ebonda and Lukutu were renamed Alberta and Elisabetha respectively. Lever appointed Moseley director general of the HCB at Kinshasa, Dekeyser director at Ebonda and Lukutu,[9] and Sidney Edkins, an Englishman, itinerant agent general. He gave orders for the HCB steamers to be fitted out as tankers, which would transport the palm oil in bulk to Kinshasa, and came to an arrangement with the Jesuits over the founding of a mission in Lusanga. The latter would be responsible for the school for Africans which, in accordance with the Convention with Renkin, Lever had promised to set up in Kwilu circle, as, indeed, he had undertaken to do in all the other circles. The mission would be founded in February 1915, at the confluence of the Kwenge and Kwilu rivers.[10]

William Lever passed in Europe for a philanthropist with enlightened views, on account of the excellent conditions under which the workforce lived and worked at Port Sunlight. It was for this reason that the socialist deputy Emile Vandervelde, during a debate in the Belgian Parliament on the Lever–Renkin Convention, had been persuaded to back the latter, being convinced that the English magnate's future concessions would not be to the detriment of Africans. Lever, for his part, reserved a proxy vote for the Belgian socialist on the HCB's Board.

In May 1911, in England, E.D. Morel[11] had reproached Lever for having negotiated a Convention with Renkin which turned Africans, who had been owners of palms, into wage-earners working for him. He had asked Lever how he proposed to get the palm fruit from the Africans if they withheld them. Lever had answered that he counted upon buying them at a tempting price. The Lever–Renkin Convention had been vague about prices, but it had on the other hand fixed the workers' wages at 25 centimes a day. Lever counted upon having the fruit cut down for him, rather than buying it, and for such hard work the aforementioned wage was wholly inadequate. To be employed as a cutter of palm-fruit clusters was no laughing matter, since it involved using a large belt in order to climb the tall palm trees to the very top, where the clusters containing the fruit grew. In order to climb the trunk of a palm tree, the cutter makes himself a belt out of two detachable pieces of vegetable material. The larger piece serves as a back, while the smaller is supposed to clasp the trunk of the palm tightly. The two parts are joined together by simple knots. At the foot of the tree, the cutter undoes the second knot, throws the free end round the tree and re-attaches it to the back. He begins his climb. He leans against the back, with his two feet on the bark. By bringing his body closer to the tree, he lets the belt hang free and is able to raise it 20 to 30 centimetres. He presses up against the tree again and moves his feet higher. The alternation of these movements brings him gradually closer to the crown. Once he has reached the top, he adopts a stable position and leans against the back, opposite the cluster of fruit that he plans to pick. A few blows from the machete enable the cutter to detach a frond (leaf) from its base. He then cuts the cluster that has grown in the axilla of the leaf, and lets it fall to the ground.[12]

When in the Congo, Lever was able to ascertain for himself that the wage he was paying for the cutting of clusters was insufficient. Indeed, in a diary entry for Christmas Eve 1912, he noted that the problem of the cutters of palm fruit "has grown as an ominous dark cloud", and that the people of Lusanga were no longer bringing fruit, after having done so for barely a year.[13] From this Lever did not conclude that it was necessary to reduce the number of clusters to be cut each day. He did not want to devote money to ensuring the fair remuneration of Africans, who, given such circumstances, would have worked quite willingly. Instead, he adopted the method generally used during this period to make Africans work, namely, coercion. In mid-December 1912, prior to Lever's arrival in the Congo, his agent general had anyway asked the governor-general of the colony to set up a State military post in the vicinity of Lusanga, with patrols travelling the length and breadth of the region.

Intent upon turning his concessions in the Congo into a personal "kingdom", Lever returned to Europe in March 1913. He was now less than ever disposed to buy the fruit at a tempting price. The Africans would have to work "his" palm trees as wage-labourers, on the pittance he chose to pay them. Where Africans were concerned, Lever would prove to be not a philanthropist but an oppressor. The HCB was not destined to be the great enterprise which Lever, who was to become Lord Leverhulme in 1922, declared it to be, and that his admirers would subsequently take it to be. He had launched himself upon the Congo in order to turn the HCB into a sordid affair of large-scale profiteering, not heeding the harm done to Africans.

First beginnings at Lusanga

The report on HCB operations for the period between 1st July 1912 and 30th June 1913 reformulated the request made in mid-December by the company's agent general as follows:

> The crucial problem of labour is still complicated by various causes . . . It would be desirable to set up, at any rate temporarily, in the vicinity of

Leverville, a military post consisting of two whites, one of whom would be an officer, and two platoons, and to let the patrols travel through the region . . . We should brook no further delay in defining the boundaries of the *chefferies*,[14] or chiefdoms, and in issuing medals[15] to the chiefs in the Leverville region.

This last observation referred to the fact that at this period a system was developing whereby chiefs supplied workers and were rewarded with subsidies paid to them by the employers.

On 28th November 1913 Jules Renkin, the Colonial Minister, forwarded the above text to Governor-General Felix Fuchs, adding that it hardly seemed possible to meet the company's request as formulated. Indeed, the request too obviously amounted to a call for a system of coercion. The real solution to the problem, the minister added, seems to him to be to occupy and administer the region as a *territoire*,[16] with Lusanga-Leverville as its administrative centre.[17] In other words, Renkin proposed detaching the post of Lusanga from Bulungu *territoire*, to which it then belonged.

In January 1914, Moseley, who had become the managing director of the HCB in Brussels, complained in an interview with Renkin that the engineers then building the railway line between the Bas-Congo and Katanga were recruiting temporary workers at "unreasonably high" salaries. Moseley expressed the hope that the minister would ensure that a more prudent policy would be followed in future, for such exceptional wages were giving Africans a false notion of the value of their labour. The engineers employed on the above-mentioned line, Moseley proposed, should be instructed not to exceed the going rate of pay in the regions in which they were operating.[18] Once one knows the wretched wages paid by the railway companies in the Congo, one may all too easily imagine what Lever's Englishmen were paying.

In a letter dated 14th April 1914, Jules Vanwert, commissioner for the Kwango district, of which the Kwilu basin formed a part, responded to Renkin's suggestion that the HCB region become a *territoire* with Lusanga as its administrative headquarters. He wrote to the governor-general as follows:

Given that the English like to remain masters in their own houses, they are not likely to relish the establishment of an administrative capital in Leverville and, as far as I am concerned, the structures that we would be able to build in this spot with the limited funds available, would cut a sorry figure beside the impressive company buildings. This issue is therefore liable to do serious damage to our prestige . . . The steps recently taken to accelerate the administrative organisation of the country will certainly help with the recruitment of workers for the HCB.

Vanwert added—and here he was in error—that the Company desired nothing more than a sub-commissariat of police with a handful of soldiers to keep the peace in its post. He then proposed to the governor-general that such a sub-commissariat be created, with one European and fifteen soldiers. Fuchs issued an ordinance to that effect on 29th May 1914. In response to a request made by the inspector of state, Auguste Gérard, he decreed that the future police superintendent would combine with his other official duties that of tax collector in the region worked by the HCB. He further specified that the company should at its own expense provide accommodation for police personnel, black and white, within its compounds.

On 7th July 1914, Moseley wrote to Renkin to complain that the police force set up at Leverville fell far short of what the Company had been requesting for the past two years. He asked that this force's role not be restricted to keeping the peace in Leverville, and that it should be authorised to conduct patrols in the neighbouring region, within a fifty kilometre radius of the station. Renkin replied as follows on 17th July:

> Our understanding is that, just as you have presumed, the local police force assigned to Leverville will be placed under the command of a white agent. As regards "patrols in the neighbouring region, for example, within a fifty kilometre radius of the station", they could be arranged, if the need arose, but only to keep the peace, and to co-operate within pre-defined limits in the implementation of due legal process and of warrants for arrest.[19]

If those running the HCB set such store by military patrols in the Lusanga region, this was because they feared they would not be able to continue with the system of forcible recruitment employed by their numerous agents, accompanied by armed auxiliaries. These agents had encountered more and more resistance during their tours, or else the villages had emptied before they reached them. Indeed, the first clashes between labour recruiters and villagers took place precisely in July 1914:

- a recruiter by the name of Buelens was met with a volley of arrows in the village of Kasamba, whose chief was Mosenge; he was slightly wounded in the chest;
- a recruiter by the name of Vanherenthals was attacked in the village of Kisimuna, one hour's journey from Leverville; he suffered serious arrow wounds in the arm and the chest;

- a recruiter by the name of Sosson was met with a volley of arrows, and the man in command of his escort received a wound in the leg;
- a recruiter by the name of Monard was also greeted with arrows.[20]

In two letters dated mid-July, the director of Lusanga circle, one Howell A. Hopwood, brought the above facts to the notice of Alfredo Bonelli, the deputy district commissioner, who was then on a tour of duty at Mitshakila. In the second of the two letters, Hopwood added:

On all sides our agents record growing hostility in the region . . . We see only too clearly that if the unrest is not promptly put down, the situation will once more take a turn for the worse. We therefore ask and request of you, as the representative of the Belgian government in the region, kindly to restore order, with as little delay as possible, and we further regret to have to inform you that, if the means at your disposal should prove inadequate, we shall ourselves take all necessary steps to protect the lives of our agents and our industry.

In writing to Bonelli, Hopwood invoked article 18 of the Renkin–Lever Convention, which stipulated that: "Police measures will be taken to guarantee the safety of the Company's agents, and to go to their aid should the need arise." When Bonelli failed to reply, Hopwood took his case, on 30th July, to Vanwert, who was based in Bandundu, the administrative centre of the district. On this occasion, Hopwood sounded a more cautious note:

We would be profoundly grateful to you if you would indicate to us just how far we may go in ensuring our own security, and what we may do to uphold the prestige of the company and of its agents in the eyes of the natives. For example, what can we do when a European is met with a volley of arrows? . . . Do we have the right to apprehend the guilty party and to convey him within forty-eight hours to the nearest administrative centre?

Vanwert answered on 4th August by forwarding a copy of his letter to Bonelli and to the territorial administrators in Bulungu and in Kikwit: "The mission with which the deputy district commissioner (2 officers, 75 soldiers) has been entrusted, along the eastern bank of the Moyen-Kwilu, will in the near future permit the recruitment of a workforce of which you have great need . . . The process will be a lengthy one and, if it is to bear fruit, it is crucial that it not be interrupted." Vanwert went on to give a glimpse of the security forces present in the region. In Bulungu *territoire*, on the right bank of the Kwilu, there were the personnel attached to the Bonelli mission, together with the 25 soldiers escorting the BCK mission. On the left bank of the Kwilu, there were the 15 soldiers allocated to Lusanga, and the escort provided for the tax collector in Bulungu. In Kikwit *territoire*, there were 3 agents and 100 soldiers.

To the precise questions put by Hopwood, Vanwert answered that, in case of attack, a European had the right of self-defence, and could safeguard his life with his own weapons. Were he able, in such circumstances, to apprehend the guilty party, he would not be committing an arbitrary arrest if he delivered up the malefactor within 48 hours to the nearest Colony post. Vanwert further added that the company should abide by the ordinance of 1st October 1913 on use of firearms, if it deemed it necessary to request that its agents be armed for the purposes of self-defence. The latter would have the right to be accompanied by five armed workers, provided that the management of the HCB had lodged a prior request for an escort permit. (The 1st October ordinance entitled each European to have three weapons, and each European establishment to have twenty-five weapons.)

Upon receiving a copy of this letter, Bonelli wrote to Hopwood that the HCB recruiters should, as they moved from place to place, take into account the state of mind of villagers whose way of life had been thrown into such turmoil. If they were to acquire a better grasp of the language of the country, and to display more patience, many conflicts might be avoided. By way of example he cited a sequence of events in Pia. He then referred to the letter by Vanwert quoted above, remarking that the latter had explained how HCB agents might move around more safely and protect themselves. "For my own part", Bonelli continued, "I also think that it would be useful, in the light of what is ordinarily done in the Compagnie du Kasai and in the Comptoir Commercial Congolais, for your staff to have legal escorts at their disposal." He added that the police post would shortly be set up at Lusanga and that proceedings would be instituted against those responsible for the attacks upon Buelens and Vanherenthals.[21]

At the beginning of September, the new director general of the HCB in Kinshasa, the Luxemburger François Beissel (a veteran of the Compagnie du chemin de fer du Congo), forwarded Hopwood's file relating to the villagers' attacks on his agents to Fuchs. Beissel asked Fuchs to issue directives to Kwango district, according his agents government protection. At the same time he asked to be granted an interview, so that they might consider the issue in more depth. Following the interview, Fuchs wrote as follows, on 22nd September, to Vanwert:

I do not doubt that immediate steps have been taken to provide an appropriate response to the incidents that have occurred, and also to protect persons at risk from any further aggression from the populations in question. I must nevertheless draw your attention yet again to the overriding duty incumbent upon us to take all possible steps to safeguard the lives of individuals, and to guarantee the smooth running of enterprises against interference and harassment at the hands of local peoples that are backward and resistant to European penetration.[22]

It is only too plain that whereas Vanwert and Bonelli, being on the spot, had grasped that the villagers' attacks were really in self-defence, Fuchs was prepared to contemplate the unleashing of military operations against them. Six months later, Renkin would in fact reproach him for the vagueness of his directives.[23]

By way of special measures for the protection of the HCB, Vanwert merely set up the police post in Lusanga on 5th October, under the command of the military agent Julien Staessens, who was advised to abide by the letter of the law. In February 1915, however, Vanwert decided to recall Staessens, after the latter had threatened to sue the HCB's managing director, Wall, for libel. Whatever the rights and wrongs of the matter, the two men had any number of grievances against each other. Staessens was within his rights, however, in deeming that Wall was overstepping the mark in banning his soldiers, along with villagers and labourers, from cutting palm fruit for their own consumption in the palm grove at Lusanga.

Vanwert replaced Staessens with the military agent Médard Devos, who took up his duties in Lusanga at the beginning of March 1915. There were no difficulties with Devos, or at any rate not to start with, but relations between Bonelli and Hopwood had soured. The latter failed to turn up for a meeting agreed upon with the deputy district commissioner, and offered no explanation. Eight days later, Bonelli met Hopwood by chance in the company of Wall. Bonelli wanted to discuss at length various disputes over policing in Lusanga. Although Hopwood and Wall professedly had no time to listen to him, they nonetheless insisted upon the need for some State presence when they were recruiting labourers, and also inquired into the possibility of banning all trade in palm fruit within the boundaries of their concession. Bonelli concluded that these gentlemen were not concerned overmuch with the issue of policing. He was mistaken. The HCB wanted a police force, but not of the kind imposed upon them, which had followed the letter of the law.

Vanwert believed that the Company wished to be rid of the police force when Beissel asked him in May to transfer it to a site opposite Leverville, on the other side of the river Kwenge. He was making this request, he said, in response to conflicts arising between Devos and his own agents. The following month Beissel, on his way to Bandundu—accompanied by three high-ranking representatives of the Company, and speaking on their behalf—told Vanwert that they all wished to see the police force partially disbanded, maintaining just four or five soldiers at Leverville to keep the peace. The district commissioner answered that he was willing, upon receipt of an official request, to have Devos and his men return to the administrative headquarters of Bulungu *territoire*.

In a letter from Kinshasa dated 28th June 1915, managing director Wall made the request, but not in terms that Vanwert had anticipated. The letter took Devos violently to task, reprimanding him, among other things, for the manner in which he collected taxes: "Instead of promoting labour recruitment by making tax-collecting trips on the periphery of our region, he does precisely the opposite, and collects taxes at our station and at posts in the immediate vicinity. Many workers are therefore driven to desert." The letter continued as follows:

> We cordially request that you have the superintendent of police transferred forthwith. We propose to ask the government for a duty picket of from four to six "policemen".[24] These men would be under the command of our head of station, who could be sworn in as a police officer. An arrangement of this sort exists in the Compagnie du chemin du fer du Congo, where it has worked well. We cordially request you to grant this provisionally, until such time as we are able to request it formally from the government.

In a lengthy report to the governor-general, dated 13th July, Vanwert summarised the history of the police post, calling it an unhappy experiment. He concluded by recommending that the post be closed down. He seemed not to realise that he had himself been responsible for the experiment, since the Company had wanted a military post capable of mounting patrols in the region which would maintain the forcible recruitment of the workforce. Instead of which Vanwert had imposed upon the Company a police superintendent who was expected to "abide by the letter of the law". He had turned a deaf ear to the notion of putting "policemen" at the disposal of an agent of the Company.[25] These policemen would inevitably be soldiers, since there were no policemen as such in the Congo at this period, but only soldiers euphemistically known as police in specific circumstances.

At the end of August, Beissel, the HCB director general, asked the new governor-general, Eugène Henry, for the "picket" described by Wall, in the course of an interview held in the presence of English directors of the Company. On this same occasion, Beissel called for the wholesale military occupation of the region by the Belgian State, and for the collection of taxes in villages and not in posts. These two measures would, it was hoped, enable the Company to increase the number of its workers in the Kwilu from the two thousand then in its employ to the ten thousand needed for the development of the concession. Beissel also complained about the concession being spread across three different *territoires*, namely, Kikwit, Niadi and Bulungu, and asked that it be incorporated into a single *territoire* with an administrative headquarters near to Lusanga. This would implement Renkin's old idea, and thereby facilitate communication between the Company and the territorial authorities.

Henry refused to grant a scaled-down police force under the command of an agent of the Company. Instead, he advised his interlocutors to use guards hired at their own expense to keep watch over their stations. He promised them that, once the war had ended, he would reconsider the organisation of the *territoires*, and the possibility of introducing an occupying column into the area. They could rest assured that numbers of government personnel would be boosted in the post-war period.

On 30th September 1915, Henry wrote to Vanwert informing him that he could definitively withdraw the "policemen" from Leverville, the management of the HCB having just reassured him that it did not wish a European police superintendent to be retained there, and that it would itself see to the surveillance of its stations by guards in its own hire, with the proviso that all infractions of the law be referred to the nearest government civil servant. Henry informed Vanwert of Beissel's wishes regarding the organisation of the *territoires*, without, however, backing them.[26] The point to note here is that Henry gave the HCB *carte blanche* to reinforce its own militias, a thing that could readily be done using black West Africans already employed by them. The above-mentioned ordinance regarding use of firearms guaranteed that it would have weapons in abundance for the purpose.

During the First World War, the Belgian colonial administration, in exile once Belgium had been occupied by Germany, was based in London, while Max Horn, for his part, had become government commissioner with the HCB. For many years, as we shall see, Horn would play a crucial role in liaising between HCB bosses in Europe and the colonial minister. He would be behind those projects harmful to Africans which the Company would implement, or try to implement. He would receive fixed fees paid by the Company to its board members, although the sums in question did not appear in the annual accounts.[27] On 5th November 1915, Horn forwarded to Renkin the report on Company dealings for the financial year 1914–1915, which stated that the administrative and political situation in the region of Leverville posed a serious obstacle to the Company's future progress. Horn offered suggestions as to how this state of affairs might be remedied. On 17th November, he brought the following extract from a letter by Beissel to the colonial minister's attention:

> Since war broke out, military occupation of Lusanga country has been reduced to almost nothing, and the natives are well aware of this. Recently in a village ten kilometres from our posts, the natives declared to our recruiting agent, when he asked them for labourers, that they would no longer go to work, having no need of money now that *Bula Matari* [the government] no longer had soldiers to collect taxes.
>
> Let me once again draw the attention of the governor-general and of the district commissioner to the need to deploy in our concessions the few civil servants and soldiers remaining in the region.

Horn commented that, in his view, the district had to be administered more vigorously.

Renkin, the colonial minister, forwarded this same extract to Henry, the governor-general, and requested that he consider whether the local authorities in the Kwango were paying due attention to all questions of native policy. He numbered among such questions the collection of taxes in the villages and the possibility of state employees providing effective support to commercial and industrial enterprises. He further added that merging all the regions of the Kwango, where the Company's activities were concentrated, into a single administrative *territoire* would be as useful to the general running of the Colony as it would be to the Company.

Henry merely forwarded the minister's message to Vanwert, without, however, enclosing the extract from Beissel's letter. In his reply to Renkin, dated 7th February 1916, he said that Beissel and the Company directors, during the interview he had had with them the previous August, had acknowledged the difficulty of introducing changes at that juncture, and that he had promised them that he would reconsider the question after the war and arrange then for an occupying column serving to guarantee the safety of "all natives wishing to work or to honour their obligations towards the State".

Let me stress here the hypocrisy of using an administrative idiom to turn a military column forcing Africans to work for Lever, into a column protecting those volunteering for Lever.

In a dispatch dated 11th February, Renkin, without waiting for Henry's reply to his previous letter, wrote to say that the more he reflected upon the matter, the more he was of the opinion that it was in the colonial administration's best interests that the various regions in the Kwango with HCB establishments be combined in a single *territoire*. He was satisfied that the existence of a single administrative unit would help the Company to run more smoothly, but such a change would also, he thought, be to the advantage of the colonial administration. Renkin continued as follows:

> The development of private enterprises of a commercial nature is one of the most important factors in the success of colonisation. But the government finds a further motive for promoting their expansion when, as is the case here, such enterprises grasp that the satisfaction of the natives and the improvement of their material and moral situation are preconditions for the development of their economic activities, and desire, on the other hand, to devote a part of their profits to realising these same preconditions.

This is astonishing use of language on the part of the Colonial Minister, who clearly did not wish to understand that the supposed humanitarian concern for the Africans, of which Lever was making so much, was rank hypocrisy. In 1911, Renkin had been criticised for granting huge concessions to the English magnate at a time when he was busy liquidating concessions granted at an earlier date by the Congo Free State. He had defended himself then by arguing that this Englishman would not exert pressure upon the Africans, and he still clung to this same argument. He imagined that the single school which Lever had built in Leverville, and the promises he had made about helping to eradicate sleeping sickness, constituted proof that he wished to devote a share of his profits to promoting the happiness of Africans. Renkin did not pause to wonder why Lever had, from the outset, insisted on the presence of soldiers in the Kwilu concession. He had not understood that the insistence upon having a single *territoire* for this same concession was motivated solely by the calculation that, on the one hand, a single administration could more easily be brought under his thumb, and, on the other, that it would make it easier to exclude from his fiefdom any rivals for palm products, as we shall see below.

Henry replied to Renkin on 6th April 1916, to the effect that, in Vanwert's estimation, Bulungu *territoire* was too big to be merged with Kikwit *territoire*, and that the boundaries of any such single, unified *territoire* could only be settled once the Company had decided precisely which blocks of land it wished to occupy. In the meantime, in a letter dated 22nd March, the management of Lever Brothers renewed its assault upon Renkin, urging him to effect a more stringent administrative control of Leverville region:

> We much appreciated the promise of assistance that His Excellency the Governor-General and the civil servants in Leverville region kindly gave us, but we now believe that, despite their sincerely held intention to come to our aid as far as was possible, they have not managed to keep that promise, on account of cuts in staffing and the many difficulties occasioned by the war . . . We therefore venture to ask whether it might not be desirable to send a special mission to reinforce administrative personnel in Niadi *territoire* [where the population is reckoned to number over 20,000 adult men].

When forwarding this letter to the governor-general, on 20th April, Renkin wrote that he could not accede to this request, and that it would anyway have been impossible to recruit the staff needed for a special mission. He added that the best possible use of existing personnel would be to reinforce the occupation of regions which were economically reliant upon the HCB, while at the same time taking into account all of the government's aims. Henry answered that using existing personnel to reinforce the occupation of Niadi region could be achieved only by abolishing a number of posts, all of which had occasioned the gravest sacrifices when originally established. He further added that, in his view, the HCB would again thrive economically, once the current staff shortages had been addressed.

The reader may well wonder just how the dispatch of two or three additional territorial administrators could strengthen the occupation of Niadi *territoire*. The answer is simple enough. Each local agent was presumed to have a detachment of soldiers at his command, and therefore to be able to play the part of a potentate, driving reluctant villagers towards Lever's factories.

In a letter to the governor-general dated 18th July 1918, Renkin informed him that, according to the management of Lever Brothers, the post at Bulungu was seriously hampering their operations, that it seemed to be of little use to the local administration, and that moving it further inland would enhance the occupation of the region. Lever had asserted that the existence of palm groves in the vast area of Bulungu obviously fostered fraudulent claims, which harmed the company, since it was manifestly hard to distinguish between palm fruit originating in that enclave, and those which, having been harvested from oil palms on land leased by the Company, belonged to it. Renkin asked the Congolese authorities for their opinion on this matter. The said authorities understood that what the HCB wanted was not so much the departure of the State from Bulungu, as the departure of the commercial firms which had set up business there, and which were buying palm nuts from the Africans. They dragged their heels for a whole year before making known their opinion, which was utterly opposed to the interests of the HCB in this regard.[28] (Renkin, for his part, was then no longer in charge of the Colonial Ministry, having quit at the end of 1918.)

The HCB management never again raised the issue of the organisation of the *territoires* in the Kwilu. While awaiting the eagerly anticipated day upon which ministerial directives in support of its recruiting would at last force the territorial service to play an active part in it, the Company continued to shift for itself.

The duplicity, and the claims of the HCB

On 2nd April 1920, the Colonial Minister sent each of the major employers in the Congo a copy of a booklet entitled *Rapport sur l'hygiène des travailleurs noirs, présenté par A. Boigelot*, to which were appended the first regulations in the Belgian Congo covering the welfare of workers.[29] Although these regulations applied only to Katanga, the Ministry circulated the booklet to employers operating outside that province, on the understanding that they could expect to see analogous legislation in their own case.

Forminière aside, the HCB was the only company to welcome the Boigelot report. Furthermore, Forminière's response paled beside the outpouring of fine phrases the HCB had lavished on the report. A similar outpouring featured in the letter that Moseley sent from Liverpool on 27th April 1920 to Renkin's successor, Louis Franck. In this letter Moseley expressed his delight at the official publicity and endorsement accorded by the minister to the report's ideas and conclusions. Much good would result, he went on, "from the awakening of a sense of responsibility on the part of those who had formerly been indifferent, for so grave a matter as the African workforce, as well as from the salutary warning given by the official reiteration of the report's practical conclusions [the penalties laid down in the regulations]". In order to demonstrate to Franck that the HCB was at the forefront of progressive employers in this regard, Moseley next quoted extensively from a letter he had just written to the governor-general, from which some extracts follow:

> We deem it necessary for the legislator to intervene, as much to formulate measures enabling the recruitment of the workforce to occur under more effective, less painful and more certain conditions, as to [develop] checks

and guarantees regarding workers' food, accommodation, wages and medical care . . .

We also reckon that it behoves everyone, and especially the employer, to contribute in a direct and practical way to the fight against sleeping sickness . . .

It is not solely by direct, medical measures that illnesses are fought. Better living conditions have a part to play also, and one should strive, as we have always had it in our hearts to do, to lavish them upon the native populations . . .

If an example were needed to illustrate the above remarks, the model villages set up between Leverville and Kitjaka will serve the purpose . . .[30]

The reader will note that Moseley here pleads for measures that would render recruitment more effective. During this period, the HCB looked fondly on the idea of officially conscripting Africans into the workforce,[31] whereas a form of clandestine conscription was already operative in Elisabetha and Alberta. There is ample evidence for this in the case of Elisabetha, as I shall show below. As for the marvellous conditions that Moseley boasted of having created for his workers, salary and ration together were 8 to 15 francs per month, that is, 25 to 50 centimes per day, which amounts to little more than the pre-war remuneration, despite the massive depreciation of the Belgian franc, which had lost three-quarters of its 1914 value. As for the model villages, we shall hear more of them below, as of the workers' food. And as far as the fight against sleeping sickness is concerned, let me simply note that it was in the hands of an anti-trypanosomic medical mission led by Doctor Jacques Schwetz, who, in the years from 1920 to 1923, practised in several *territoires* in the Kwilu basin and in the neighbouring region of Kamtsha.[32]

We have seen how the HCB claimed that territorial organisation in the Kwilu had to be altered. They also claimed the right to regulate the price of provisions they were buying in Kinshasa to feed their workers in Lusanga. In a letter of 5th October 1920, Beissel asked the governor-general to fix a maximum price for the sale of rice produced locally (in Orientale province and Sankuru district, in particular), smoked fish and *chickwangue*.[33] Beissel explained the motives for his request as follows:

. . . formerly, rice could not be sold to the Africans for more than 15 centimes a kilo; at present, it is sold to them in Kinshasa and in Matadi at 2.50 or 3 francs by small retailers concerned to speculate; the maximum price should be pegged at 0.50 francs in the major centres; an African's ration is generally reckoned to be 0.50 francs a day; daily consumption of rice being as much as half a kilo, at 25 centimes, a black would still have 25 centimes to buy himself oil, fish, seasonings, etc.; as for fish, it is necessary to stop the products of the Pêcheries du Congo being hoarded by small traders; it is also necessary to establish a market price-list in the major centres for this product, and for *chickwangue*.

The governor-general told Beissel that he could not stop middlemen operating between producers and consumers, that the requisitioning of rice had never been successful, that establishing a monopoly over the products of the Pêcheries would only be possible if the latter agreed to it, and that market price-lists stipulating a maximum sale price would force primary producers to abandon their crops. There was nothing to stop major employers, the governor-general added, buying directly at the point of production. The real solution to the problem lay in an increase in production.

The Ministry of Colonies approved the governor-general's response. It saw that Beissel's request implied a curtailment of all trade in the three products mentioned, and it knew that the Company would itself hardly relish such regulations if applied to the sale price of palm oil. The employers, they concluded, could anyway produce a part of their workers' food themselves.[34]

The HCB also laid claim to the right to have villages relocated at its own convenience, to position them close to its own factories (but outside of their compounds), under the authority of chiefs answerable to the Company, in order to extract the maximum possible labour and food-crops. It began by enticing individuals, in the hope that whole communities would follow suit.

In April 1921, the Company complained to the minister that the colonial administration in the Congo had begun to send back Africans from the various encampments which had formed around its factories to their *chefferies* of origin. Franck wrote a letter on this subject to the governor-general, probably at the Company's prompting, pointing out that the colonial administration should try to relocate whole groups, and that the constitution of encampments containing men of diverse ethnic origin in the vicinity of European centres ought certainly to be avoided. Nevertheless, Franck continued, there was good cause to take existing circumstances into account, for the presence of a certain number of Africans might well be desirable so far as the recruitment and feeding of a workforce were concerned. Franck therefore ordered that individuals be left where they were, until such a time as whole groups, to be designated by the HCB, should join them.[35]

There is a revealing paragraph on the situation in Lusanga in the political report on the Congo-Kasai for the second quarter of 1921: "The Company is finding it hard to recruit a workforce in Niadi *territoire*, on account of deaths which are supposed to have occurred at Leverville and during the return journey of certain workers. For this reason, the natives feel some fear at the thought of enlisting."[36] This represents a typical example of the sort of administrative veil that tended to be drawn across painful events. Max Horn, for his part, in his report on the HCB for the financial year 1920–21, described the situation at 30th June 1921 as follows:

- oil production for the financial year: 5,413 tons, three-fifths of which in Lusanga region;
- daily wage (wage plus ration) for an unskilled worker: 1 franc;
- the factory at Kwenge is operative; a factory is under construction at Brabanta, the centre of operations for Basongo circle;
- three "locomotives" are in service on 59 kilometres of narrow-gauge track;
- the school at Alberta is run by Father Albert Dereume, that at Leverville by Father Sylvain Van Hee.

In the same report, Horn vaunts the efforts made by the Company in the fight against trypanosomiasis, noting that "thousands of cases of sleeping-sickness have been treated in villages in Lusanga region by our doctors and their black medical assistants, who have worked with the Schwetz mission".[37] Schwetz himself made the following assessment of the efforts made by the Company in this sphere:

Setting aside the lazaret in Leverville, which holds 50 to 100 patients . . . the Huileries have deployed in Kwilu for a whole year, from May 1920 to May 1921, a second doctor, who has devoted himself almost exclusively to sleeping-sickness. The outcome of this work has, unfortunately, been poor . . . If the Huileries wish to have a serious impact upon sleeping-sickness, all they have to do is . . . to hire some doctors and put them wholly at the disposal of the head of the medical mission. But, instead of that I have been informed that, for reasons of economy, the Huileries do not propose to increase their medical staff in Kwilu. The members of the medical mission have therefore begun to treat sufferers from sleeping sickness in the Huileries posts themselves.[38]

A letter from Liverpool dated 13th December 1921 indicated that the problems affecting recruitment were on the way to being resolved. In this letter, Moseley informed Franck, the Colonial Minister, that the most recent mail from the Congo had brought heartening news as regards the workforce.

The recent tour of the governor-general through the HCB regions would seem to have had a real impact. Moseley continued as follows, in a tone astonishingly obsequious for a business letter:

> It is our wish that this admirable initiative should soon bear fruit on all sides and it is with the utmost confidence that we anticipate the benefits it may bring the whole Colony. We have the honour to express to you our profound gratitude and to beg you kindly to transmit to his Excellency the Governor-General the high esteem in which we hold the assistance that he has deigned to give us.[39]

On 8th May 1922, Horn confirmed the good news announced in Moseley's letter. He wrote that palm-oil production had risen steeply in the month of March, because territorial civil servants, apparently on the governor-general's orders, had "applied themselves more to encouraging natives to work for the Company". The governor-general in question was Maurice Lippens, an advocate of forced labour in the Congo—as is plain from his 1922 circulars, from which I have quoted elsewhere.[40] In the circular dated January 1922 he particularly deplored the fact that, in the course of his journey across the Congolese provinces, he had been compelled to acknowledge that the authorities were not always lending adequate support to the colonists, traders, agents and directors of the commercial and industrial firms, large or small. He added that all government agents and civil servants should realise that it was their paramount duty to uphold such efforts.

Horn's report commented upon another important issue, namely, the discussions broached a fortnight before between the Colonial Minister and William Lever regarding the granting to the latter of a monopoly over the oil and palm-nut trade across the whole of his five circles, which measured 5.5 million hectares, or almost twice the surface area of Belgium. This monopoly would be created through the formula of tripartite contracts, concocted by Horn. (I will return to this issue in chapter 3.) A decree of 16th March 1922 recast and consolidated the measures to be taken concerning Africans' labour contracts in the Congo. It remained in force, albeit with a few modifications, for the remainder of the colonial period. It placed the employer under an obligation to furnish the hired man with, aside from his wage, sufficient food, suitable accommodation, bedding, and medical care in case of sickness. It empowered provincial governors to determine, through ordinances on health and safety, the conditions to be observed regarding food, accommodation, bedding and medical care. It authorised the employer to deduct fines from workers' wages due on the day on which they had been incurred. It made provision for prison sentences for workers who reneged upon their obligations, namely, sentences of from two to three months for dishonesty, and of a fortnight for violations of work discipline.

Beissel, however, was dissatisfied with a number of the measures laid down in this decree. In a letter dated 22nd November 1922 he made known his dissatisfaction to Doctor Albert Duren, Inspector of Industrial Hygiene, who had come to explain to him the nature of the obligations incumbent upon employers as regards food, accommodation, bedding (blankets, *pagnes*)[41] and medical care, by virtue of ordinance no. 58 of 23rd July 1922, adopted by the governor of Congo-Kasai in execution of the above decree. Beissel wrote to Duren that certain aspects of the decree constituted an idler's charter, in particular the clauses which stipulated that the sum held back by an employer for a day's absence from work could only come from the daily wage. The sum withheld—in the form of the daily wage—amounted to 40 centimes, whereas the worker received an advance of 1.60 francs per day in the form of ration, accommodation and equipment. Other measures aside from fines were needed, Beissel went on, to combat absenteeism. "As the man hired could not renege more seriously upon his obligations than by abstaining from work without a plausible excuse, I would venture to hope", Beissel concluded, "that the prison sentences recommended would be applied with all due rigour in the case of unjustified, repeated absences. I would be glad to receive some reassurance in this regard."

Beissel forwarded to the provincial governor a copy of his letter to Duren, and likewise asked him to combat absenteeism with prison sentences of from two to three months. (As if to counter Moseley's fine phrases, Beissel emphasised that what the workforce needed, first and foremost, was prison and a crust of bread.) Writing on the provincial governor's behalf, his deputy, the commissioner general Alphonse Engels, answered that a sentence of two months could be imposed, but that a fortnight seemed more appropriate, given that, for it to be applied, the employer did not have to prove that the worker had been dishonest.[42]

A note on the relocation of the Luba of Kasai
to the Tshikapa diamond mines (Forminière) (1919–1920)

From 1918 onwards, the HCB tried to persuade the State to have villages relocated nearer to their factories and installations. They would pursue this same aim for twenty years, as the remainder of this narrative will show. The HCB was, however, not the only firm to have done so. Indeed, Forminière (Société internationale forestière et minière du Congo), a huge company mining for diamonds at Tshikapa in the Kasai—half-owned by the Belgian state but under American management—had for ten years pursued the policy of resettling the Luba near to its mines.

The Luba people, fixed since time immemorial between the Lubi river and the great Lualaba lakes in Katanga province, had suffered greatly from razzias, perpetrated at first by Ngongo Leteta, a vassal of Tippu Tip, and latterly by Mpania Mutombo and Lumpungu, who were prominent auxiliaries of the Belgian state.[43] Consequently, from 1895 onwards the Luba were to be found scattered across the Kananga-Dibaya region, and also at various points along the Lulua river. Being now dispersed, without land of their own, and often treated as slaves by the other native peoples, the Luba tended to see in the European a harbinger of better times. They were industrious, and therefore willing to collaborate, whereas the native peoples of the country between the Kasai and the Lulua rivers were full of mistrust.[44]

It was from among the Luba that Catholic missionaries from Scheut found, at Mikalayi, Bukonde, Tshilundu and Tshilomba, the thousands of adults and children who entered their missions in the years before 1900.[45] The colonial administration for Kasai district (its administrative seat in Luebo) likewise chose Luba to be workers for Forminière, once that company commenced operations at Tshikapa in 1912, while the local Tshokwe population kept its distance. As a consequence, Forminière had 3,000 workers at its disposal in 1916, brought from the banks of the Lulua, in part from the area surrounding the post at Luebo, to where the Luba had earlier been led in search of a better life. The Forminière settled them on the edge of its concession, in villages on the right bank of the Kasai. From 1917 on, the company sought to settle yet more Luba contingents inside the concession, especially upon the Tshikapa–Angola motor vehicle road which it had built along the watershed between the Tshikapa and Longatshimo rivers.

The relocation had been completed by the end of 1920. At the beginning of that same year, Maurice de la Kethulle, the director of the department for economic affairs in Boma, went on a tour of inspection to Tshikapa and noted that the workers' food rations were inadequate.[46] At the beginning of the following year, he went again and drafted a report incorporating his findings, which has not been preserved, but which must have been utterly damning so far as Forminière was concerned, to judge by the commentary on it made by acting Governor-General Martin Rutten on 8th May 1921 in his biographical notes on Maurice de la Kethulle. The commentary reads as follows: "de la Kethulle has produced a very interesting and very useful report. My only criticism concerns his tendency to formulate his judgements in too cutting a tone, so that he risks causing offence when he would do better to persuade."[47] Towards the end of 1922, the Colony's chief medical officer, Alphonse Rhodain, noted that the dietary situation at Forminière had improved a little, but not enough.[48]

How many workers did the relocation of the Luba in 1919–20 bring to Forminière? In order to make an estimate, I have only two figures, namely, the number of men at work in 1918 and in 1921: 4,000[49] and 10,000 respectively.[50] Since the difference amounts to 6,000, I presume that the greater part of this difference derives from the relocation. Between 1921 and 1924, the workforce at Forminière would increase from 10,000 to 20,000 men, chiefly on account of some 6,000 workers supplied by the Bourse du Travail du Kasai.[51]

In November 1923, the Belgian journalist Chalux visited Forminière's Tshikapa concession and gave what was, generally speaking, a very flattering account. He was especially full of praise for the so-called roadside villages, that is to say, workers' villages built along the roads. When he passed through, there were already some twenty of them. The whole of his narrative strikes one as improbable in light of the following remark: "the crucial point is that these roadside villages have not been created solely for the profit of Forminière, but in order to reward those of its workers who have been in its service for a minimum of eight years." It is plain enough from the archives that the construction of these villages was only embarked upon in 1919, during the relocation of the Luba of Dibaya. Furthermore, the same system was still being applied in 1923, since Chalux tells us that newcomers supplied by the Bourse du Travail du Kasai were offered "a spade, a machete and six months' worth of rations".[52]

The resettling of the Luba on Lulua land in the vicinity of the Scheut missions, on Tshokwe land in the vicinity of the Scheut missions, and on Tshokwe land in the Forminière concession, had a bloody sequel in 1959–61, when the *pax belgica* in the Congo broke down. The Lulua attacked and hunted down the Luba living in the vicinity of the missions, while the Tshokwe fell upon those settled in the "roadside villages". There were thousands of deaths, and Forminière had to withdraw from its Tshikapa concession.[53]

The Lejeune Report (1923)

The moving of villages

As mentioned in chapter 1, from 1918 on the HCB was attempting to move villages towards its factories, against the wishes of the local administration, but with the blessing of Minister Franck. In July 1923 the governor of the Congo-Kasai, Léon Bureau, warned Sidney Edkins, recently appointed managing director of HCB in the Congo, against any further such initiatives. In response to this warning, Edkins replied on 3rd August that the government's attitude towards the locating of African settlements in the vicinity of HCB posts was more or less identical with what the Huileries professed:

> so much so that we cannot discern any obstacle to our projects being realised. Indeed, we have never dreamed of constituting small groups, which could only have been formed through the dismantling of neigh- bouring collectivities, around our industrial centres, but, on the contrary, we have always supposed that any groups settling within our concessions would be constituted by these same collectivities, under the authority of their traditional chiefs.

Edkins went on to reassure Bureau that the company was minded to permit these collectivities the use of all the land they required, and to build model villages for them.

It fell to Alphonse Engels, Bureau's successor as provincial governor, to respond to this letter. In a missive of 11th August, he stated that he could see no objection to a group, if it enjoyed political independence, moving to an HCB concession, on condition that it had the use of land of surface area and value equivalent to what it had possessed before, and that it could exercise the same hunting and gathering rights, in particular, the right to grant products it had picked to whomsoever it pleased. He noted, however, that the labour power of such a group was not the exclusive preserve of the company. Engels then advised Edkins to deal not with collectivities but with individuals, who would be under an obligation to lend their services to the Huileries in return for the advantages granted to them by the company, advantages arising out of the fact of having model villages at their disposal. He continued as follows: "We would recommend that, where necessary, our territorial personnel should conduct an active and unremitting propaganda campaign to persuade chiefs and natives that each village in *territoires* bordering upon your factories should send a contingent of men, and for preference whole households, to these agricultural and industrial villages."[1] Edkins replied as follows on 16th August: "From now on we shall do everything in our power to guarantee natives wishing to come and settle with their families in the immediate vicinity of our industrial centres a comfortable house [in dried brick] and a plot of land suited to market-gardening . . . We have no doubts that the government will lend us the [promised] help."

Edkins enclosed with his letter the standard contract that the company was planning to have candidates for the model villages sign, and asked Engels to approve it. He pointed out that this contract would allow the Africans the option of returning to their village for periods of several months, at least twice a month. On 30th August, Engels replied to Edkins. He was calling upon the commissioner of Kwango district, he said, to recommend that the territorial administrators in the vicinity of Lusanga should launch an active and unrelenting propaganda campaign aimed at chiefs and villagers, to the effect that each village should send to the Huileries a contingent proportionate to its size. The proposed contract met with his approval, with the proviso that during the periods of leave the men would still be free to work, either for themselves or for third parties. On 8th September, Edkins thanked Engels effusively, in a letter several paragraphs long, one of which read as follows: "We will spare no sacrifice in order to set up . . . these settlements of workers' families which should, in our opinion, wholly transform the living conditions of the workforce, by providing it with . . . comfort, security and a uniform standard of living which will certainly constitute a major advance."[2]

After Engels had informed him that Sören Sörensen, the district commissioner of Kwango, would travel round checking that chiefs and their subjects were acting upon the administration's recommendations,[3] Edkins reassured the interim governor on 3rd October that the necessary arrangements for the construction of the model villages were now in place. He further added that it was his intention to provide his workforce with good moral and material living conditions, as rapidly as possible and with the help given by the government to the Huileries.

The general government in Boma was increasingly irritated by this correspondence, which had been forwarded at regular intervals by Engels. On 4th October, the secretary general, Henri Postiaux, sent the following note to the interim governor-general, Léon Bureau:

> The HCB is not as yet asking us altogether to take its place in furnishing it with the workforce it needs, but the assistance that has been requested of our territorial heads seems to me already appreciably to exceed what we have so far agreed to do for private enterprises.
>
> I ought to make it plain that I am no supporter of a system that involves favouring the settlement of families, bound by contracts, on HCB land, where, once they have planted their crops (and abandoned those they had planted in their villages of origin), they will be more or less at the mercy of their employer.
>
> The proposed system raises real dangers, which might be exacerbated when its implementation is entrusted to persons whose treatment of the natives has not always been above reproach. (How many times have we had to remind them of their obligations?)

On 11th October, Bureau informed Engels that he in no way supported a system which would impel several families from each village to settle in the immediate vicinity of the industrial centres in Lusanga circle. Bureau asked him to tell the Société des Huileries that the government could not look favourably upon the creation, within its concessions, of workers' villages populated by emigrants from neighbouring *chefferies*. He stressed that in any case the local territorial authorities would have to play a part in suggesting or facilitating such transfers, whether collective or individual. Bureau's order was based upon a whole series of reasons, the main ones being as follows:

- The system as defined risks inflicting irreparable damage upon the *chefferies*, for it is obviously altogether out of the question to accord the HCB the exclusive right to create industrial settlements at the expense of native sub-groups.
- The HCB deceives itself in supposing that the mere existence of such villages will guarantee it a reserve of workers in the vicinity of its factories. It is incontestable that, for the native to undertake labour which is fairly hard, or from which little pleasure is to be had, a degree of coercion will have to be used. This coercion is more or less legal

when it emanates from the colonial authorities, and above all from native chiefs. Such authority cannot be vested in a company.

- The inhabitants of the new villages will have been removed for good from the already existing collectivities. This is bound to displease the chiefs, and will cause them to lose interest in, or even to thwart, subsequent recruitments. Now, the Huileries is not the only company in need of labour, and in the light of legislation prohibiting forced labour in the strict sense, there are very few [territorial] administrators who, without the effective help, freely given, of the chiefs, could hope to arrive at a satisfactory solution to the problem of supplying workers in sufficient numbers to meet the ever-growing need.
- The new villages will become places of refuge for men and women who have clashed either with their chief or with the administrative or judicial authority. By virtue of what rights could the Company co-operate in handing over such fugitives? One may well suspect the impartiality of its employees in performing such an action, which would represent interference by a private body in functions that the blacks know perfectly well are the exclusive preserve of the colonial authorities.

In his letter Bureau also touched upon the question of land for "candidate-workers", a term used by him to refer to the future inhabitants of the planned villages. Closer examination of this question seemed pointless, Bureau observed, in light of the reasons listed above, and would serve only to demonstrate still more conclusively that the creation of the aforesaid villages was impossible. In a marginal note on this same subject, Boma Land Registry wrote: "If the native does not own in his own right the land on which he is to be settled, and which is necessary to him, it would be slavery."[4]

In a letter dated 29th October, Engels notified Bureau that he had immediately informed Edkins and the district commissioner of the Kwango of his point-blank refusal of the HCB villages project. In later passages of the same letter, however, he intimated that he had taken this decision reluctantly. "I have the impression", he wrote, "that this question has been dogged by serious misunderstandings. Large-scale industries, when they are well organised, should lead to the creation of worker settlements around them. Large-scale industry cannot coexist with native sub-groups as they now are." Engels went on to say that something other than the system currently in use was needed to supply the HCB with labour. Long-distance, short-term recruitment was eminently harmful to the race. Ceaseless movement, he continued, or the shuttling of men between village and factory, spread disease, imposed arduous journeys, and sundered traditional ties. It left a worker without a home as such, and often kept him apart from his wife for long stretches of time. Continual recruitment was costly, and therefore prevented private companies from providing their personnel with good wages, diet or accommodation.[5]

Engels' concluding remark echoes the opinion voiced by Edkins during an interview with Bureau on 14th July: a long-term contract was the necessary corollary of the employer's obligation to provide good accommodation, diet and medical care for his workers, an opinion challenged by Bureau. As far as policy towards the HCB was concerned, Bureau would certainly prove to be a more critical governor than Engels. Both men, however, failed to put their finger on the real reason for the repugnance felt by Africans for Lever's enterprise, namely, the utter inadequacy of the wages. I am convinced that the paying of decent wages would have rendered the use of coercion in recruitment superfluous, and would have given rise quite naturally to longer terms of service.

It was in a letter of 26th October that Engels had informed Edkins, in no more than a few words, of the governor-general's decision to reject his project for "model villages for workers". Edkins responded with a vigorous defence of the scheme, three pages long, which closed with the assertion that the rejection was surely based upon a misunderstanding, the underlying reasons for which he would be glad to know.[6] On 22nd November, Engels forwarded this response to Bureau, observing that he, for his part, reckoned that the Company was entirely in the right. Nevertheless, he added, "if your position on this question is still unchanged, I will tell the company why you have decided to condemn the creation of industrial villages and I will request it to let the matter drop".[7] Thus, the affair was concluded, at any rate for the time being.

The Lejeune report

In his copious correspondence on model villages, Edkins was forever vaunting the efforts of the HCB to improve the living conditions of Africans in the Kwilu. How things really stood we shall see shortly, through the report that the medical officer for Congo-Kasai province, Dr. Emile Lejeune, drafted at Kikwit on 8th December 1923, after a six-day tour of inspection in Lusanga circle, between 25th and 30th November. In order fully to understand this report and its repercussions, it is necessary to appreciate that ordinance 58 of 23rd July 1922 on healthcare provision for workers had been replaced, after the employers had exerted some pressure, by ordinance 47 of 12th August 1923. The new ordinance was not as strict as the earlier version had been. Whereas, for example, ordinance

58 had laid down that the ration should be paid in kind, save to workers earning a daily wage of at least 1.50 francs, to whom one could tender its equivalent in money, ordinance 47 stipulated the same thing, while adding that as an interim measure the employer could guarantee the supply of food to his workers by tendering cash, which would enable them to buy the quantity of foodstuffs necessary to feed themselves. In the covering letter sent with his report, Lejeune wrote to Governor Engels as follows:

> I trust that my visit will have more tangible effects than that of Chief Medical Officer Rhodain, almost a year ago. Mr. Rhodain identified many shortcomings and errors, and made various suggestions, but aside from a small improvement in the ration, which is anyway still decidedly inadequate, no serious steps have been taken since his visit. I therefore make so bold as to insist that you use your high authority, and oblige the HCB to perfect its methods for improving the wretched situation brought to your attention here. I know that large sums have been spent, but this seems to me not to be enough. The organisation of frequent and regular inspections by well-informed provincial inspectors on behalf of [the Department] of Trade and Industry, seems to me to be a necessity that I take the liberty of suggesting to you. It is difficult, it seems to me, for local administrators to take action, their authority being slight by comparison with the massive influence wielded by the Mbila Company which, although all its agents assert its profound wish to obey the law, seems to go no further than voicing its good intentions.[8]

I now present lengthy extracts from the Lejeune report itself, with my comments and clarifications added in square brackets:

The HCB employ 3,000 workers in Leverville and its environs, 1,500 in Kwenge and its environs and 2,000 in Tango.

The company itself differentiates between workers who are local, and workers who have been imported. It defines as local all those whose villages of origin are not more than around ten hours from the workplace, and as imported all those who come from further afield. It is on this distinction that rules governing the payment and rationing of men, as also accommodation, are based.

Local workers are not issued with rations and earn a little more; the imported workers are issued with rations and earn a little less. Camps are built for imported workers, whereas local workers house themselves, often in the neighbourhood of work centres, where they set up pseudo-villages. It is there that their relatives and friends come to bring them whatever provisions they need.

This distinction between imported and local workers does not seem to me to be always consistent with the decree on labour contracts. [In fact the decree on the labour contract does not make this distinction, which was probably dreamed up by the HCB, in the context of its plan for relocating villages, so as to persuade local workers to move nearer to company posts.] The attached lists concerning Leverville and Kwenge give the approximate number of workers in each category. [The lists give 2,004 locals and 961 imported (a total of 2,965) for Leverville, and 1,515 locals and 330 imported (a total of 1,845) for Kwenge.] These figures are not wholly accurate, as I was able to discover when checking the figures for post 8 in Leverville, where I was informed that there were 298 workers, when in fact there are almost 400.

Recruitment
The recruits are hired for three months, generally speaking, and are given neither blanket nor *pagne* [the equipment stipulated in ordinance 47]. Nights are cold in the Kwilu, however. Sometimes a thick mist covers the river bed until late in the morning and the Europeans for their part have to wrap up warm. Furthermore, the majority of deaths are due to respiratory ailments. I regard blankets as an absolute necessity.

The workers are not always adults. A very large number of adolescents, and even children, are employed by the HCB. This work of healthy non-adults is permitted in certain circumstances in the agricultural enterprises. But I have observed children or young adolescents, at Leverville itself, pushing wagons, and on boats on the river Kwilu loading timber and fruit. They are not of an age to do such work.

The issuance of rations to the imported workers
The four types of ration stipulated in the terms of service, consisting of rice (or millet, manioc, maize), dried fish, meat and oil, all provide far too few proteins, carbohydrates, fats and calories. I have discovered that, generally speaking, oil is not issued. Furthermore, the ration is not issued on Sundays, and this diminishes the value of the types of ration by one seventh. After each type I have specified how far it is deficient, and what elements would therefore be needed to supplement it. Examination of the four types of ration seems to indicate, on the part of the company, a concern to give the different blacks the type of food which is to their taste. In theory this is commendable, but in practice the blacks do not have a choice. They receive whatever provisions are to hand.

On the other hand, the blacks lack the pans and utensils needed for the preparation of their food, so that preparation is often unhygienic or unpleasing.

Each team of 20 men is looked after, in theory, by a "kook", who cooks the daily ration, the rice, in a large iron pot. At midday, the cooked rice is handed round on palm leaves, and consumed straight away in the open air, with a little dried fish, which the blacks eat raw, probably because they have no pan in which to cook it. The oil, when there is any, is poured over the rice.

The blacks have just this one meal a day. Some of them keep a portion back, and eat it cold in the evening.

Sometimes, there is no cook. This, I found, was the case in the experimental palm grove, where 200 workers are employed.

I have also seen the [imported] Yanzi receive nothing else but 750 grams of *chickwangue* and 100 grams of fish.

At Leverville, the Europeans generally claim that the ration is quite sufficient! I discovered that the Yanzi arrange for caravans of provisions to be brought from home, so as to compensate for the shortcomings of the ration issued to them, and the same is true of the imported workers at the agricultural posts, as I learned in particular from M. Cotton at post 5.

Anyone familiar with the abundant portions the blacks ordinarily consume, and the hygienic conditions under which food is prepared in the villages, will not be surprised at their dissatisfaction with the diet offered at the company posts.

Accommodation

In Leverville there is a brick-built camp, which would be good if there were latrines, kitchens and a rubbish pit, and if it were fenced in, cleared of brushwood and regularly whitewashed. Besides, this camp is only large enough for a very small fraction of the workers currently at the post.

I have seen the camp of the imported Yanzi [whose overcrowding had been particularly criticised by Rhodain during his inspection in November 1922, but later put an end to, according to Horn, in a statement to the minister].[9] The camp consists of straw houses in which from 10 to 20 men sleep in cramped conditions, on pallets upon which 7 or 8 at the most should be accommodated. The camp is in reality little better than a simple night shelter of poor quality.

The workers living in this camp, 400 in number, have to carry all their valuables with them when they go off to work, for nothing can be locked up. They therefore set out in the morning, around six o'clock, with their sacks and without having eaten. They get THE MEAL at midday, and return in the evening. They have the whole night to chat and to sleep, but nothing to get their teeth into. If they came with their wife, they would not be given any suitable accommodation. Finally, newcomers often have no shelter, and have to fend for themselves. One may readily understand how it is that, given such conditions, they refuse, after a first stint of three months, to re-enlist . . .

Local workers settle in the vicinity of the central posts or of the agricultural posts. Some elders have installed their Penates, and others, who are their "kith and kin", may then cluster around them, on a more temporary basis. These small villages are very dirty, unplanned and unhygienic. If this way of proceeding is accepted, it is at any rate incumbent upon the entrepreneur to take in hand the setting-up and the upkeep of these villages.

An analogous situation is to be found in the agricultural posts: houses that are neither clean nor cared for, too small for the number of men who live there, and camps without latrines, fences, incinerators, etc.

Generally speaking, the workers live in cramped conditions.

Clothing
In the HCB, no clothes are provided for the blacks.

Conclusions
Rations, accommodation and clothing are inadequate, and on each count the company is to blame. Whilst it is true that a few former workers, installed with their families, close to the camps, live comfortably, the imported workers, who are single, cannot do the work that is asked of them and still remain healthy under existing conditions.

I am persuaded that these imported workers, when they complete their term of three months, have lost weight, when they ought to have gained some, and I can well understand workers shunning work with the HCB, where they find nothing to attract them, and where nothing is done to render their leisure more pleasant.

The district has instructed administrators to help the HCB with recruitment. Personally, if I were an administrator, I would not send a single worker to the company. I understand, and I strongly favour, the notion of government coming to the aid of companies, but I think it is impolitic, and that we do not have the right not to defend the native, by demanding for him a minimum which would guarantee to some extent the existence of his wretched race.

What the HCB plan to do

– Recruitment: construct barns on the roads usually taken by recruits, and a rest camp at Leverville.

– Ration: the company says that it wishes to comply with the existing regulations. Yet the most recent directives issued by the managing director in Kinshasa specified rations consisting of 420 grams of rice a day, plus 1 franc 80 centimes a week. (An erroneous or mischievous interpretation of article 19 of ordinance 47.) [This article authorised, as an interim measure, where rationing was partly in kind, the tendering of cash allowing the purchase of what was still needed.] For guidance, in Leverville a kilo of fish costs 3 francs.

– Camps: the company has allotted a substantial sum towards the con-struction, in brick, of permanent agricultural camps. It seems that the scheme is to be implemented immediately. I have seen several brick-making machines arrive from Leverville.

What should be done

Ordinance 47, which seems to have been wholly disregarded, should be rigorously applied.

1. The recruits should, if possible, be adults who do not suffer from sleeping sickness. They should be properly dressed. They should be examined by a doctor on arrival and when they leave. It is crucial to determine which are local, and which are imported workers, and the diet should be adjusted to suit workers in each of these categories.

2. A statutory ration, which is adequate, should be issued to all workers.

3. The camps should be fitted out without delay so as to comply with the recommendations [of ordinance 47] and *chefs de camp* appointed solely in order to look after the blacks. The villages of local workers should themselves be built under European supervision. When one is employing 7,000 men, and one plans later to use some 14,000, it makes sense to introduce a European service of some size to take responsibility for these men. I would ascribe all current difficulties to the lack of such a service.

4. Children should not be burdened [with adult work].

Lejeune rounded off his report with a note on the organisation of the HCB medical service in Lusanga circle. Here are some extended extracts:

The centre of operations is in Leverville, where a doctor is resident, and is responsible for a hospital for Europeans, a hospital for blacks and a lazaret. A second doctor resides in Tango, but the HCB is proposing to send him very soon on a tour of the agricultural posts. At present, he is tied to Tango, and is responsible only for a very small infirmary.

In principle, sick Europeans in Leverville and in Kwenge are treated in Leverville, while those in Tango, if they do not need to be hospitalised, are treated on the spot.

Things are much the same with the blacks. There are about 25 agricultural stations or posts around Leverville and Kwenge. Some have black nurses, while others have none. The sick and the slightly injured should in theory be treated on the spot, but serious cases can be conveyed within a few hours to the doctor in Leverville.

In practice, however, the few nurses attached to agricultural posts are wholly insufficient and inadequately equipped; even those agricultural posts with a European in residence lack the basic necessities. The sick are given either minimal treatment or no treatment at all. They are full of mistrust and, if their condition is somewhat serious, disappear and return to their villages to be cured or to die. Indeed, the doctors in Leverville see only a very small proportion of all cases.

It may be objected that one has no right to retain sick people by force, in order to treat them, but to this I would reply that the natives, when they are well cared for, come of their own accord, immediately and in significant numbers, to ask for treatment. If the blacks in the HCB lack such trust, this is because the necessary steps have not been taken to win it . . .

Hospital for blacks

This hospital is brick-built, with wooden beds for 30 patients, a surgical ward—set up in one of the sick-rooms, which, though gloomy, can be, and is used—a dispensary and some kitchens.

The wards, very good when all is said and done, were very badly looked after and inadequately cleaned, in spite of improvements already introduced by Doctor Moncarey.

The dispensary is too small, and was dirty and badly organised. It seemed to me impossible to do serious work there.

The kitchen was not in regular use, and the ration was inadequate. I saw a worker with a fractured thigh, still not mended after three months, who since his accident had been fed a diet without any vitamins!

There are three latrines, with "Arab trenches", very badly built, and a morgue which ought to be knocked down and re-built: its floor is of beaten earth, across which infected fluids flow, and the see-through partitions attract flies.

The hospital has no perimeter fence.

It is worth pointing out that, for the 4,500 workers employed in the Leverville-Kwenge complex, there should be 225 beds in the hospital. Yet the plan is now to increase the number of beds to 60.

When I visited, there were only a dozen or so patients.

Lazaret

It is still the old, wretched lazaret made of corrugated iron, as described a year ago by the chief medical officer. Nothing has changed. There is not even a small dispensary for preparing and giving injections.

There is no real supervision; the patients sleep on the ground, without blankets, and the cooking is not properly organised. I therefore imagine that advanced cases receive little treatment. This lazaret leaves a very painful impression.

The infirmaries in the agricultural posts

I have seen the nurse at post 6 in the Kwilu. He has no shelter-infirmary and has the most rudimentary equipment and dressings. In such circumstances, the medicine he practices is obviously laughable, and to settle, for form's sake or in order to abide by the law, for such basic care is to end up with an outcome the precise opposite of what we seek. At post 8, which is maintained by a European, there was not even the means to dress a wound. No register of the sick was kept in either of these two posts.

I saw in the village behind post 8 a patient in the advanced stages of sleeping sickness who was dying, abandoned even by the natives. Even though he was a former HCB worker, no one had even thought to send him to the lazaret. This had not been the custom!

The organisation of medical work at Leverville

Blacks who are wounded or sick visit in the morning, in a dispensary on the river bank. The doctor then sends those patients in need of special treatment to the hospital dispensary. Whites are examined and treated at the Europeans' hospital. The existence of several different premises seems to me to hamper the smooth running of the service.

Deaths, cemeteries

Leverville has one cemetery for those blacks who die in the lazaret and another for those who die of other conditions in the hospital. There is a need for both, since the lazaret lies on the other side of the Kwenge, and since transportation of the dead from the lazaret to the general cemetery is inadvisable. The latter is twenty minutes at least from the factory.

The general state of the cemeteries leaves much to be desired. They are not fenced off; some tombs have no number, and the burial registers are not kept correctly.

The cemetery for the lazaret contains 150 graves, the other almost 500.

In the past, the doctor was not even informed of deaths occurring in the agricultural posts. More recently, the medical service has begun to insist that it be kept informed, but, as I said above, many people, when they fall ill, go back home to die.

Mortality and morbidity

Given what I have said above, there is no need for me to enlarge upon these topics. It is not possible to ascertain with any degree of accuracy what rates of mortality, still less rates of morbidity, are among the workers in the Huileries.

Certain missionaries have complained of very high mortality rates among the recruited workers, but these cannot be confirmed, for want of documentation.

A report drafted by His Excellency Governor Bureau indicates, among certain groups of workers, a mortality rate of 9% in three months, which is huge, but once again, for want of reliable documentation, it is impossible to pin it down precisely.

I have found the most frequent causes of death recorded in 1923 to be bronchial infections and pneumonias. The hospital register also refers to 5 septicaemias and 1 tuberculosis.

Conclusions

To sum up, I have found things to be in a deplorable state, and I have been deeply disillusioned by the flagrant practical shortcomings of the HCB's medical service so far as the treatment of its blacks in Leverville and Kwenge is concerned. There is a very long way to go before we achieve medical care for natives throughout the circle, workers or otherwise, or active intervention in the fight against sleeping sickness.

It is deeply to be regretted that, after so many years of work, and probably after so much money spent, the real situation in Lusanga is not more satisfactory.

The improvements [to be made in order to achieve an adequate medical service, improvements listed by Lejeune] and the smooth running of the service, once the proper organisation is in place, cannot be effected by just two doctors, the current staff. We need at least one itinerant doctor answerable to the doctor in Leverville, with the doctor in Tango staying put and assuming responsibility for the neighbouring agricultural posts . . .

I have called for the suppression of the 1916 convention with the HCB, which was designed to extract from this company a commitment to providing general medical care for the natives in the circle and to participating actively in the fight against sleeping sickness. The government should not demand from the company things which it cannot give; but it should demand that it provide medical care for its employees.[10]

On 22nd December, Engels informed Edkins that he had just received the Lejeune report, a copy of which had been forwarded to Wilson, the director in Leverville. He asked him to acquaint him as soon as possible with any measures taken to ensure observance of the decree of 16th March 1922, and of ordinance 47 on workers' health and safety. He added that it was his intention in the near future to check that they were being strictly applied, given the utter lack of any effective response to the observations and suggestions made the year before by Chief Medical Officer Rhodain.[11]

Lejeune had good cause to write to Engels, in the above-cited covering letter sent with the report, that one ought not to hope for too much from the steps taken by territorial administrators to improve the treatment given to HCB workers. When asked by their superiors to provide information on this topic, the administrators simply fed back to them the data furnished them by company agents. The best proof of this fact is supplied by two responses dated 20th December 1923, given by the territorial administrator of Bulungu, Jacques Kevers. In the first response Kevers pointed out that, according to information supplied to him by HCB agent Symons, the company had recruited around 400 workers in the Gobari region; that 5 of them had died; that 4, having fallen ill and returned to their village, were simply waiting until they were cured before resuming work; and that all of them, being housed and fed by the company, were content with the way in which they were treated, and with the payment they were receiving (on average, 50 francs per man at the end of their three months' period of service).

In the second response, Kevers alleged that credence had to be given to the claims made by the director general of the HCB in Lusanga, Elso Dusseljé, a Dutchman, who had entered the company's service in 1916 after a career of fifteen years in the concessionary companies of the French Congo. Among these claims, the following falsehoods were to be found:

- All the imported workers received a ration of 500 grams of rice, 10 grams of salt and 100 grams of smoked fish or meat. (The terms of service mentioned by Lejeune refer to 450 grams of rice or to 200 grams of millet, manioc or maize to make up the quantities.)

- The fruit cutters were housed in their own villages and offered their labour in the immediate vicinity of the latter.
- The Huileries doctors gave free medical care not only to their own workers, but also to all Africans who were not employed by private companies. The latter were also treated, but the employer had to pay the cost of treatment.[12]

Furthermore, the territorial authorities would sometimes draw erroneous conclusions from the information which they passed on to others. Consider, by way of example, the case of Vanwaeyenberge, the territorial adminis-trator of Kikwit, who stated on 4th January 1924 that, of the 60 workers supplied by the chiefs of the villages of Kasendji and Lumbi, 13 had died. Sörensen commented as follows: "the chiefs seem to have exaggerated greatly, and one should not set too much store by their declarations". Engels, however, came to the opposite conclusion: "the terms of service being for three months, the mortality rate would rise to 13 x 12 x 100 divided by 3 x 60 = 86.66%".[13]

In the meantime, Edkins, having received notice of the governor-general's decision to reject his plan to shift the villages towards his posts, raised the recruitment issue once again. In a long letter of 18th December 1923 to Governor Engels, he had set out to prove that his company's failure to recruit could not be imputed to the manner in which it treated its workers. Indeed, Edkins claimed:

natives in our service are better fed than they would be in their own villages. The rates of pay accorded to our personnel are the highest in the district. Ordinary workers are paid 1 franc for their ration and 50 centimes for their wage for each day's work. The cutters, who are entitled to 1 franc for their ration and 50 centimes per crate of fruit cut, can easily supply two crates per day. The reason for the failure of our recruitment is purely and simply the repugnance felt by blacks for every kind of work and every kind of sustained effort. The villagers even refuse to carry the luggage of civil servants, as our agent Geno and myself have observed. Our agent Cotton has reported that tons of rubber, grass and palm–nuts rotted in the villages, simply because of a reluctance to transport them . . .

I would readily concede that the villagers' repugnance is heightened by the fact that work for the HCB generally entails separation from wife and family, and chiefs tend to be opposed to the departure of the women, for fear that those under their jurisdiction might definitively abandon their group, and settle in the vicinity of the Huileries posts. Yet you would surely allow that the labour shortage, which cannot be corrected by us, cannot endure for long without *compromising the very existence of our interests*, which represent so large a part of economic activity in the Colony.

Would the government not agree, Edkins asked by way of conclusion:

to take measures in our favour which have enabled, and still do enable us, to assemble in other regions sizeable quotas of workers? Since the government, without infringing upon existing legislation, has acted thus in favour of numerous enterprises whose work regime is often harsher than that of the HCB, could we not hope to benefit from similar assistance?

Engels replied to Edkins on 26th December:

I am forwarding your letter to the Governor-General, given that I cannot comply with your request for special assistance with the recruitment of your workforce. Like you, I believe that the labour shortage from which you suffer is liable to compromise, if not the existence, at any rate the further development of your interests, but I cannot go along with your assertion that the cause of this situation has nothing to do with your own practice.

I continue to believe that the Société des Huileries du Congo Belge has not done everything that it should have done—everything that can be done to attract the native to its concerns, and then to retain him. You will probably tell me that considerable sacrifices have been made for the workforce. I will refrain from discussing this matter, but would simply note—in the light of Dr. Lejeune's report—that they are insufficient, or that they have not produced the desired results.

Arguments, to the effect that the worker is better fed by you than in his own village, are hardly persuasive, since the native is not obliged, when in his own village, to do the work that you ask of him . . .

In his report on Lusanga, Dr. Lejeune suggested a procedure whereby the health of the workforce to be retained would be supervised, through weighing workers both upon their arrival and upon their departure . . .

That the laziness of the native constitutes a very grave obstacle to recruitment, I would readily allow, but the Government has done its duty once it has loyally sought, through persuasion, to steer the native towards work. Reforming the temperament and mores of a population is not the work of a few years, and the economic aspects of colonisation should serve to reinforce governmental action by awakening needs in the local population that work alone can satisfy.

The Government deeply appreciates all [your] industry has done to transform working conditions in this country, by making the best of a scanty workforce and by avoiding the waste of raw materials. But it considers itself [unable to] treat your industry as a special case, by intervening to guarantee it a workforce at rates and under conditions which are not strictly determined by the local market.

The head of the province's medical service, being mindful of the conditions under which your workers live and work, writes that in all conscience the territorial administrator should refuse to advise the natives to go and work in your concerns.

This declaration, the seriousness of which will not have escaped our civil servant, will receive, I do not doubt, your closest attention. If it has not led me to alter my directives to the territorial authorities forthwith, this is because I know that I can place my trust in you and that, once you are aware of the real situation, you will not hesitate to do everything in your power to render it easier for us—to make it possible for us—to continue with the assistance which has been accorded to you up until now.[14]

Reactions to the Lejeune report

In a letter of 4th January 1924, interim Governor-General Bureau wrote to the Colonial Minister, informing him that he was forwarding the Lejeune report, to which he attached the following commentary:

In order to assess the true value of the statements made by Dr. Lejeune, one should compare his report with chapter 2 of the report drafted by Dr. Rhodain, which was conveyed to you during his period of office, and after his journey in the Kwilu.

Comparison of the two documents serves to show that, except in the case of the ration supplied to workers, which has been somewhat improved, the situation described by Dr. Rhodain has not altered . . .

It seems, then, that we ought not to expect the Société des Huileries to go to any great expense to improve the situation of its workers.

Bosses in Africa persist in blaming their failure to recruit workers on the indolence of the blacks, when the real cause is to be sought in the fashion in which they treat those in their employ.

It is crucial that the Board of the Huileries du Congo Belge at last realises the real situation in its enterprises in the Kwilu, and intervenes vigorously and rapidly. The Lusanga enterprises are becoming more and more unpopular with the natives, and it would not be rash to claim that, if radical steps are not taken, their prosperity will before long be irremediably compromised.[15]

On 12th January, Engels forwarded to Bureau, without further comment, Edkins' defence against the Lejeune report. The defence, dated 1st January, consisted of a memorandum of 26 lengthy pages, rounded off with appendices dozens of pages long. Here are the key passages, stripped of their aggressive and arrogant tone:

The Blacks' hospital
In September 1923, orders were given for the construction of two new wards (30 beds), as well as for the construction of a huge dispensary. The equipping of the annexes is also anticipated.

As far as the upkeep and diet of the patients are concerned, no limit has been decided upon.

According to the minutes of the meeting of the Kwango labour commission (18th December 1923), Deputy Public Prosecutor Colin declared that, as regards the medical service, the HCB aside, no firm and no commercial enterprise in the whole district was in compliance with ordinance 47.

Lejeune alleges that the number of beds is insufficient. The norm laid down in ordinance 47 has not been achieved by any enterprise in the Colony. The figure of 4,500 workers quoted for Leverville-Kwenge is anyway inaccurate. There are only 2,000 workers as such. The 2,000 other men in our service live in the villages. [In response to this claim, Lejeune would object that it seemed to imply that the company was not obliged to provide medical care for local workers.][16]

The Lazaret
It was still defective because Doctor Rhodain had been planning to transfer it to Kikwit and have the mission responsible for running it. But the treatment of the sick had not been in any way impaired by this delay. In June, the company decided to build a new lazaret, to be run by the Sisters of Saint-Mary. Father Van Hee has just had the plans sent to us.

Infirmaries
The *médecin provincial* complains that our nurses in the agricultural posts are not up to their jobs. We would answer that, since we have failed to persuade the government to send us qualified nurses, the best we can do is to train our coloured health workers ourselves. Besides, we are not

obliged to employ a specialised staff. Article 44 of ordinance 47 stipulates that employers should allocate just one employee performing the function of nurse for each locality of 50 men.

If there is a shortage of medicines in the infirmaries, this is because the black nurse lacked the foresight to order what was needed in time. Furthermore, when the *médecin provincial* visited, ordinance 47 was no more than a month old.

Reviving a proposal formerly made by Rhodain, Lejeune has voiced the opinion that a third doctor should be sent by the HCB to Lusanga circle. We have already explained to the government that the company's financial situation does not permit such a measure.

Besides, the 1911 Convention between the Colony and the HCB specifies just one doctor per circle.

Recruitment

The *médecin provincial* complains about our employing non-adults for hard work. In February 1923, we instructed the head of Lusanga circle to ensure that our recruitment relied as little as possible on non-adult labour.

Accommodation

We have an extensive building programme, which will provide workers' houses made of baked or sun-dried bricks (costing 600 francs per house) . . .

All of these houses should be built in 1924, save for 65 at Leverville, to be built in 1925, and 40 at Kwenge, to be built in 1926. I will end here by noting that in the whole of Kwango district the HCB is the only body which has so far acted purposefully to provide accommodation for its workers. At the above-mentioned meeting of the Labour commission, Cominex, Interfina, the Compagnie du Congo Belge, Spoiden and CK, employing 125, 500, 1,000, 600 and 5,000 workers respectively, each undertook to build 10 houses by 31st July 1924 (in the case of the CK, the houses were to be in brick, while the others opted for adobe).

Dress

To provide a *pagne* and a blanket for men hired for just three months, would be tantamount to doubling their wage, and thereby ruining any enterprise having to honour such an obligation.

At the time when Lejeune visited Lusanga, the HCB was not under any legal obligation to provide blankets for men recruited prior to the publication of ordinance 47. [Ordinance 58 of July 1922 had imposed this obligation.]

Rationing

When Rhodain visited Lusanga, he judged the ration provided by us to be inadequate: 200 grams of rice, 100 grams of meat, with oil available on request. During this period no text specified the quantity of foodstuffs the statutory ration should have. [In actual fact, ordinance 58 had done so.] Rhodain fixed it at 500 grams of rice, 100 grams of fish, 100 grams of oil. From March 1922, we adopted this standard ration, and we informed the chief medical officer of the fact, further specifying that, for making the oil required for the ration and for picking manioc leaves, we were allocating 1 picker for each team of 20 men, and that, in addition, we were allocating 1 cook per team. [Lejeune would answer here that he had not seen the aforesaid picker anywhere.]

In a letter of 19th June 1923, a copy of which is in the appendix, we wrote to the manager of Lusanga circle to tell him of our plans to introduce a mixed ration, consisting of 500 grams of rice, maize or millet, and 0.35 francs in cash. Lejeune was mistaken when he wrote that these instructions recommended a ration of 420 grams of rice per day, plus 1.80 francs a week. He was mistaken again when he claimed that at Leverville a kilo of fish is worth 3 francs. [Lejeune would reply that Wilson had shown him the letter recommending 420 grams of rice and 30 centimes in money, and that the employee of Sedec had informed him that fish was worth 3 francs.]

But we have not yet managed to introduce the mixed ration, because the outlying stores, where we will distribute the fish at 2 francs a kilo, have not yet been built. While waiting, we have temporarily increased the daily portion of rice to 800 grams, and that of salt to 14 grams.

Lejeune voiced the opinion that the necessary steps had not been taken to feed the native in a manner befitting his tastes. Our attempts at growing crops have met with serious obstacles, and we have had to abandon them. On the other hand, we have tried in vain to buy local crops from the natives. We need to organise periodical markets, although the administration doubts whether such a thing would be feasible. According to the minutes for the meeting of the labour commission of 18th December last, the weekly ration is limited to 2 francs in cash at Cominex, Interfina and Spoiden, and 2.50 francs at the Compagnie du Congo Belge. The current weekly ration costs our company 4.80 francs (rice) + 1.80 francs (fish) + 0.10 francs (salt) = 6.70 francs, without counting the oil, which represents 0.50 francs. It is therefore a ration nearly four times as large as that provided by the other employers in the district.

Discrepancies between the labour regime and the guidelines contained in the labour contract

In order to avoid any possibility of contravening the law, we have sub-mitted the text of our employment contracts and of our work-books to the government. The governor-general has just replied [letter of 21st Decem-ber 1923]. We were waiting for this reply in order to render the formulae used in contracts and in work-books consistently the same, in all of our concessions.

The memorandum written by Edkins in defence of his position ends with a peroration of four pages predicting bankruptcy for the HCB if the govern-ment were to fail to compensate it for the financial obligations imposed upon it by ordinance 47, with measures serving to stabilise the workforce and to increase its output.[17]

On 11th February 1924, Bureau forwarded Edkins' memorandum to the minister, together with a note commenting on it written by Chief Medical Officer Rhodain. Bureau wrote to say that he wholly endorsed the conclusions arrived at in the note, which brought to light the HCB's duplicity. He continued as follows: "the HCB's management in Africa is persisting with the attitude adopted by it in the earlier rounds of corres-pondence forwarded to you. It seeks to deny the most incontrovertible facts, by invoking directives it has given to its own staff! It tries to justify, in spite of everything, the defective medical care provided for the workforce employed in its agricultural enterprises in the Kwilu. I feel no need to comment further on this question."

Here are the key passages in Rhodain's note, dated 24th January 1924:

In the letter of 1st January 1924, the HCB's managing director and his secretary say "we seek to demonstrate in the most spectacular fashion not only that the *criticisms to which we have been subjected are not well-founded*, but also that we really have done all that it was humanly possible to do in order to meet our obligations under the law".

What the letter in fact demonstrates: . . .

As regards *the blacks' hospital*:

Already in the course of my visit in November 1922, the HCB doctor, Dr. Cripps had informed me that the hospital was to be improved. Monsieur Seidelin had confirmed that this was the company's intention. By the time of Doctor Lejeune's visit, nothing had been done. He found the situation to be still as I had described it, and *he quite rightly criticised it*. The Huileries reply that improvements are going to be made.

Doctor Lejeune calls for the number of beds to be precisely as laid down in ordinance 47, that is, 5% of the number of workers. As it is an agricultural concern, this is perhaps excessive.

The future will show *exactly how many beds are needed* . . . , but it is plain enough that 30 beds are not sufficient. The number should be raised to 60, and then one should wait and see.

As regards the *lazaret*:

The HCB admits that it is *defective*; they claim that, if it has not been modified, that is because of a proposal I had made to build a lazaret in Kikwit, to be run by nuns. In reality, it was the HCB which blocked this proposal, because they were awaiting nuns in Leverville. But they change the terms of the question.

The lazaret as such was not to be rebuilt, for what remained of it was not worth the trouble. On the other hand, it was, in my opinion, badly situated. The HCB could, however, have immediately improved its *internal organisation*. At the time of my visit, the supervisory staff, whether nurses or workers, was insufficient: the patients very probably received their injections, but those in the final stages of sleeping sickness and the crippled were not cared for. Beds did not exist, and the sick had no blankets. M. Lejeune said much the same. His criticisms were well-founded . . .

As regards the *infirmaries in the agricultural posts:*

Rapid though my progress through the HCB had been, I had found that workers in these posts did not receive medical care, and I had called for a regular medical inspection of these posts.

Mr. Lejeune finds, a year later, the same situation. Indeed, he clarifies how things are, noting that at post 8, where almost 400 men are employed, there are not even the materials to make up a dressing. The HCB replies that they are short of nurses. This is no excuse, and Mr. Lejeune's observations are accurate.

In asking the Government for more nurses, here too the HCB is avoiding the issue.

The HCB has received some nurses already; it should have trained still more itself, and long ago, and failing that, it should not have taken on so many workers. As an enterprise expands, so too should its medical care.

The company is quibbling about the obligation imposed upon it by article 44 of ordinance 47 to provide medical care. It is immaterial whether such care is given by a company employee or by a nurse, the point is that it must be provided. Where there is not even the wherewithal to dress a wound, although there are almost 400 workers, *medical care is evidently not being provided*. . .

The company is again quibbling when it states that ordinance 47 came out just a month before Dr. Lejeune's visit. They forget that I criticised their set-up at the outset [1923], when ordinance 58 was in force, and they thus acknowledge that, had the law not exerted pressure upon them, they would have permitted a state of affairs to continue which, from a purely humanitarian point of view, was highly reprehensible.

As regards the *organisation of the medical service*:

Dr. Lejeune, like me, has found that, given the scale of their operations in the Kwilu, the HCB's current medical service is no longer adequate. He naturally calls for the introduction of another doctor, responsible for tours of duty, and for the treatment of those suffering from sleeping sickness within the circle conceded to the HCB. Treatment of this sort seems to me to be an obligation, at any rate morally speaking, imposed upon the HCB by virtue of the decree ratifying the 1911 Convention concluded between the Colonial Minister and Lever Brothers, which stipulates in article 4: "The company will endeavour to improve the conditions of populations settled in the vicinity of its factories, and to provide them with medical care".

How will it bring medical care to the numerous sufferers of sleeping sickness living in its concessions if the doctors do not visit the villages? I venture to ask what treatment the HCB will offer in place of the itinerant system which I advocate and from which *they do not really anticipate significant results* . . .

Up until this point the HCB has in no wise shown that Dr. Lejeune's report is not *rigorously accurate*. On the contrary, the report is highly accurate, and the HCB cannot contest it. In his report, Dr. Lejeune was supposed to state the facts, and this is what he did. The HCB's proposals were really no concern of his, for they had not even begun to be implemented.

In the next 13 pages, the HCB once again do not refute any of Dr. Lejeune's statements of fact, as regards the age of the workers (statements reiterated by me), children on the night shift, accommodation, clothing or food.

My conclusions are as follows:

Dr. Lejeune has outlined, and described in detail a state of affairs for which I too can vouch. The sole improvement effected after my visit to the Kwilu, at the end of 1922, consisted in increasing the food ration, which had previously been a starvation ration. This increase is insufficient.

Those arguments advanced by the HCB that are founded upon *what they are going to do and upon what others have not done* in no way refute what has been duly stated by myself and by Dr. Lejeune. Indeed, they reveal a duplicity which should rightly render the government suspicious.

The major dispute between the HCB and the administration in the Congo regarding the Lejeune report did not make waves in the Ministry of Colonies in Brussels. This was in part because the General Secretariat in Boma had failed to enclose the report with Bureau's covering letter of 4th January 1924, which reached Brussels on 1st February. Franck wrote a note on the latter, with reference to the commentary it contained, "to be forwarded to the Huileries". The director general of the Department of Industry and Commerce, Guillaume Olyff, decided to wait for the report before writing to the HCB. In a letter of 5th February, Olyff asked Boma to send on the missing document, which as a consequence only reached Brussels two months later.

Towards the end of February, when the government was in open crisis, Stubbe, the director of the HCB in Brussels, submitted a copy of Edkins' memoir of 1st January 1924 to Franck. This copy was scrutinised by the relevant departments within the Ministry, but they could not give a final opinion, for want of the Lejeune report. On 10th March, Franck was replaced by Henri Carton de Tournai, a Catholic. Two days later, the Ministry received the memorandum in question, together with Rhodain's highly critical note, from Boma. Olyff forwarded Rhodain's note to Carton, who apparently did not have the time to attend to it. Three weeks later, on 9th April, the secretary general at the Ministry of Colonies, Nicolas Arnold, sent Rhodain's note to Stubbe, with the following comments:

> You will no doubt see that this note, whose conclusions the Governor-General declares that he fully endorses, does not confirm the information supplied by your company, regarding the provision of health care for its workforce in the Kwilu.
>
> Consequently, I cannot do otherwise than urge you once again to give your staff in Africa the order to comply at the earliest possible date with the directives issued by the local authorities.[18]

The matter was thus concluded.

3

The Establishment of a Monopoly
in the Circles (1924–1926)

Monopoly achieved through the swindle of tripartite contracts

We saw in chapter 1 that from 1918 on Lever Brothers' management in Liverpool had called upon Minister Renkin to close down the post at Bulungu, so as to drive off the merchants who had been vying for the purchase of palm nuts. The 1919 annual report for Equateur province highlights the HCB's efforts to acquire a monopoly over the products of the palm trees in and around their Ebonda and Ingende circles. In Ebonda circle, sentences convicting villagers for having picked palm fruits on land monopolised by the company had been quashed by the public prosecutor's office. A letter on the same subject, sent by the HCB on 4th November 1920 to Minister Franck, demanded that Congolese justice prosecute those villagers who were harvesting palm nuts on land leased out to the company, or who were harvesting nuts though paid a wage, and selling them on to third parties.

On 9th December, Franck, by way of the governor-general, asked the public prosecutor to alert his subordinates, and especially the magistrates, to the need to display the same vigilance in prosecuting these infractions as in curbing theft or embezzlement committed against persons. He continued as follows:

> The obligation of magistrates to grant protection to the Huileries, regardless of any personal opinions they may have as to the disadvantages of large concessions, is self-evident . . . Certain legal difficulties have, I know, been raised. This is the case when the natives have taken, for their own profit, palm-nuts from palms growing on blocks leased to the company, although its cadastral survey has not yet defined any boundaries where they adjoin *terres indigènes* . . .[1]

The undemarcated state of the *terres indigènes*, or "native lands", raised difficulties for the palm-nut trade. These lands—which, according to the 1911 Convention, could not be included in the territory leased out to the HCB—represented a stumbling-block to the implementation of the latter's plans. They were to be demarcated by the State, following a procedure outlined in the pamphlet of March 1917 on the 1911 Convention. The procedure, anticipating the work of a boundary commission, involved a good number of surveyors measuring the innumerable blocks which the HCB were supposed to choose within their five circles. The State did not intend to abide by its own regulations. It was supposed to pay the surveyors, although the company was responsible for their board and lodging.[2] This explains why the demarcation process—which, according to the agreement, as modified by the decree of 4th March 1920, was supposed to have been completed by 1926—had barely made any progress by 1922. In that year the plots already demarcated and leased out to the company amounted to no more than 10,334 hectares in Lusanga and 41,600 hectares in Ebonda.[3]

Elsewhere no progress at all had been made. In Barumbu circle, however, some attempt at demarcation had been undertaken. In 1918, the government surveyor, Albert Deridder, had demarcated to the south of Isangi a huge block within Yaboloko *chefferie*, including *terres indigènes* which chief Bula would hand over, or so it was presumed, in exchange for other plots. But the chief wanted none of it. In January 1919, appearing before the boundary commission—which consisted of the surveyor, the territorial administrator and the director of the circle, and which was looking into the question of the *chefferie's* rights over this block—Bula was unwilling to relinquish his rights over Lileko forest, and protested that he had already handed over Mokolongo, Ingelete and Lefelele palm groves. Yet it was all to no avail; he had to give up the forest, in compensation for which he was offered a tract of land elsewhere. On 22nd September 1919 he was compelled to sign an agreement with the HCB regarding this exchange of plots.

In February 1920 the governor-general had the documents concerning this affair sent to the minister. The director general, Albrecht Gohr, rejected the exchange in June, for the following reasons:

> The agreement is in principle legitimate: directives recommend that the territorial authorities should promote such exchanges. It is clear, however, that the territorial authority, which is responsible within the Commission for protecting natives' interests, cannot force the chief to give his consent. I must express my regret that pressure has been applied to the chief in order to obtain his acquiescence . . . The minutes recording the exchange

left some doubts regarding another point: Yaboloko *chefferie* is in reality handing over plantations whose output will continue for several more years; in return it is getting fields that have still to be cleared. It is to be presumed that the concessionary will allow the natives to harvest the produce from the surrendered plantations until they are wholly exhausted . . . Once again the minutes ought to mention this clause.[4]

In fact, in 1922 the HCB no longer set great store by state demarcations of land. They were concerned instead to corner a monopoly over the purchase of palm-grove produce growing on all five of their circles, an area almost twice that of Belgium. The leasing of fields, later to become property according to the 1911 Convention, was of scant importance compared to the supplying of factories with fruit. These factories were anyway supposed to be able to process 6,000 tons of fruit per circle per year, for the leases to be financially viable. After the original investment in the factories, what counted was the acquisition of fruit, not the leasing of the land. Moreover, that acquisition was best guaranteed by having a monopoly over all purchases. There was nothing new about such a circumstance in the Congo: the Compagnie du Lomami and the Société Anonyme Belge (SAB) in the Busira[5] had already obtained a monopoly over all natural products in their vast concessions.

In the latter there was the same problem of *terres indigènes* that were enclaved, and not demarcated, in the case of the Compagnie du Lomami, or not equitably demarcated, in the case of the Société Anonyme Belge. It was therefore impossible to determine the origin of natural produce delivered up by the villagers to be traded. Both villagers and purchasing traders risked being charged with theft and receiving of products belonging to the concessionaries. In order to avoid these difficulties, the government had granted the latter a monopoly over the purchase of all products harvested within the concessions. This grant was based, for appearance's sake, upon the concluding of so-called "tribal accords" between the companies and the Africans, guaranteeing the latter, at any rate on paper, a suitable price for the produce delivered.

On 20th April 1922, in Brussels, Lord Leverhulme conferred with Minister Franck regarding the problem of monopolies within his circles. He began by complaining about competition from traders:

Where is the counterpart to the obligations imposed upon me by the Convention? I have to commit large sums of capital to the building of factories, and produce oil continuously and in ever increasing quantities . . . to found schools and hospitals, and to make purchases in Belgium that I could perhaps effect more cheaply elsewhere; and what advantage do I then have over traders who come and buy from the natives, when, and only when, the prices on the European market are favourable, palm-oil and palm-nuts originating in land leased out to me, indeed, in palm groves in which the harvest is only possible thanks to arrangements made by me? They divert both labour and products from my factories with all the more ease since, not having the same obligations as myself, they can temporarily offer higher prices. The counter-prestation granted to me by the Colony must perforce consist of an exclusive right to the palm fruit.[6]

In order to obtain this exclusive right within the five circles, while still aspiring to lease out plots of land, Lever proposed to Franck a highly complex and indeed eccentric legal arrangement, involving the concluding of three different kinds of accord. They consisted of the following:

a) An accord between the HCB and the State to halt the demarcation process, and to grant the company on a provisional basis large blocks (dozens of square kilometres) of its own choosing within its circles; blocks in which it could appropriate plots to be leased.

b) Accords between the State and the native communities to place these blocks under joint ownership, with the joint ownership to be managed by the Colony, that is to say, with the latter approving or rejecting the aforesaid appropriation of plots.

c) Accords between the HCB and the native communities acknowledging the HCB's exclusive right to the palm fruit growing on such blocks.

Lever suggested combining accords b) and c) so as to produce single contracts to which the Colony, the Africans and the HCB would be party, and which could be termed tripartite contracts.[7]

Lever's proposals had been dreamed up by Max Horn, who was never short of ideas that might please the Liverpool magnate. Within the Belgian Ministry of Colonies they prompted a brisk exchange of notes between the heads of the Department for Native Policy and the heads of the Department for Industry and Trade. The proposals fostered confusion, and were soon forgotten. Horn, however, had an eye for the main chance. He drew up a draft for a tripartite contract, which, in the spring of the following year, Managing Director Beissel submitted to Rutten, who at this time was acting governor-general in the Congo. The latter was flabbergasted. He knew that Governor-General Lippens, who had just retired, had entered into negotiations with the HCB with a view to framing an arrangement similar to that conceded to the Compagnie du Lomami and to the SAB—an arrangement which was, moreover, very concise. But the lengthy document sent to him by Beissel in no way resembled these "tribal contracts". On 27th April 1923 Rutten telegraphed the Minister as follows:

> Beissel has sent me, and is insistent that I grant my approval to, the text of a tripartite contract to be concluded between the Colony, the HCB and the native communities, the terms of which the Governor-General, the Huileries, Denyn and Gohr [legal adviser and director general of Native Policy at the Ministry respectively] are supposed to have agreed in Brussels. Be so good as to let me know if this draft has indeed been accepted by the last two named above. If so, be so kind as to send me text of contract.

On 2nd May the director general of Industry and Trade, Olyff, forwarded a copy of this telegram to his colleague Gohr, together with some related documentation submitted by Horn. On 4th May Olyff forwarded to Gohr the copy of the tripartite contract which, according to a letter from Stubbe, director of HCB in Brussels, Rutten had been asked to approve. Olyff commented that, if Gohr accepted the text of this contract, the latter might, as Rutten requested in his telegram, be sent to Africa by the next post.

Gohr was not prepared to give an inch. It seemed that he had no faith in the scheme for a tripartite contract. In response to Rutten's telegram, Franck said that he had had some talks at the Ministry but had not reached an agreement, that no opinion had been voiced by the legal adviser and that Gohr had expressed some reservations. "I will not take a decision", he went on, "without knowing what your feelings are, and without you being in agreement". He continued:

> While you are scrutinising the text of the tripartite contract, we should continue to grant this company effective support with recruiting and with the development of its workforce. It would be an error to skimp on such support in the case of the major enterprises, and I am gratified to note that recently steps have been taken to guarantee the various huileries, in several different regions, a larger quota of workers.

This letter brought it home to Rutten that it was up to him to concern himself with the implementation of the tripartite contract.[8]

The HCB returned to the attack. In a letter dated 4th September 1923, managing director Moseley and director Stubbe wrote to Franck to say that they were confident of reaching an understanding very soon on the issue of the tripartite contract, which would allow the difficulties raised by the question of native rights within the company's concessions to be resolved. They expressed the hope that the latest negotiations with the department and with Rutten, who had recently returned to Belgium, would lead to a definitive agreement on the matter.[9]

During his period of leave in Belgium, in November, Rutten, in collaboration with Victor Denyn, Gohr and Stubbe, drafted the definitive version of the tripartite contract, covering four large pages and consisting of a preamble and nine articles. The contract, which defined the boundaries of the huge block to be placed in joint ownership, specified that the *chefferies* would grant the company, up until 1936, rights over fruits present and future from palms growing within this same block. The *chefferies* were allowed to sell such fruits solely to the company. The company, for its part, had to pay for the fruits delivered by the villagers a remuneration so calculated that an adult man could earn, for a day's harvesting, a sum equal to the wage and to the daily ration in force in the given region. Where palm nuts offered to it by villagers were concerned, the company was supposed to pay a price at least equal to the going price in the region's trading-posts. The size of the wage and of the daily ration serving as a basis upon which to calculate the price of the fruit, together with the average price for the palm nuts, were to be decided upon by mutual agreement between the district commissioner and the local director of the circle. When they failed to agree, the final decision would rest with the governor of the province.[10] (I would emphasise here that the basis upon which the price of fruits was calculated worked very much to the detriment of the Africans. For, by selling one day's harvest of fruit on the open market, they could in fact earn three or four times more than a worker hired by the company earned in a day.)

On 3rd December 1923 the minister sent to Bureau the definitive version of the tripartite contract, together with the reasons used to justify it, namely, the credit due to Lever for having introduced the palm-oil industry to the Kwilu; his investment of considerable amounts of capital; delays in the demarcation of the *terres indigènes*; the fact that the expiry date for choosing which lands to lease after the provisional marking of boundaries (1926) was imminent; the onerous obligations arising out of factory capacity and the quantity of produce to be exported, etc.[11]

No sooner was he installed as governor-general of the Congo, in March 1924, than Rutten decided how the tripartite contracts with chiefs and notables were to be concluded. The conclusion was to be effected in the presence of the governor-general's special delegate, a delegate who, in accordance with the ordinance of 30th September on agreements to be made with Africans, was entrusted with the task of explaining to the chiefs, sub-chiefs, notables and elders featuring in the deed the precise scope of the document, of ensuring that the text reflected the agreement of the parties involved, and of checking whether, so far as customary law was concerned, the said parties had the right to enter into the commitments specified in the deed. This staging was designed to prove to the wider world that the contracts were above board. In order to lend them a still greater air of respectability, they had to take the form of deeds authenticated by a magistrate from the public prosecutor's department, acting as a notary.

Some tripartite contracts were "concluded" in mid-1924 in Lusanga and Ebonda, and the following year in Boteke and Basongo. To say that they were "concluded" is, however, to beg the question, for in reality they were imposed upon the Africans, who did not dare oppose them, with an impressive show of ceremony. The introduction of the tripartite contracts was delayed at Barumbu-Lukutu, on account of the opposition of the governor of Orientale province, Adolphe Demeulemeester. The latter judged—and in this he was backed by the magistrates in Kisangani—that these contracts, since they eliminated competition for the purchase of palm-oil products, were against the Africans' best interests.[12]

The Portuguese of Bumba protest

The compulsory tripartite contracts were not forwarded to the Department in Brussels, which had no notion as to what was happening in this respect in the Congo. Only in 1934 did the Department ask for information on this matter.[13] Such contracts are therefore only very rarely to be found in the African archives. I chanced upon a copy "concluded" in the Ebonda circle, regarding the region located in Modjamboli *territoire*, in the triangle formed by the river Congo and the river Molua. This particular contract caused much disquiet in Bumba, the administrative centre of a *territoire* extending beyond the Itimbiri. The post in question, only twelve kilometres from Alberta-Ebonda, was located on the left bank of the Molua, which served as a boundary with Modjamboli, and likewise as an eastern boundary to the block monopolized by the above-mentioned tripartite contract. During this period the *territoire* of Bumba formed part of Orientale province, but it was about to be re-annexed to the district of the Bangala (Equateur province), to which it had formerly belonged.

The dynamic traders of Bumba, all of whom were Portuguese, regarded this tripartite contract as a harsh blow dealt by Equateur province. They bitterly regretted having been transferred to this province, and all the more so given that they knew that Demeulemeester in Kisangani had been wholly opposed to contracts of this kind. On 22nd August 1924, in Basoko, they sent the following telegram to the minister: "The traders of Bumba take the liberty of protesting against the HCB's assault on free trade, which is preventing the natives from selling their products in Bumba. A letter of explanation follows." Extracts from this same letter, dated 10th August 1924 and sent from Bumba, now follow:

> The traders from the trading post in Bumba respectfully take the liberty of apprising you of their claims regarding the situation that has arisen due to the implementation of the tripartite contract agreed between the Government of Equateur province, the natives and the Société des Huileries du Congo Belge.
>
> This contract concluded on 5th July last prohibits anyone purchasing in whatsoever fashion products deriving from the elaeis palm, be it nuts, kernels or oil, in the concession granted to this company, and what is still more detrimental to our interests, this measure also covers products harvested on land occupied by the natives . . .
>
> The natives have strictly defined rights over their fields and plantations, and over the products harvested there. How then could it be acceptable for them to be forced to surrender their palm produce to just one company? Does this obligation not deprive them of the benefits of competition? What authorized representatives of the natives could ever have concluded, in their own name, a contract which brings them only disadvantages? What price the commercial liberty guaranteed by the Charte Coloniale in a contract such as this?
>
> For the above reasons the merchants of Bumba beg you to take due account of their petition, and will be deeply grateful to you, Your Excellency, if you could intervene and use your lofty authority to have the contract of 5th July formulated in such a way that it no longer damaged the interests of private traders, who remain
>
> Your devoted servants,
>
> [eleven signatures]

Having received no answer to this petition, the most prominent of the Bumba merchants, one Cunha Melo, presented their grievances to Kinshasa Chamber of Commerce on 23rd October. His compatriots, he declared, had set up rice fields, built their brick houses at the administration's request, and paid 100,000 francs in taxes the previous year. Now the black women who used to make their way to Bumba with palm nuts were stranded. Trade in this product risked being banned as far as Lolo and Moenge, places located on the river Itimbiri and included in the HCB circle of Ebonda. Melo added that the chiefs had been coerced by the authorities into signing the contract, and that the traders were now calling for a further meeting of the chiefs in the presence of a delegation of some of the traders.

A Kinshasa weekly entitled *L'Information Coloniale* published the above grievances together with the letter to the minister. On 1st November it also published the following appeal, which was directed at similarly affected traders in other circles besides Ebonda:

TRADERS OF BUMBA,
of Kikwit, Basoko, Mbandaka, Ilebo, etc.
Because our vital interests have been damaged by the tripartite contract, we count upon your total solidarity in order that we may resist with all our might and by all legal means the enactment of a ruling that is so detrimental to us. Send any relevant information to us.
   For Ferreira, Melo and Co.
   Partner: Cunha Melo—Kinshasa.

The appeal, which was in bold type, took up half a page.

At the 11th December meeting of the Chamber of Commerce, Melo unleashed a violent diatribe against the Modjamboli tripartite contract, and in its December issues *L'Information Coloniale* published the following telegram: "Bumba traders express gratitude for your successful defence of their interests; since your paper highlights situation, improvement noted here, and many new traders plan to set up business. The traders." In the meantime, the president of the Chamber of Commerce had asked the governor-general for information on the tripartite contracts. The latter had given it, while at the same time emphasising that the contracts were not immobilising the entire surface area of the five circles but only specific blocks. On 26th November the Chamber thanked the governor-general for the information, adding that it had been passed on to M. Melo.

In January Beissel appeared before the Chamber and gave a talk on tripartite contracts. He declared, among other things, that the administration had not managed to demarcate within a reasonable length of time the plots of land chosen by the company, and that it was for this reason that the government had authorised the conclusion of the contracts. When questioned by the president of the Chamber regarding the above-mentioned talk, Secretary General Postiaux sent him, on 30th January 1925, a lengthy defence of the tripartite contracts. In concluding them, Postiaux declared, the government was seeking to prevent the Africans from fraudulently taking palm produce from land belonging to the company, either for their own gain or for that of third parties other than the HCB. The Compagnie du Lomami and the SAB had found themselves in the same situation. If the Chamber, Postiaux went on, had concrete information proving that blacks had been subject to coercion, it ought to bring it to the attention of the authorities. Furthermore, the traders of Bumba had to take into account when starting up in business the necessarily precarious nature of a part of their operations. The HCB's rights were after all widely known, for the Convention of 14th April 1911 had been published in the *Bulletin Officiel*.[14]

But the Portuguese of Bumba had not protested in vain. They managed for a long time to block the imposition of tripartite contracts in the area to the east of Bumba, while in the case of Modjamboli the colonial administration allowed the villagers to profit from some palm oil and palm kernels slipping through. No matter how adamantly the advocates of tripartite contracts insisted that the latter did not grant them a monopoly over the circles in their entirety, in practice traders often found themselves barred from trading in palm-oil produce in all villages within a sixty-kilometre radius of the centre of the circles.[15] The same advocates insisted that the Africans too derived some benefit from the contracts, namely, the selling of their products without fear of being charged with theft or receiving stolen goods, and at a price set by the colonial administration.[16] As regards price, it is clear that it was what the company was ready to pay, and no sensible person will claim that the elimination of competition guarantees a fair price. As for proceedings for theft and receiving stolen goods against Africans selling palm-oil products from their own forests, this was nothing short of a scandal. The palms belonged to them, the State had arbitrarily awarded them to Lever, who was the real interloper, as will become apparent in the following.

Hyacinthe Vanderyst and the ownership of the palm groves

The priest and missionary Hyacinthe Vanderyst, one of the Jesuits' collaborators in the Kwango-Kwilu, protested at the terrifying death rates suffered by the Mbunda, who had been dispatched to Lusanga as forced labourers. Vanderyst is known in Congolese history for his scientific activities, which were of a practical nature, and which resulted in countless publications. It is no surprise then to find that, being an engineer and agronomist, he took an interest in the Kwilu palm groves, devoting an article to the question of their origin in the *Bulletin agricole du Congo Belge*, published as early as 1919. During the controversy in the press over the imposition of tripartite contracts, Vanderyst published, in 1925, in the December issue of the periodical *Congo*, a remarkable article entitled "Les

concessions de forêts secondaires et de palmeraies congolaises". Here are
some lengthy extracts:

Hundreds of thousands of hectares of palm groves and secondary forests
with *elaeis* palms scattered through them have been, or are about to be,
granted by the State to companies, despite the public or private protests of
natives, who claim full and untrammelled property rights in them . . . There
is a danger here, and one worth pointing out.

The facts of the case are anyway serious enough. The natives believe
themselves to be wronged: they often make themselves out to be the
victims of an injustice; they claim that the State deprives them of immobile
property created or preserved through their agricultural labour or by that of
their ancestors; in short, they accuse the State, or specific companies, of
dispossessing them, of despoiling them and, not to mince words, of
robbing them . . .

If their protests are well-founded, they ought to be taken into account,
their entitlements to property should be examined, the damages they have
suffered should be assessed, and they should be granted a just and
equitable compensation for expropriation effected for the sake of the
public good. The State and the companies are alike responsible for
repairing the injustices committed, committed indeed, until such a time
as there is any proof to the contrary, in good faith . . .

The crucial question

Can the Belgian State dispose of the palm groves as if it were their owner?
The State answers in the affirmative. But is this affirmation not purely
gratuitous? Is this not the decision of the master who imposes his will
upon subjects who cannot make their voices heard in Europe, or have their
rights acknowledged? Has this question been scrutinised, has it been
seriously studied, while taking into account all the elements necessary for
a proper assessment? . . .

At any rate, no serious, rigorous investigation has been held, to my
knowledge, in the Congo, by a responsible commission appointed specifically for this task. No document has been published, to my knowledge, by
the administration such as might justify the expropriation of the palm
groves without just and prior compensation. These lacunae are much to be
regretted . . .

Native customary law is not familiar with the notion of prescription!
Every dispute persists and subsists indefinitely until such a time as a
settlement is arrived at through friendly discussion or through a trusted
arbiter chosen jointly by the interested parties. The question of the palm

groves, if it is not resolved according to native customs, will remain open forever, because of its great material significance . . .

Are there natural palm groves?

In the debate between the State and the natives, this is a question of the utmost importance. The natives claim in the most formal sense that they— they or the ancestors—are the creators of the palm groves in the Congo. They deny the existence of natural palm groves, at any rate so far as their own observations extend. Conversely, with a remarkable display of unanimity, the interested parties, both the State and the companies, assert that the Congolese *elaeis* palm groves are natural formations, that is to say, formations which arose of their own accord in nature, and without any human intervention whatsoever.

Who is right? This is the question that must be resolved. All of my own observations, researches and studies confirm in the most positive and absolute fashion the argument espoused by the natives. For this very reason, I hold it to be my duty to intervene on their behalf. Conversely no one has so far openly attempted to prove that the palm groves are natural formations. This is no more than an assertion, wholly lacking supporting arguments . . .

The natives declare themselves to be owners of the palm groves, and perhaps of the secondary forests, and this on several grounds:

On the grounds that they were the original occupants of the country, in terms of stable settlements, hunting, fishing and the harvesting of natural products;

On the grounds that they were farmers who cleared and exploited the savannahs, which were thereby turned into forests, and later into palm groves;

On the grounds that they were clearers of virgin forests which, being periodically exploited for the production of food, gradually turned into palm groves;

On the grounds that they were creators of palm groves thanks to their direct and deliberate intervention, which had entailed introducing the *elaeis* palm into the country . . .

For what reasons does the State deny these grounds, or refuse to take them into account? . . .

Certain steps ought now to be taken. I propose in fact that a special commission of enquiry be set up, consisting of three members, a botanist, an agricultural engineer and an ethnologist qualified in law, in order to investigate thoroughly this question in the field, in Africa, and thereby to settle it in conformity with the dictates of Right and Justice.

Lode Achten and the tripartite contracts

The district commissioner for the Kasai, Lode Achten, having arrived at the end of his career in February 1928, published some critical remarks in November that year, in the periodical *Congo*, in response to an article that had appeared in the same periodical some three years earlier.[17] The original article, entitled "L'application du contrat tripartite", had been written by Théodore Heyse, the director of the Department of Industry and Trade within the Ministry of Colonies and a professor at the Antwerp Colonial Institute. As its title suggests, the article was a defence of the tripartite contract, although Heyse had never set eyes on one.[18] The remarks (in Dutch) made by the man on the ground, Achten, carry the same title as the article by the theorist and bureaucrat, Heyse, namely, "Over de toepassing van het drezijdig kontrakt". The issues were familiar to Achten, since Basongo circle lay within his jurisdiction. Here are some lengthy extracts from this article:

Heyse's article is clear and succinct, but the subject seems to me to have been viewed too much through juridical spectacles . . . Do the natives know what the tripartite contract commits them to, and have they given their agreement voluntarily? In fact, there are some regions in which they have accepted the contract while there are others in which they would not hear of it. In Equateur province, for example, they at first accepted, and then refused it. One might suppose that to mean that the natives . . . had acted independently and in full knowledge of what it is that they were doing. There is good cause, however, to wonder whether the blacks, despite all the efforts expended with this aim in mind, are capable of understanding a contract which the whites themselves only grasped after reading numerous directives, circulars and reports, not to mention the many appendices. How many whites, even among those personally involved in the affair, how many of them would dare to claim that they had understood the ins and outs of the question? . . .

Were the natives in a position to act independently? Admittedly, they were not subject to any direct coercion. In all conscience one may say that civil servants and magistrates, the only persons to hold real influence and power over the natives, performed their allotted tasks conscientiously. Yet a man's a man for all that, and who among us manages wholly to set aside his own personal preferences? The blacks, with their acute sense of observation, quickly grasped what we wanted from them. Furthermore, is not Bula Matari [the State] their lord and master, their natural and legal protector? Who, then, could deem what it proposed bad, or worse still, refuse it? . . . Anyone who is acquainted with the frame of mind of the blacks, and who is conversant with the controversy surrounding the conclusion of the tripartite contract, will assume that the natives had but a very slender grasp of the meaning of the contract. If anyone thinks otherwise, he has but to go to the villages within the circles, and keep his ear to the ground, and observe what is happening around him. If only one could start again!

What advantages did the natives acquire through the arrangement they came to with the whites, and did these advantages offset the abandonment of a part of their rights over the earth and its products?

In M. Heyse's opinion, the advantages consisted of an increase in general well-being benefiting the inhabitants of the circles, the founding of schools and the provision of medical aid. As for the increase in material well-being, it has proved more apparent than real. The oil mills can only work with the help of the natives, which is acquired reluctantly, with or without the assistance of the administration, and ordinarily whether the natives like it or not. Remuneration for services rendered is also not commensurate with the efforts demanded, and the inhabitants of the circles have no opportunity to seek other, better-remunerated work. It is indeed stipulated that the district commissioner must oversee the prices paid for palm fruit, and in reality he does intervene when the payment seems to him to be truly inadequate, but in fact the concessionary is the sole master in such matters, and it obviously tries to exploit its monopoly by all sorts of means which elude observation.

Not a great deal of teaching goes on, and really it is little better than a dressing on a wooden leg. I know of one school which is not attended by a single child from the villages in the region. For such an institution to bear fruit, the concessionary has in the first place to be persuaded of its usefulness, and therefore has to see to it that the teaching is well done. There is precious little sign of such interest being shown.

The medical service, for its part, is well organised and renders the working population a real service. The villagers derive far less benefit from it, and sometimes they wholly lack adequate care. Even in the most favourable of circumstances, it is still doubtful whether the benefits of medicine offset all the ills that exploitation of the palm groves causes the population . . . The compulsory labour is generally too onerous . . . The time devoted to collecting and to transporting the fruit is often excessive, and the contribution made by the women and the children often puts impossible demands upon their physical strength. As regards the freedom to choose one's work, there is much to be said. Indeed, both persons directly involved and outsiders have several times denounced intolerable situations and outright abuses. In such circumstances, a medical service, even if it is one of the very best, cannot measure up to the daunting task with which it is faced.

Even taking account of every good, in all conscience one does not dare to answer in the affirmative to the question put regarding the advantages arising for the blacks from the exploitation of the palm groves by the whites . . .

As M. Heyse explains, the State had undertaken to demarcate the company's lands by a given cut-off date [1926]. The task proving to be impossible, the State revoked the demarcation process and put the land under joint ownership. Now, however, another question arises, namely, by what right does the State bind the rights of the natives to the property titles of a private enterprise. The natives have nevertheless not concluded any agreement with the company. The State claims that it itself assumes the responsibility for ensuring respect for their rights, and furthermore that it is not imposing the tripartite contract on them, that they are free to accept or to reject it.

Even if this reasoning holds good and the law is not broken, it is still the case that the law may sometimes be a dead letter, and it is indeed against the hypocrisy of such a legality that I wish to protest here. [Here Achten lets it be clearly understood that the contract was compulsory.]

Let us now consider the situation as far as the land itself is concerned.

Through the tripartite contract the company has acquired the right to take over land, while acknowledging the rights of third parties and requiring the agreement of the authorities. In reality, the concessionary has long ago taken over vast tracts of land answering to the many requirements of its enterprise, for building trading-posts for the whites, camps for the workers, jetties for boats and outposts in the woods; for the exploiting of natural palm groves; for the growing of food, the creation of new plantations and the building of roads. The occupation of such land occurred without the administration having a hand in it, and without taking into account the rights of natives. The latter anyway withdrew as far as possible from the environs of the white establishments . . . It did not occur to them to resist the monopolising of their land by the whites, whom they anyway feared too much. Besides, what is an earthenware pitcher next to an iron pot?

The much-discussed question of the origin of the palm groves, and of ownership of them, was again up for grabs here. Anyone who has studied even in a cursory fashion the distribution of the *elaeis* is forced to acknowledge that there are no natural palm groves or, at the least, that they are extremely rare, that their proliferation is due to man, even if indirectly, through the spread of seeds and the enhanced opportunities provided for the latter to germinate and to develop around villages and in fields. The blacks are therefore in reality, in nine cases out of ten, the owners of the palm groves and their rights are customarily confirmed by their working of them [for fruit or for wine]. There is no mention whatsoever of this right, neither in the 1911 Convention nor in the later dispensation, both of which speak only of land.

Proof that this right is disregarded and trampled underfoot is furnished by the fact that the concessionary does not even take it into account, and simply takes over all the palm groves.

I am in no doubt whatsoever that the palm groves should be considered the property of the natives. It does not follow, however, that the palm groves should be tabu for the administration and for the colonists. There are in fact palm groves and vast tracts of land which are not used by the blacks and from which they derive very little profit. It would obviously be illogical not to exploit these riches when the occasion arises, but in this case the property rights of the first owners should nevertheless be recognised and expropriation could only be in exchange for appropriate compensation. The agreements and settlements ought to mention this fact.

Given such a failure to recognise native rights on paper, they would naturally suffer still more in practice. At present, the situation closely resembles that prevailing in the concessions of the Congo Free State, which were so fiercely denounced. Far from "avoiding whatever would be likely to undermine the confidence of the native in the equitable nature of the contracts to which he has subscribed" [a quotation from Heyse], the concessionary, or at any rate his agents, seems determined to achieve precisely the reverse. Not only the question of land and palms, but also the more or less compulsory work in the forest or in the enterprises of the whites, the *corvées* of various kinds, humiliations such as the ban on hunting, on tapping the palms for wine, on holding ceremonies, all of these innovations and humiliations have disrupted the natives' existence and embittered them. They no longer feel at home "on the land sold by Bula Matari to the company", and their trust in the justice of the whites has been deeply shaken.

4

In Barumbu Circle (1917–1930)

Forced labour in wretched conditions (1917–1924)

In 1916 in Barumbu circle labour recruiting went like clockwork, thanks to
the cooperation of the commissioner for Aruwimi district, who resided in
Basoko. In that year Elisabetha could rely upon a daily average of 1,831
men, who were serving for two-month stints. In the month of April 1917,
the daily average fell sharply to 1,106 men, a figure which dropped still
further in the following months. The attention paid by the colonial service
to the HCB would seem to have flagged.

During the first days of August 1917, the director of Barumbu circle,
Dehees, went with Beissel to Kisangani in order to beg the governor of
Orientale province for help. There they found the commissioner general,
Alexis Bertrand, acting as governor. They explained to him that recruitment
of cutters of palm-fruit clusters was alarmingly low. They needed 600
cutters, men who knew how to climb palms, and yet had only 127. Their
approach seems not to have had any immediate effect, since Dehees wrote
on 2nd October to Bertrand:

> I would consider it an honour if you could kindly use your undoubted
> influence to help with the recruitment of our cutters of palm-nut clusters . . .
>
> I take the liberty of explaining to you how such help might take the
> form of the following measures:
> 1 Tax collection staggered across the whole year in the palm-tree areas.
> 2 Moral assistance from the territorial authorities who, by using their
>   influence with the chiefs and by proffering their considered advice to
>   the natives, may persuade the latter to come and work with us.
> 3 Increase in rates of tax in the palm-tree regions . . .
>
> The moral assistance granted us by the territorial authorities, should
> they be willing, is certainly the most important, and would be the most

effective, of such measures. In requesting such assistance, I believe that I am defending the best interests of the black man. The natives in our region are apathetic and lazy; in order to persuade them to work, it will be necessary to exert moral influence upon the authorities they respect and heed . . .

Bertrand wrote back on 10th October, stating that the question of providing the various enterprises with labour still concerned him, that for the time being he was asking much of the Africans as far as rice cultivation and the raffia harvest was concerned, but that he would attend to the business of recruitment just as soon as circumstances allowed him some respite. Bertrand left Kisangani a few days later.

Dehees returned to the attack with the titular governor, Demeulemeester. In a letter dated 11th January 1918, he repeated the gist of his letter of October 1917, while adding a number of further details: the daily average of workers had fallen to 1,327 in 1917; by 1st January 1918 only 706 men were left. "Our situation is genuinely critical", he concluded.[1] Demeulemeester reacted more positively than Bertrand had done to Dehees' plea for help. He raised the question in a letter sent on 7th February to the governor-general, enclosing with it copies of the Dehees–Bertrand correspondence. In his letter he pointed out that the severe labour shortage in Elisabetha had already been raised in a correspondence between the governor of Kisangani and the general government in Boma. The commissioners of Kisangani and Aruwimi district had been instructed to encourage those administered by them to enter into labour contracts of at least six months. Since coming to Kisangani, Demeulemeester went on, "I have raised the question once again, and I have asked the commissioners for Kisangani, Aruwimi, Lowa, Maniema and Ituri districts to investigate the possibility of recruiting cutters of clusters for the HCB." It was not only the Huileries that suffered from labour shortages, Demeulemeester continued, but other companies too. The natural laziness of the Africans was to blame, and, in addition, in Aruwimi district, the senseless competition from traders paying up to 45 centimes a kilo for palm nuts. The result was that Africans could meet their fiscal obligations without having to go and work for the HCB.

As these letters from Demeulemeester were reaching the acting governor-general, Charles Tombeur, the latter received a letter from Braham, the managing director of the HCB in Kinshasa. This letter, dated 14th March, asked him to do his utmost to back HCB recruitment in general. Tombeur forwarded Demeulemeester and Braham's letters to the Colonial Minister on 23rd March. He emphasised the critical nature of the situation in Elisabetha, comparing it to an analogous situation in the Kilo-Moto gold mines. As regards Braham's request, he wrote to say that he had instructed the territorial authorities to give the HCB's recruiting expeditions all the assistance that was compatible with existing laws and regulations. He added that there was little hope of achieving an appreciable improvement in the difficult recruiting situation, which had earlier been pointed out by the titular governor-general, Eugène Henry. He concluded his letter by noting that "provincial commissions for the recruitment of workers are to be set up".[2] (This last sentence indicates that Tombeur thought to solve the problem by setting up recruitment commissions, which he did through the ordinance of 22nd April 1918.)

The directives issued in pamphlet form in March 1917, mentioned above, stipulated that Africans' rights over their land lying within the circles were restricted to those already in existence in 1911, when the Convention came into force. The correspondence regarding this stipulation has something unreal, indeed repugnant, about it, once one knows that the so-called natural palm groves were in fact the property of the Africans. One such item of correspondence consists of a letter sent by Beissel on 20th September to the governor of Orientale province, after discussion with him at Kisangani. The letter bears witness to the greed and determination with which the HCB sought to grab almost all the palms growing within their circles. Here are a few extracts:

> Since the building of the factory in Elisabetha, the natives are supposed to have been informed that they cannot plant new crops on domainal land which our company has asked to lease; yet they continue nonetheless to encroach on the *territoires* granted to the Huileries du Congo Belge, they destroy the palm trees growing there and they settle in new regions which are often very distant from any village, without the administrators preventing them . . .
>
> You have been kind enough to tell me that these acts of taking possession were precarious and that we could reoccupy the land thus occupied as and when the harvests on the plantations had been completed. I have duly noted your rulings but I am hereby anxious to establish that the Société des Huileries du Congo Belge will never be able to recognise these occupations as rightfully maintained for the benefit of the natives and perpetrated in good faith, considering that our rights should be recognised and definitively fixed from the time of our settlement in the circles, or at any rate within a reasonable and not too distant lapse of time.
>
> It is up to the government to take such measures as it may deem useful in order to avoid the encroachments in question . . . it is crucial that the palms which have been conceded to us, and which constitute the basis of

our original settlement here, should be left intact and that encroachments upon them do not continue as they have been . . .

At the end of this letter Beissel confirmed that it was his intention to occupy in perpetuity land in the locality of Bomaneh, which is situated on the northern bank of the river Aruwimi, and which had been abandoned for many years. He proposed to ask to be allowed to lease the tract of land in this locality extending outwards from the zone of 1,500 metres requested by the company along both banks of the Aruwimi.[3]

There is good cause to be astonished by the arrogant tone of this letter, written on behalf of a company which was wholly dependent on the government for its manpower, given that it was not paying its workers an appropriate wage. There is also good cause to be surprised that those governing the colony were prepared to tolerate such a tone when the workers in Barumbu circle were suffering from hunger.

The workers' hunger appears plainly enough in the following passage from the economic report on Orientale province for 1920:

HCB: there are two thousand mouths to feed and the region is not producing enough to satisfy them. The commissioner for Aruwimi district declares moreover that, with the company paying only one franc for the weekly ration, its workers cannot sustain themselves as they should; he backs up this claim by noting that in this district a soldier's food costs at present 3.50 francs a week in this district, while food for the sick and for prisoners costs 1.50 francs.

This is the chief cause of the drop in the size of the native work-forces in Elisabetha circle. There is only one remedy to this situation, namely, large-scale cultivation of foodstuffs . . . We have noted that the Belgika company, in its enterprise on Bertha island [near to Kisangani], commits 1/10 of its personnel to cultivation of foodstuffs, without which it would be impossible to feed everyone. Why does the HCB not follow its example?

On 30th September 1921—after, it is worth noting, a delay of nine whole months—Minister Franck forwarded this text to the director of the HCB in Brussels. The latter sent it on to the company's headquarters in Liverpool, from where Managing Director Irvine drafted a long reply on 14th October. He wrote to say that the weekly ration had been raised at the start of the year to 1.75 francs per week, 25 centimes per day being the amount that had been fixed at this period in Alberta by the Deputy Public Prosecutor Jadot. "The wages of our workforce", Irvine went on, "are very satisfactory; doing piecework, our cutters and porters can very easily guarantee themselves a daily wage of 1.50 francs". He continued:

> May I make so bold, Your Honour, as to respectfully remind you of how, in the course of the visit you did us the great honour of paying to Alberta [around mid-1920], you had the opportunity to see a cutter climb a palm and cut off its clusters? This allowed you to grasp on the spot just how few minutes are needed to cut three or four of these clusters. Now, the native only has to cut twenty or so a day, in order to be sure of earning the high monthly wage of 40 to 45 francs, let alone the ration. The porters who transport the clusters from the collection point to the agricultural post are paid on the same basis. As for workers employed in the factory and in our stations, their remuneration is also at least adequate . . .

Where the cultivation of foodstuffs was concerned, Irvine maintained that the company had made many attempts, but unfortunately with little success. For this reason, it was buying rice, meat and fish, often preserved, which it sold to the workers at below cost price. He ended his letter by rejecting the comparison with the Belgika company, because the latter employed only a small fraction of the workers in the pay of the HCB.[4]

Towards mid-1923, the provincial doctor for Kisangani, René Mouchet, a man who had shown concern for the welfare of African workers throughout his career, carried out an inspection in Barumbu circle. In the relevant report he supplied more details, which had been lacking in Irvine's letter of 14th October 1921, concerning wages, rations and food supplies. They read as follows:

- ration: 1.20 francs per week in cash, plus 1.75 francs in free provisions (2 kilos of rice and kilo of fish per week), or in total 2.95 francs, or 42 centimes per day;
- wage: for cutters: 0.12 francs per cluster; for non-cutters: 0.55 to 0.65 francs per day, ration included.

On the basis of these figures, I would conclude that the cutters had to cut a dozen clusters in order to reach the daily wage of 1.50 francs recorded by Irvine. (In 1928, 7 clusters per day was considered to be a difficult task to execute.) This suggests that the 1923 wage was approximately 90 centimes. As for the non-cutters' wage, it was calculated on a daily rate, although it included a weekly ration. It seems to me that this was done deliberately in order to obscure the low levels of remuneration involved. In order to grasp what the daily wage really amounted to, one has to reduce it by 1.20 francs divided by 6, or in other words by 20 centimes, which gives 35 to 45 centimes. This sum falls far short of the twice 25 centimes written into the Renkin–Lever Convention, dating from before the First World War, while by 1923 the cost of living had quadrupled. This observation renders all further comment regarding wage levels superfluous.

Here is some more information from the Mouchet report on the workforce in Barumbu:

There are between 2,500 and 3,000 workers, distributed across small camps of 200 men maximum.

The dwellings provided are adobe huts measuring 4 by 3 metres, with verandas in front. These buildings are of good quality, but there are not enough of them. Although designed to hold 3 single men or one married man, there were, when I visited, overcrowded dwellings, as at Eboro, where there were dwellings containing 6-8 single men.

Sanitation in the camps is very poor. Either there are no latrines, or there are wretched "Arab ditches", which are poorly maintained, and which the natives do not use, probably for this very reason.

(The free distribution of the rice and fish ration is theoretical only.) In reality, the sole food that the blacks can obtain is *chickwangue*, and once again provisions often run short.

In certain posts (Eboro, for example), workers receive about half of their ration.

It must be acknowledged that the HCB management makes no attempt to remedy the situation, and simply asks the colonial administration to help it with recruitment and food supplies.

Supplies of *chickwangue* are very irregular. Some days the market is plentiful, on others not. There are never supplies in reserve. It would, however, be a simple matter to build a mill and to buy manioc roots, in order to have stores of flour, to set up food-producing plantations, to set aside reserves of rice . . .

In reality, it is a hand-to-mouth existence, and the workers suffer from this. Given such conditions, it is in no way surprising that many desert.

The medical service consists of a doctor in Elisabetha and seven to eight nurses distributed across the various posts. The manager of the enterprise plans to set up small infirmaries in each camp that is some distance from Elisabetha.

Mortality among the workers does not seem to be high . . . The number of deserters being high, and the sick often deserting for fear of the hospital, the recorded death rates probably do not reflect the real situation.

It was not until 28th December 1923 that the minister communicated the salient points from this report to Stubbe, drawing his attention to their very real importance. Stubbe, who had just got wind of the scathing report submitted by Doctor Lejeune on the situation in Lusanga, answered immediately, on 29th December. The HCB recognised, he wrote, that sufficiently comfortable accommodation was still lacking in some of their posts, but the authorities would find a very clear improvement in this sphere in the near future. The Eboro region had only been occupied relatively recently, and this was why accommodation still left something to be desired. "We were surprised to learn", he went on, "that there is a shortage of rice in Elisabetha, given that our management at Kinshasa had entered into a special contract six months ago for the supplying of rice to this circle." Stubbe concluded as follows: "We are grateful to you for having kindly drawn our attention to the above points, and we shall endeavour to draw the appropriate lessons from these criticisms."

This constitutes a clever answer from the HCB in Brussels to observations on Elisabetha, more shrewd certainly than that given by Irvine in Liverpool two years before. But Stubbe's cheerful demeanour could obviously in no way alter the concrete situation in the year that had just ended. The 1923 annual report for the Service des affaires économiques of Orientale province indicated that the company's black personnel were undernourished. This report had been drafted after a delay of nine months, so that Governor-General Rutten, upon receiving it in Boma in November 1924, wondered whether in the meantime the dietary situation had stayed the same in Elisabetha, or if the HCB had finally managed to triumph over the difficulties they had encountered in providing their workforce with food. On 22nd November 1924 he wrote to the governor of Orientale province to say that one should first of all suggest that the HCB take on the production of foodstuffs itself.[5] This represented a lame response to a situation which for some years had been intolerable. It would have been both simpler and more satisfactory to put a stop to the state's supplying of workers. But this would have been out of the question at this period, when it was a matter of implementing the 1922 circulars issued by Rutten's predecessor, Governor-General Lippens, which had instructed government officials to support the companies unconditionally.

In a letter dated 18th June 1924, Major J.E. Tinant, the director of Elisabetha, informed Demeulemeester that he was going on leave, and that he was to be replaced by Charles Dupont, the company's secretary general in Kinshasa: "I want to take this opportunity", he wrote, "of thanking you for the precious help you have kindly given me in enabling the company to flourish, while at the same time guaranteeing the populations collaborating with us a well-being whose effects are making themselves felt among the natives whom we employ." He then asked the governor to go on offering support to his successor, without which it would be impossible to realise the industrial development of Elisabetha. He added:

> It is clear that as the natives come to appreciate the advantages to be had from working in Elisabetha, the company will be more able to extend its activities, and will no longer require the same degree of involvement from government officers, but I regard it as my duty to alert you to the fact that at present their support is as indispensable for maintaining and further developing what has been achieved at Elisabetha as it is for the further progress of the natives.

Tinant's emphasis upon the material well-being and progress procured for the natives by his company sounded grotesquely false to a governor whose agents were year after year delivering up forced labourers to it. Demeulemeester answered as follows:

> Permit me to tell you in all sincerity that you have in no wise convinced me that such material well-being, the beneficial effects of which, your letter implies, have already been felt by the natives in your employ, has been attained. If this were the case, the government's support would certainly no longer be indispensable. You know on the other hand that certain guidelines in my own ordinance on health and safety have not always been spontaneously observed at the HCB.

Demeulemeester tempered this pertinent observation by adding that he recognised that Tinant's relations with the provincial government had been dominated by the concern to serve the company's best interests while not neglecting those of his African personnel.[6]

In his own flattering style, Dupont asked the commissioner for Aruwimi district, on 7th September, to let him know, *territoire* by *territoire*, the number of temporary workers available for stints of three months for the HCB in the district, together with the chiefs and sub-chiefs of the *chefferies*. He needed the information in view of the impending visit to Barumbu circle of Lord Leverhulme, who planned to set up two new factories there, one at Basoko, the other at Barumbu, where the state was still running its old coffee plantation, although it had been partly turned into an *elaeis* plantation.

In a letter from Basoko dated 31st October, the acting district commissioner, Emmanuel Schmitz, sent Dupont two tables containing figures for

74,039 men surveyed, and detailing their ethnic group and *territoire*. He noted that 30,000 men had to be subtracted from this figure, namely, those from the distant *territoires* of Lokilo and Opala, the Lokele and other peoples living on the water, and the Mombesa of Mondimbi who had only recently been subdued. There remained 44,000 men, from whom one had again to deduct 20%, because they were either too old, too sick or too young, which reduced the potential workforce to 35,200. On the other hand, 5,000 men were employed in the (HCB) enterprises, although the upper limit to recruitment had been fixed by the governor of the province at 10%. Consequently, Schmitz concluded:

> The maximum figure for the quota of temporary workers to be supplied by the district has now been attained, unless further legislation allows us to . . . [a word is suppressed] persuade the natives to become in greater numbers workers for your company. [The word suppressed is undoubtedly "force", or some synonym, because the word "persuade" is preceded by the interjection "suppose we write".] The figure for HCB workers is now as high as 4,000, of whom almost 3,000 are supplied by Aruwimi district . . .
>
> Your management ought to bear in mind the unpopularity the work that you impose enjoys [sic] . . . and should not exaggerate its appeal to the workforce.[7]

In a report dated 22nd June 1925, Schmitz wrote to the governor of the province: "Recruitment of workers for the HCB has been for many years so unpopular with the natives that the moral pressure exerted by the territorial administrators barely prevails." Later in the same report, Schmitz wrote:

> The whole of Aruwimi district is rich, and a worker gathering the natural produce of the forest (palm nuts especially) may readily earn a living and create resources not available to him through labour in industry or trade. Nevertheless, personnel for the trading sector are easily found. The same cannot be said for workers in industry, who are hard to recruit. The only way to effect an easy transition between [forced] labour and free waged labour would be to pay the worker a wage that is at least equal to what he can earn without leaving his village or changing his habits. The only industrial firm established in the district [the HCB] offers its workers a wage that in no way compensates them for their sacrifices—I refer here as much to the monetary question as to the changes in the way of life of the person hired—which they are "persuaded" to accept. Up until now recourse has been had, in order

to accustom the native and to bring him gradually to commit himself to the above-mentioned enterprise, to short-term contracts (3 months). Even for so brief a stint, the workers would no longer commit themselves if the administration were to refrain from interfering. The situation is exacerbated by the fact that this industry has no facilities for growing its own crops. The workers' principal grievance against the firm is the fact that they do not receive a ration in kind.

In response to the above remarks, acting Governor Moeller noted on 16th November 1925: "I would point out that, at my prompting, wages have recently been doubled and that the ration is to be improved by reintroducing meat paid in kind."[8] Here Moeller took his wishes for reality. Wages were in fact only raised in August 1926. Nevertheless, by 31st December 1925 the number of requisitioned workers had risen to 5,500, of whom 3,605 were from the Aruwimi and 1,895 from other areas.

The Mill Hill Fathers against the State and the HCB (1925–1926)

The Mill Hill Fathers, who were for the most part from the Netherlands, had been proselytising in Lulonga district since the time of their arrival in the Congo, in 1905.[9] Father Théodore Vanderlinden belonged to the group arriving in that year. In 1907 he had founded the Baringa mission, and had been its Father Superior for many a long year. On 18th June 1925, in Baringa, he took up his pen to denounce the requisitioning of his flock, who had been compelled to hunt, in order to supply the military garrison of Basankusu, the administrative centre of the district, with fresh meat. He addressed his complaint to Monsignor Camille Vanronslé, apostolic vicar of Kinshasa, beseeching him to bring it, by way of the Commission for the Protection of Natives, to the attention of the relevant authorities, in order that requisitioning might cease forthwith.

The archives no longer have the original version of the complaint. There is just one copy, whose accuracy as regards the numerous figures quoted may well be doubted. Here are the main passages, in abridged form, from the copy:

The populations of Befale *territoire* have been absent from the villages since January. Up until mid-March they were collecting copal-resin[10] in the forest in order to pay taxes. Since April most of the *chefferies*—following a directive from the Basankusu district commissioner—have been supposed to furnish between them 500 kilos of dried meat each month for the soldiers of the administrative centre. Each *chefferie* has to furnish seven baskets of meat monthly, that is, about 140 kilos. [Which would suggest that three to four *chefferies* were involved in furnishing this compulsory labour.] Each basket holds around thirty portions of meat representing five animals, that is to say, of pig, of "*isoko*", of "*benbende*" and of "*befale*". In order to furnish the quantity of meat demanded, 500 of these animals have to be killed each month. In order to furnish 500 of these animals, one has to shoot at least 5,000. Since this intense hunting by the entire population, the two hunters at the mission have not killed even the smallest game.

It is utterly impossible for the blacks to furnish the quantities assigned.

The administrator pays 10 francs per basket containing 20 to 30 kilos of meat. A pig, when freshly killed, has a market value of 100 francs. A basket is therefore worth from 400 to 500 francs.

The soldiers of Basankusu receive so much meat that they sell some of it on to the tax collectors at a high price.

Cultivated crops are out of the question when the population is always absent. There is good cause to suppose that a general famine will not be long in coming. Simba *territoire* too is supposed to furnish 500 kilos of meat, as are various other *territoires*. This therefore means that each month 500 baskets of meat are requisitioned for the soldiers of Basankusu.

In no village has the catechism been given since January. Christians are prevented by the chief from attending Mass. I have protested to the district commissioner, but to no avail. The government has no right to deprive the natives of food that they sorely need, and all for a derisory price. It is not permissible to mobilise an entire population in order to supply 150 soldiers. The latter could see to it themselves. The roads in the *territoire* are becoming impassable and the villages are falling to rack and ruin. Continual camping in the forest cannot be good for health.

The apostolic vicar forwarded the above complaint to the public prosecutor, Victor Vandenbroeck, who on 21st August passed it on to the governor-general, with the following comments:

> Setting aside the harmful consequences of, and the injustices inherent in, the above-mentioned requirement the compulsory labour thus demanded of the local population represents an abuse of power, given that it not on the list of tasks that may be required of the *chefferies* in the ordinary course of things, above all if, as is claimed, the remuneration provided is below its local value.
>
> The actions denounced being therefore liable in themselves to legal proceedings, I would be much obliged to you if you would let me know if

the public prosecutor should set up an enquiry to investigate them, in order to rule judicially on their illegality.

On 22nd September, Demeulemeester, as acting governor-general, answered Vandenbroeck as follows:

> I see no need to call upon the public prosecutor's office to instigate an enquiry. I am inviting the governor of Equateur province to check the truth of Father Vanderlinden's assertions. The improbabilities and contradictions in his letter cause one to doubt the well-foundedness of his complaint.
>
> Having said that the *chefferies* are supposed to furnish 500 kilos of meat, he says further on that 500 pigs, *isoko*, *benbende* and *befale* have to be found to satisfy this monthly requisition of 500 kilos of meat. So, in order to furnish this quantity, 5,000 animals have to be slaughtered! Further on the 500 kilos . . . become 500 baskets weighing around 20 to 30 kilos each. [Here Demeulemeester is being disingenuous, since the 500 baskets refer to several *territoires*, including that of Simba.].
>
> You will perhaps reckon that there is good cause, in your role as president of the Commission for the Protection of Natives, to caution Monsignor Vanronslé against supporting complaints which, whilst tending to cast suspicion on the fashion in which our civil servants and agents treat the natives, seem at first glance to be if not pure phantasy at any rate marred by blatant exaggeration. Complaints of this kind are bound to damage the good relations which should prevail between missionaries and civil servants.

On this same 22nd September Demeulemeester sent copies of the complaint, and of the public prosecutor's comments, to the governor of Equateur province, drawing his attention to the improbable nature of Vanderlinden's allegations, while at the same time asking him to decide which of them should be addressed, and to curb injustices, if indeed there were any.

The file was then forwarded by the governor to the commissioner for Basankusu district, Henri Dupuis, whose predecessor, François Jorissen, was at the origin of the whole affair. For the latter had in fact written on 11th March to the territorial administrator of Befale to the effect that he had read in his correspondence that he could easily provide 300 kilos of meat for the black personnel in Basankusu. Jorissen had therefore asked him to deliver to the district's administrative headquarters by canoe, and on a monthly basis, all the dried meat that was available in his *territoire*.

On 2nd November Dupuis forwarded a copy of this letter to the governor, commenting that most of the points raised by Vanderlinden would have to be examined on the spot, which he would do forthwith. But, he asserted, on the basis of accountable receipts in the district, between March and the end of September Befale had sent 1,666 kilos of smoke-dried meat, on average 238 kilos per month. This indicated that the soldiers, who needed 23 kilos of meat per day for themselves and for their families, had not sold any of it. (This was faulty reasoning since Simba was also supplying meat.)

Eight months later, on 6th July 1926, Dupuis filed a report on his local investigation. His findings were, in outline, as follows:

Vanderlinden's allegations were unfounded. Jorissen had stipulated that 300 kilos should be supplied monthly, not 500 kilos. [Partly inaccurate because he had also mentioned "all the dried meat available".] The territorial administrator divided up this quantity between the sixteen *chefferies* mentioned by Dupuis, which represented 9,782 tax-payers all told. The latter had between them supplied 1,801 kilos in 6 months, or 185 grams per tax-payer. The *chefferie* of Loma-Moke, situated in the region of Lingunda, which was very rich in game, had supplied the most, namely, 185 kilos, representing 1,330 grams for every adult man. [This calculation, which seeks to prove too much, is certainly not truthful.]

As for the price paid, it was not 10 francs a basket but 1 franc a kilo, the tariff accepted by natives for supplying smoked meat to the state. It is true that the wild pig sold to the Europeans fetches 100 francs or even more, but an African who has grown rich through copal-resin, will readily agree to supply the state with food at a moderate price. [Here the African is credited with a generosity that defies belief.][11]

I think that one can conclude from this affair that, while Vanderlinden may have exaggerated the number of animals killed, given the price paid for the fresh meat the Africans were required to supply, the State was robbing them blind.

In the meantime Elisabetha HCB and the Mill Hill mission in Simba had begun to fight tooth and nail. The area of activity of this mission, like Simba *territoire*, extended from Djolu in the west to Yahuma in the east, on either side of the river Lopori. Father A. Gutersohn, who had founded the mission in 1921 and served as Superior from that time on, had in particular incurred the wrath of Director Dupont because he was preaching to his flock that they had the right to refuse to work for the HCB. On 7th April 1926 Dupont duly wrote to Beissel that the only obstacle to recruitment in the region of Simba lay in the at times overt, at times covert, but certainly unremitting opposition of the members of the Catholic mission established there. By way of illustration of this claim—which the territorial administrator Jean Thorn would, according to Dupont, readily confirm—he quoted four cases of opposition recorded by his labour recruiter Munchen during his trip in Simba in the previous February–March. These cases were chiefly attributable to Father Gutersohn, who was advising those recruited not to go and work in Elisabetha. He concluded: "At any rate the opposition of the missionaries in Simba, which grows livelier by the year, has aroused such prejudice against us that I reckon that it is no longer possible to tolerate it without protest, nor without having recourse to government intervention."

On 28th April Beissel forwarded an extract from Dupont's letter to the governor of Equateur province, with the comment that it did not sit well with a mission, and a foreign one at that, to thwart the development of an industry. He requested the governor to intervene in the most prompt and effective manner possible with the Mill Hill missionaries in Basankusu, with a view to curbing without delay the prejudices aroused against his company. (The reader will have noticed that Beissel, though the boss of a wholly English enterprise, did not scruple to emphasise the foreign nature of Gutersohn's congregation.) The commissioner-general for Equateur province, Walter Parker, simply forwarded Beissel's letter to the governor-general, on 5th June.

On 12th July, Territorial Administrator Thorn sent the district commissioner in Lulonga a long report referring to Dupont's letter mentioned above. Here is a first extract:

> During my last visit to Elisabetha in January last . . . I let Dupuis know what I had anyway informed him of in my annual report for 1925, under the heading HCB recruitment, namely: "that we meet with very determined opposition from the Christians, which sometimes leads to flight from a village as soon as a recruiter appears. The natives, upon seeing that the Christians categorically refuse to commit themselves to the HCB, follow the example of the latter and take to their heels."

In the later parts of his letter, Thorn told what he knew of the four instances of opposition mentioned by Dupont. From this account it transpired that the administrator was often doing the rounds with the HCB recruiters, at times compelling the Christians to leave for Elisabetha. It also transpired that the Protestant missionaries in the Congo Balolo Mission at Yoseki did not wish to align themselves with the Mill Hill

Fathers in their opposition. Here is an extract from the later part of the letter, which amounted to a virulent attack upon Gutersohn:

> During a conversation I had at the beginning of 1925 with the Reverend Gutersohn, I pointed out to him that his attitude towards HCB recruiting was very far from neutral. He replied to me that the Mill Hill mission did not forbid its natives from going to the HCB; but that it considered it to be its duty to inform its adepts that HCB work is free and that no one can force them to go there.
>
> This assertion is perfectly right and proper, but anyone familiar with the native mentality will see where such advice leads, since it clashes with the efforts made by the colonial administration to show the native the usefulness and necessity of work, and to show that his moral and material improvement is simply a result of work.

It was startling hypocrisy on Thorn's part to speak of the "moral and material improvement" of the Africans, when he was himself requisitioning them for work to be done far away and in wretched conditions.

On 22nd September Parker forwarded Thorn's letter to the governor-general, with a view to his making some representations to the Mill Hill missionaries, and particularly to Father Gutersohn. In Boma one of Rutten's collaborators reckoned that the governor of Equateur province very often had recourse to the governor-general when having to take a disagreeable step. He suggested to his superior that he inform this governor that it was up to him to act. But Rutten was just as ready to write directly, he noted, because the attitude of the Mill Hill Fathers could not be condoned. If they had criticisms to make, they should at least make them openly, and not encourage the Africans to remain idle.

Rutten wished to respond personally to the attack levelled by Gutersohn at the sacrosanct entente sustaining the triangle of State, Catholic missions and companies. In a letter dated 22nd October he therefore wrote to G. Wantenaar, the Father Superior of the Mill Hill mission in Basankusu, to say that, according to the local administration and the HCB management, the adepts of his missions were putting up a strong opposition to the recruitment of workers for Elisabetha. In the later sections of his letter, Rutten reproduced almost word for word the passage from Thorn's report quoting his conversation with Gutersohn, and the latter's declaration that no one could force the Africans to go to the HCB. Rutten continued as follows:

> Assuredly in speaking thus Father Gutersohn is saying nothing that is not wholly the case, but you will allow that stating this principle in the

presence of natives who are only too prone to laziness can but serve to confirm them in their idleness. Without tendering advice serving to encourage them to work, and even when this precaution is taken, it can sometimes be imprudent to speak of their rights to primitives who are ignorant of their duties. Yet Father Gutersohn would seem to have failed to take such precautions: several natives have declared that, *on the express advice* of this missionary, they had refused to leave, even after having entered into a contract . . .

Permit me to hope that no further intervention on my part will prove necessary, and that the observations which you will not fail to make to your missionaries, will be enough to alter their attitude.

Father Superior Wantenaar answered on 13th February 1927 to say that he was astonished to learn that the adepts of the mission in Simba were not content simply to refuse for their own part to enrol with the HCB, but were also advising the villagers to abstain. He had in fact, he wrote, used his stay in Simba on 15th August 1926 to question the catechists, who had assembled for the feast of the Ascension, as to where their Christians stood. It transpired that, of a total of 1,311 tax-paying Christians, 239, that is to say, 18%, had enrolled with the oil mills in Elisabetha. He enclosed with his letter a table giving for each village, of which there were 64 all told, the number of Christians, and of those the number working for the HCB. Wantenaar commented on these figures as follows:

Either these 239 Christians enrolled in the oil mills, are volunteers, or they have been recruited by force.

If they are volunteers, it seems to me that the Christians of Simba have done their duty, and even more than their duty towards the oil mills, and that the complaint directed at them and at their missionary, Father Gutersohn, is not well-founded.

If this high number of contracts is the outcome of forcible recruitment, it did not have the approval of the Government, given the declaration made by the right honourable Minister of Colonies to the effect that . . . "in no case and in no region, could more than five per cent of the adult, able-bodied men in any community be recruited" . . .

Also I know that, where the recruitment of married Christians in the region of Simba is concerned, the husband often sets out on his own for Elisabetha while the wife, especially if she has children, remains in the village, for fear of having nothing to eat in Elisabetha. I also know that this abnormal situation has destroyed monogamous marriages sanctioned by religion. It seems to me that in such cases the missionary has the right, and even the duty, to intervene, to oppose recruitment, and, should the need arise, to inform the natives concerned that no one can force them to enter the oil-mills.

I have already asked Reverend Father Gutersohn to be prudent and not to interfere with recruiting, save in cases where the moral or religious interests of Christians are at stake.

On the other hand, and with all due respect, may I take the liberty of asking you to protect the Mongandu population in the region of Simba. During my visit, in the month of August, I had the impression that too much pressure is put on this population. The natives are continually being forced to leave their villages, either to serve for a term in the oil mills or to go hunting—if I am not mistaken they are supposed to supply the soldiers at Basankusu with 700 kilos of meat—or to porter this meat from their own village to Simba, or from Simba to Mompono, or again to carry out repairs to roads, etc., sometimes very far from their own village. When I travelled from Simba to Befori I found almost all the villages abandoned; the entire population was in the forest, hunting for Basankusu, and Father Vanderhelm of Simba, who was accompanying me, assured me that this situation, with almost wholly deserted villages, was normal for 10 to 14 days each month.

Wantenaar's response made an impression on Rutten, who commented on it in a letter sent on 9th February 1927 to the governor of Equateur province. While obviously taking care to skirt around the crucial question of recruitment, voluntary or forced, he made the following observations:

- The missionaries' interference in recruitment could only be tolerated if it was shown beyond dispute that in practice a wife with children could not accompany her husband. Where the opposite was the case, it was the duty of the missionaries to urge the men to get their families to accompany them.
- Admitting as likely the claim that a wife would stay in her village for fear of not having anything to eat at Elisabetha, was tantamount to concluding that in this circle the HCB were not doing their utmost to give their workers healthy and plentiful food.
- The assertions regarding demands for game imposed on the Mongandu of Simba seemed exaggerated. They resembled those made by Father Vanderlinden in 1925.

In other respects, Rutten clearly showed that as far as he was concerned the affair was closed. He asked his correspondent to draw the attention of the

HCB management in Elisabetha to the question of the purportedly insufficient food and to inform it of the other complaints made against it by the
Mill Hill Fathers. On the other hand, he asked him to draw the Fathers'
attention to the serious and inevitable repercussions for the future development of the HCB, should they persist in thwarting this company's
recruitment of its workforce.[12]

Alexis Bertrand in Barumbu circle (1930)

At the turn of the year 1930, Alexis Bertrand, commissioner general of
Kisangani, arrived in Barumbu circle in order to conduct an enquiry into the
repercussions of various intensive recruitments on the population in Orientale province.[13] In the introduction to his report, Bertrand described the
situation in Barumbu circle as follows:

> In the course of the debate within the provincial labour commission (session
> of 15th to 20th August 1930), the governor of Orientale province declared:
> "We take direct involvement to mean the government substituting itself
> completely for the recruiter. Direct involvement still exists in the case of the
> recruitment of 1,200 cutters of fruit for the Huileries du Congo Belge and for
> the Régie des Plantations de Barumbu . . . We take indirect involvement to
> mean a situation in which the administration does not actually recruit but
> merely provides moral assistance, and moral assistance only, to the recruiter,
> with territorial administrators almost invariably doing no more than indicate
> those *chefferies* in which, because of availability, recruitments can still be
> effected. In the Aruwimi, there is a more concrete kind of assistance, since the
> administrator is present alongside the HCB recruiter . . ."
>
> If the administrator accompanies the recruiter of a particular enterprise
> in order to assist him, there is no doubt at all that he is directly involved in
> the process; for the fact of leaving the completion of the formalities of
> recruitment to another does not alter the essential nature of one's activity.
> If the natives were more compliant, and if their sense of the inevitable
> were deeper, it would be enough for the administrator to use an
> intermediary, a "messenger", to intervene with the parties concerned,
> but that would still constitute direct involvement.

In the body of his report, under the heading "economic zone no. 3",
Bertrand considered the situation in Barumbu circle at greater length. He
began by considering two villages (Ya-Mokanda and Ya-Bibi) located in the
angle formed by the intersection of the Congo and Aruwimi rivers, to the
east of Basoko. He wrote as follows:

At all times they have resisted corvées, recruitments and various taxes . . .
About three years ago, the Huileries du Congo Belge decided to exploit
the region. The inhabitants agreed to play a part in the building of a road
intended to permit the transportation by lorry of palm fruit brought to
their villages. Success, which was rapid to start with, grew still more
intense and is tending now to even out. There was a veritable renaissance.

Bertrand then considered the case of two villages (Ya–Uma and Mokake)
located on the south-eastern boundary of the zone exploited by the HCB.
Of these he wrote:

In the last few years the HCB have taken the road up to where they live,
and now ask them simply to collect the fruit in their palm groves. Success
here was much the same as among the Turumbu [in the village of Ya-
Mokanda, mentioned above] . . .
   On the boundaries of its concession, the company has been engaged for
the last two or three years in the noble endeavour of advancing civilization, by involving the natives in its activities. The agreed remuneration, 5
francs for every 30 kilos of fruit [16.6 centimes a kilo], a remuneration
which moreover has not been undermined by the fall in the price of palm
oil products [as a result of the Great Depression], is adequate, since it is
welcomed by the sellers. It is the bringing of automobiles into general use
which has brought about an improvement in what had been a very bad
situation . . .

Bertrand then went on to describe the last two villages in the circle, Ya-
Mbenene and Ya-Mboloko, located in the centre of the concession, and to
take some demographic soundings there:

The situation is unfortunately very different in the centre of the concession, where the company first set out to exploit the palm groves.
Because it regarded the inhabitants, who were already few in number, as
undesirable rivals, it sought first of all to remove them. At the same time,
given its need for labour, it subjected them to urgent and unrelenting
requests to become wage labourers, who would have to gather produce
they regarded as their own for others, and who would work as porters, etc.
The effect of overworking may plainly be seen: they complain about
everything, even of suffering from hunger, which is manifestly not the
case. Their huts are in an utterly dilapidated state. They reek of demor-
alisation. If at present they are allowed to draw breath—relatively speaking, moreover, for the factories have to turn—a heavy past still weighs

upon them. In the two villages, the 198 women have only 174 children between them.

Bertrand then went on to consider in more general terms the HCB's activities within the circle. He wrote that, on average, a quota of 6,000 industrial workers was stationed there, whereas the specifically agricultural zone (involving the creation of new plantations) was still embryonic. He continued as follows:

> In Elisabetha circle, the palm groves are located in specific regions and have different degrees of density. The central zone, the first to be occupied and exploited, is sparsely inhabited: hence the major difficulties in feeding the mighty factories of Elisabetha. Factory work in the strict sense of the term, construction work and plantation work, which occupies around three quarters of the total workforce, is done by workers enrolling of their own free will. Sometimes, when the demand for labour is especially great, during the full harvest around March and April, administrators will send messengers to alert the chiefs to the fact that the quotas need to be boosted.

On this last point, I cannot agree with Bertrand. For he classifies as enrolling of their own free will those who had been recruited by chiefs following the orders of administrators as relayed by messengers, whereas he has told us in the introduction to his report that the mediation of a messenger amounted to the direct involvement of the administrator in recruiting, an involvement implying coercion. Bertrand's general remarks continue as follows:

> The natives dislike picking more than other tasks. The work is tiring, even dangerous, since it entails exploiting all the palms, even the giants, which in the forest may grow as tall as 15, 17, 18 metres. The natives therefore refuse to commit themselves continuously to so exhausting an occupation. When working at home, they would be able to choose when to exert themselves, and which trees to exploit. The requisite quota of cutters numbers around 1,500. The involvement, aptly termed direct, of the administration is necessary in the recruiting of over half of them . . . All able-bodied natives know how to climb palm trees; those who feel particularly threatened by the possibility of being summoned to Elisabetha take refuge in forms of employment which are despised elsewhere, such as those offered by an entrepreneur who supplies wood fuel for the steamers. So it is that, in order to obtain 700 or 800 men, a vast region is disrupted. About half of the production of the factories in Elisabetha circle depends upon this forced labour.[14]

While drawing attention to the use of coercion in relation to fruit cutting, the Bertrand report says many positive things about the exploitation of a part of the circle by non-waged villagers. He depicts the situation of the Turumbu in Basoko *territoire* as happy: the villagers, he claims, freely bring fruit in return for an appropriate remuneration. Bertrand does not breathe a word about the monopoly created by tripartite contracts or about the struggle against the latter waged by the merchants of Basoko. This fact is all the more astonishing given that in Belgium, four years later, he would lead the campaign against this monopoly, as we shall see later. We have no choice but to conclude that Bertrand, when strewing flowers in the path of the HCB, had been less than wholly sincere.

In Brussels at this period one pretended to know nothing of the forced recruitment carried out on behalf of the HCB. For their part, the English, the compatriots of Lord Leverhulme, guessed what was going on. In his report of September 1926, entitled *Visit to West Africa*, the Under-Secretary of State for the Colonies, William Ormsby-Gore wrote:

> It is perfectly clear that the type of concession from which Lord Leverhulme benefits in the Congo, is unthinkable in a British protectorate . . . There can be no doubt that the system existing in the Congo is accompanied not only by monopoly rights, but also by some elements of coercion. And the problem with coercion in any form whatsoever, is that it only succeeds in the long term when it is employed in a consistent and thoroughgoing fashion. It is pointless to imagine that one can combine a voluntary system with a slight element of constraint. Every programme of the kind fails if you are not prepared to take obligation further.[15]

As the years passed, Brussels pretended to know nothing and took offence whenever the expression "forced labour" cropped up. This was the case around October 1927, on the occasion of a visit paid by Thorn to the Ministry of Colonies. The minister Henri Jaspar wrote of it to the governor-general as follows:

> Thorn has assured me that in the Simba territory 28.5% of the adult, able-bodied men, in the aftermath of recruitments, were working some distance away . . . When questioned as to the possibility that he might be mistaken, the above-mentioned civil servant stuck by what he had said. More particularly, he specified that he had had to supply 1,000 men each quarter for the HCB. He added that the contracts were only voluntary in a very relative sense, and could indeed be said to be forced.

Jaspar asked the governor-general to check with the district commissioner as to the well-foundedness of the above declaration, and, if the situation really was as had been represented to him, to ascertain who was responsible.[16]

Such words were merely for public consumption, and were clearly not followed up.

5

In the Basongo and Lusanga Circles (1923–1930)

At the beginning of 1926, at the time of the ban on the colonial administration recruiting directly for private companies, the HCB bosses had found themselves in the forefront of the protesting employers, and had threatened to shut up shop in the Congo if the state stopped supplying them with workers enrolled by force.[1] Stubbe and Edkins had obviously not brandished this threat in too crude a fashion, but had presented it in the flowery and verbose terms habitually employed by the company, during an audience they had requested with the administrator general of the colonies, Arnold, in order to give voice to the "disquiet" they had felt upon learning of the circulars recently issued on the topic of recruitment.

Upon leaving the audience, Stubbe and Edkins wrote Arnold a letter, dated 8th June 1926, in which from the outset they expressed their doubts as to the wisdom of persevering with their vast projects in the Congo, which they now judged to be under threat. They outlined their case as follows:

> Rest assured that we deeply appreciate the lofty ideal from which the principles underlying the proposed modification of the system of labour recruitment take their inspiration, but we refuse to believe that the Government would deliberately decide to halt the economic development of the Colony by launching too suddenly a labour policy which would mean the authorities in the near future playing no part at all in the recruitment of workers for private industry and trade.
>
> If we may be permitted to express an opinion, . . . we believe that the extraordinary development of the Congo, due to the marvellous efforts of Belgium and of the wise and vigorous administration bestowed upon the Congo by the Belgian Government, was realised in a period not exceeding ten or fifteen years, that this rapid progress imparted in the main by the industrial and commercial enterprises which have proliferated

in every district of the country, has not been matched by a corresponding advance in the mentality, mores and needs of the natives. The Congo has achieved more in this short space of time than other colonies have achieved in fifty, or even in a hundred years. In these latter colonies, the natives have had the time to grasp, in stages, the great advantages that the law of work will procure for them, and therefore prove readier to work willingly and to participate loyally in the shared task of colonisation and progress. In the Congo, such an evolution, of necessity slow, has not occurred, and the conclusion must in our opinion be, at any rate for some years to come, that the natives should be guided and invited by every possible means of persuasion, to lend their services . . .

You will, I hope, forgive us, if once again, . . . we point out to you, aside from the contribution we make, or so we believe, to the Colony's prosperity, all the good, both physical and moral, that our native policy on recruitment, food and accommodation, and our social institutions, in-cluding hospitals and schools, guarantee to the black populations living in a context shaped by our activities.[2]

There should be no need for me to comment at length on the comparison advanced here between the Congo and the other colonies. If less coercion proved necessary in the latter, the reason was that something closer to an appropriate wage was paid. As for Lever's claim, repeated again here, to be guaranteeing the physical and moral well-being of the black populations, it strikes me as being too absurd to merit further consideration.

Even before Stubbe and Edkins had broached the question of recruitment with Arnold, the general management of the HCB in Kinshasa had obtained an audience with the governor-general, with a view to putting the same question to him, and had taken care to confirm in writing, on 4th June 1926, its purpose in approaching him:

The Colonial Minister has sent you a circular stating that there are good grounds for depriving the employers of the active support of the territorial administration, which is, however, in our opinion INDISPENSABLE, if they are to be successful in hiring the workers needed for their enterprises. It is plain enough that in districts such as Aruwimi, Kwango and Kasai, the local populations are not as yet sufficiently subdued or accustomed to work, for private parties, disposing neither of the means nor of the prestige of the state, to obtain either satisfactory or even significant results in recruitment.

We have been most gratified to note that you share our views and that you have readily admitted that the application of the anticipated measure by the minister is liable to give rise to the gravest difficulties.[3]

The reader will already know from the previous chapter that the aforesaid measure was not implemented, and that the colonial administration continued to recruit directly for private companies, and in particular for the HCB.

Echoes of Basongo circle (1923–1927)

If we wished to assess the relative importance of the various circles, measured in terms of the tonnage of palm fruit handled in 1933, Lusanga would have been the giant (56,000 tonnes) and Basongo the dwarf (1,200 tonnes). Barumbu and Ebonda would have come in second and third (22,000 and 19,000 tonnes respectively), while Ingende was in fourth position, with 8,400 tonnes.[4] In 1932 Lusanga boasted eleven factories, Barumbu and Ebonda three each, and Ingende and Basongo one each.

I have found virtually nothing on Ingende in the African archives. I have discovered some information, however, on Basongo, regarding the beginning of Lever's activities in 1920 and the building of the factory in 1921. This late start was probably due to the low density of the palms, which in its turn accounts for the low output of the factory.

Brabanta, the headquarters of the circle, situated on the river Kasai a dozen or so kilometres upstream from Basongo, had been built on land belonging to a village by the name of Mapangu. In November 1923, a journalist by the name of Chalux, who sang the praises of Belgian colonisation and of the roadside villages in Tshikapa, went on to Brabanta. He described it as a miniature paradise:

> Results in two years: the clearing of a vast area; *elaeis* planted (for ten metres in every direction) among the existing *elaeis*; a fine road; paths, several houses built on a model that is not merely comfortable but actually quite charming—a veritable "home"; a huge village of workers who are *in good health and therefore well-nourished* [Chalux's italics], and a future village under construction—consisting of brick houses, with small verandas, if you please; plantations; a general sense of satisfaction; a water-tower; a tennis court (to be sure!); a doctor, a dispensary for Europeans, another for blacks, a hospital for blacks, a sanitation team; many children—a revealing indication of the stability of the workforce; and finally, a large model factory.[5]

Before the publication of the book containing this idyllic description, an embellished version of the latter had been published in Chalux's own paper,

La Nation Belge, on 18th January 1924. Stubbe took pride in drawing this article to the attention of Arnold, who was secretary general at the Colonial Ministry during this period. Chalux had in fact written it after a long evening spent as the guest of Sidney Edkins on board the *Lusanga*, one of the HCB's luxurious boats.

Arnold replied to Stubbe on 25th January 1924: "I have noted with satisfaction the excellent results achieved by your company in this circle. I was particularly struck by the good impression the workers' village and the development of new plantations made on the author of the article."[6] Was the workers' situation in Brabanta really as good during this period as Chalux would have us believe? The relevant shreds of information in the archives suggest otherwise. They also mention Lode Achten, already encountered in chapter 3, who was serving as district commissioner of the Kasai when Chalux visited Brabanta. According to a report by Achten, the HCB's agent, Lemaire, went in February 1924 to the regions of Dibaya and Luisa, and succeeded in recruiting 613 men for a period of six months. Towards the end of 1925, their situation was as follows: 415 repatriated, 55 deserters, 50 dead at Mobendi and Sanga–Sanga, 90 had re-enrolled and 3 were in the hospital at Brabanta. The death rate there exceeded 9%. These 613 forcibly enrolled workers had arrived at Brabanta between March 1924 and the beginning of 1925.[7] Managing Director Beissel acknowledged that there had been 51 deaths, all in 1925.[8]

Achten greatly blamed the managers of Basongo circle for the sad fate to which they had condemned the workers recruited by them in 1924. The following year, he must have deplored the manner in which these same managers interpreted the imposition of the tripartite contracts. Governor Engels wrote on this subject as follows:

> In Brabanta they came very close to regarding the tripartite contract as compelling the native to devote all his labour and all his time to picking and supplying fruit for the factory. A table of prestations had been drawn up and the administrator was called upon to intervene whenever they were not supplied. Company sentries were posted in the villages and harassed the natives until the prestations were supplied. It was verging on forced labour, and there was bound to be a reaction.[9]

One can see from the above that Achten, in his article quoted in chapter 3, had been very careful not to tell the whole truth.

In 1926 Brabanta circle instigated the hunting-down of forcibly enrolled workers in the district of Mai Ndombe, performed by three white agents aided by the territorial administration. This fact can be deduced from the following extract, taken from the annual report for Equateur province that same year:

> Bakutshu *territoire* [administrative centre, Lokolama]:
> Following arrests made a little hastily by a young territorial agent, a native from the village of Isombo, in the region of Ila, wounded a soldier with an arrow. The public prosecutor was informed and his ruling is still awaited. Complaints were lodged with the public prosecutor against three Europeans from Brabanta HCB, who were accused of making arbitrary arrests and of striking natives, and the charges have been drawn to the attention of the managing director of the HCB.

A document from the beginning of 1927 sheds some light, albeit with a delay of two years, on the situation of the workers in Brabanta. This was the court record of the judgment delivered on 3rd January 1927 by Alphonse Wauters, presiding magistrate at the magistrate's court in Luebo, in the case of the Dane Erik Zeberg, HCB agent in Sanga-Sanga. On 25th November 1924, the latter had dealt an elderly worker, Tshisimbi, about whom no other details are known, a mortal blow. In his defence, Zeberg claimed that he had merely given Tshisimbi a slap, which could not have caused his death. The latter was due, in his opinion, to the wretched state of the workforce at Sanga-Sanga: all the workers were ill-fed, wretched and suffered from an average monthly death rate of 4 or 5 men out of a total of 450; of 520 men, around 50 had died in the course of eight months.

The court found in Zeberg's favour. It ruled that Tshisimbi's death was due to the wretched state of the HCB workforce. It acquitted the Dane of the charge of having inflicted blows and wounds without intending to cause death, having nonetheless caused it. It could not then condemn him simply for the blows, the fact being covered by the charge. Here is an extract from the summing-up:

> Whereas a regime, of the kind described by Zeberg, in which there is an annual mortality rate of over 10% . . . in which natives, of advanced years, sent far from their own villages, are dealt slaps and punches to force them to work, should be described as murderous; whereas the indications given by the accused, to explain in terms of great age, weakness and inadequate food a death occurring in overwhelming circumstances, should earn him, for his share of responsibility, severe reproaches, it would nevertheless not be permissible to maintain that through the mere fact of participating in such a regime, the accused should be pronounced guilty of any specific murder . . .

Given the lamentable conditions suffered by the workers at Brabanta, the colonial personnel in the Kasai were not prepared to carry out every act requested of them by the circle's management. Proof of this point was furnished by the administrator in Kananga who, in response to a request made in a letter of 25th September 1926, refused to dispatch to Brabanta the wives of workers who were asking for their spouses to come to their side. On 19th January 1927, the administrator in question, Emile Vallaeys, phrased his refusal as follows:

> The chiefs of the workers asking for their women are opposed to the idea of the latter going to rejoin their husbands, and claim that the latter are well past the end of their terms of service. I would in fact point out that it is over a year since these men left the *territoire*. It would be politically advisable to send them back to their *chefferie* on the expiry of their term; they would then be able to enter into a new contract and set out again with their wives.

This answer, which was full of good sense, provided managing director Edkins in Kinshasa with yet another reason to beat the drum for Lever's progress-boosting mission in the Congo. In a letter dated 13th April 1927 he sent Engels a copy of the correspondence exchanged between the director of Brabanta circle and Vallaeys regarding the sending of women to the circle, condemning the chiefs' attitudes and urging the governor to intervene. He took care to inform the governor-general of the affair, and added the following comments:

> While we fully respect the laws governing native areas, we nonetheless reckon that the latter cannot rightly serve as a pretext for obstructing the economic advance of the colony. Thus we reckon and we dare to hope that you will share our opinion that the stabilisation of the workforce indubitably constitutes the crucial factor in ensuring the economic progress of the Congo.

The governor instructed Achten to have the women sent.

Having received the public prosecutor's ruling on the Zeberg affair, on 10th May 1927 Rutten forwarded a copy to Engels with the following order:

> As the judge of the first instance would appear to have accepted the statements of the accused as the plain, unvarnished truth without having checked the accuracy of what he has said . . . I would be grateful if you

would hold an enquiry into this matter and let me know the outcome as soon as possible.

On 1st June Engels answered that he had asked the district commissioner to inform him of the workforce's circumstances. He enclosed an extract on the health and safety statistics for Brabanta which, he wrote, showed a marked improvement in 1926, as against 1925. He added:

> During my last visit to Brabanta, in February 1927, I found the situation as regards health and safety to be very satisfactory. Doctor Clémen, who is in charge of the medical service, gave the impression of taking good care of the workforce; the camps were suitable and well-kept, the workers well-fed and well-treated.

On 4th June 1927 Edkins sent Engels a letter six pages long protesting vehemently against the Zeberg ruling, which, according to him, wholly destroyed the good name of his company, although it concerned an affair dating back to 1924, and to that old story of the ill-fated recruitment of Lemaire, the chief of Sanga-Sanga plantation. Since then, Edkins insisted, everything had changed for the better in Brabanta, where the ninety men who had re-enrolled in 1925 had renewed their contracts each year. The current situation was equally satisfactory in the other circles. He continued as follows:

> We have in our enterprises in Alberta 3,700 permanent workers, who have renewed their contracts on a yearly basis for the last five or six years. Only two months ago the governor of Equateur province, Duchesne, awarded the bronze medal to 197 men among our personnel in Alberta who have been in our service for over ten years. Governor Moeller of Orientale province has expressed his satisfaction to M. Dupont at seeing the number of permanent workers in Elisabetha reach the figure of 2,599. In Lusanga too we have several thousand permanent workers who have been in our service for many a year.

For the reader's sake I ought perhaps to express some reservations as to the reliability of the above figures. We saw in the previous chapter how things really stood in Elisabetha, and we shall see how in Lusanga contracts were for life, and renewed automatically. The limited information in the archives on workers' conditions in Alberta does not readily lend itself to the idea that re-enrolments were voluntary.

In concluding his letter of 4th June, Edkins asked Engels what steps he should take to protect the good name of his company. Zeberg had said to him in writing that he had never declared to the court what Judge Wauters had attributed to him in his summing-up. "I am quite prepared", Edkins added, "to institute proceedings against Zeberg, but I do not see upon what grounds I could act." Engels would later reply that he could not say what he should do, and advised him to consult his lawyer.

Rutten, for his part, did his utmost to save the honour of the Brabanta HCB. He wrote to the interim public prosecutor, Charles Leynen, on 27th June 1927:

> M. Beissel informs me that the mortality rate at Brabanta in 1926 is not as high as nine per thousand. Furthermore, he assures me that never at any moment has a regime permitting brutality existed in the firm's enterprises run by him. These claims have been corroborated by the territorial authorities and by the governor of Congo-Kasai province.
>
> Under these circumstances I would be much obliged if you would forward to me the file on the Zeberg affair, so that I can acquaint myself with the testimonies collected by the judges, upon which criticism of the HCB's general policy towards the natives has been founded.

On 8th August Leynen sent the Zeberg file to the governor-general, who had it examined by the acting director general of AIMO (Affaires indigènes et main-d'oeuvre du gouvernement général), Robert Reisdorff. The latter presented his conclusions in a note dated 12th September 1927, the essence of which reads, in abridged form, as follows:

> In support of the reasons adduced for the ruling, there are only two declarations by Zeberg and those of the four workers at the post of Sanga-Sanga, namely, Tumba, Ganga, Tshimbwabwa and Sasa. The declarations of the four could be summarised as follows: "Zeberg often used to hit workers; the diet was bad at Sanga-Sanga; recruitment had been effected by means of administrative pressure; many workers died." These four witnesses belonged to the same ethnic group as the victim.
>
> One can therefore concede that the severity of the ruling, as far as the Huileries du Congo Belge is concerned, is out of proportion to the testimonies collected in relation to this affair.
>
> Yet it should be borne in mind that the events described took place in November 1924, that the ruling was only made in [January 1927] and that, in the intervening period, the HCB's reputation as regards the

treatment of its workforce had remained bad (high mortality rates, unhappy experience of recruitment, lack of a medical service, etc.).

It therefore seems reasonable to conclude that the severity shown by the judge towards the Huileries du Congo Belge was due to the fact that he took the Zeberg affair to provide confirmation of fairly notorious procedures attributed to this organisation in the past.[10]

This was the end of the whole affair.

In Lusanga circle (1927–1930)

While forced labour continued implacably in Lusanga circle, the situation as regards medical care and accommodation was improving. There are signs of such improvement in the report written by the Colony's chief medical officer, Giovanni Trolli, after his journey of inspection to the Kwango during the months of August and September 1927. The report contains the following passages:

Hospital for blacks at Leverville

Operates under the management of Dr. Schmit. Two large new wards of 20 beds each and two outbuildings, all made of brick and cement, have recently been built. The general plan of this hospital complex has been well thought through and the building work well done. At present it can hold 84 iron beds with sufficient space between them, so that if the need should arise one can hospitalise around 120 sick persons.

Lazaret at Leverville

Those with sleeping sickness, some 69 in number, are still hospitalised in the former corrugated iron lazaret. They are treated by the sisters in Leverville.

Medical services in Tango

A new dispensary in brick and cement has recently been built. A hospital for blacks is under construction, a ward containing 20 iron beds has been finished. The doctor holds 60 consultations a day.

Medical staff

The presence of a doctor in Kwenge and in Pindi is indispensable. The doctor in each sector should also be flanked by a health officer, who should be responsible for the prophylaxis of sleeping sickness in the surrounding area.

Accommodation (according to a table compiled by the management of the circle)

Sector	workers	brick-built houses	adobe houses	posts
Leverville	4,500	253	308	12
Kwenge	2,000	29	30	6
Pindi	400	30	36	1
Kunga	400	–	–	1
Tango	3,200	117	126	8
Total	10,500	429	500	28

The brick houses are built according to the standard HCB plan and provide fairly comfortable accommodation for the workers. The construction of the annexes, kitchens and fumigation ditches [deep trenches covered with planks with holes in them—from which a steady flow of smoke, designed to keep flies away from faeces, issues] is behind hand. In Kwenge the number of houses is small by comparison with the number of workers.

Provisioning of food

The typical ration consists of rice, fish and oil. A part is given in the form of cash. The diet is not varied enough. In Kwenge the company has begun to create plantations growing food crops (manioc, bananas, beans), so as to vary the ration, and 9 hectares have been planted so far.[11]

As is apparent, the tone of this report differs markedly from that of the Lejeune report, drafted almost 4 years before. Trolli fails to mention certain questions, among them that of the infirmaries in the agricultural posts. He comments on the very real progress made in building brick houses in the posts through which European visitors tended to pass (Leverville and Tango). The size of the workforce had increased from 6,500 to 10,500. In Pindi a factory had just gone into production.

A year after Trolli had made his report, his deputy René Mouchet made a more complete inspection of Lusanga circle, in the second week of September 1928. He wrote about it as follows, on 20th September, in a note commenting on the situation in the oil-mill zone of the northern part of Kwango district:

> In order to assess what work is required of the natives, one merely has to note that the HCB in Leverville circle handled 4,800 tonnes of palm fruits in the course of a month. Where the HCB is concerned, the circle employs at present 10,000 men, of whom 6,000 are local and 4,000

imported . . . If one bears in mind that the zone worked by the HCB contains 20,000 inhabitants and if one considers that, all in all, able-bodied adults constitute one quarter of the population, it is plain that the 6,000 locals represent ALL the available manpower, including those who are only partly able-bodied.

Industrial development demands that not merely the men but practically the ENTIRE population works. The men cut fruit or are at work in the factory; the women carry the fruit . . . 9 out of 10 porters are women. On the road it is predominantly women that you see carrying baskets of nuts.

The demand for labour even affects the children. Thus, in the factory at Kimbinga, the construction of which is now in its final stages, I have seen 30 or so children 6 to 8 years old, boys and girls, busy carrying bricks. Each load comprised 5 to 6 bricks, each of which weighed at least two kilos.[12]

On 23rd September Mouchet drafted a report specifically on his inspection, from which the following extracts are drawn:

The imported workers are brought by road. For the recruits from Niadi and Idiofa, rest-posts have been set up, although nothing similar exists for those arriving by the road from Kandale. The factory work is light. The occupation of cutter obviously presents some dangers.

Rations
The daily ration is 100 grams of dried meat, 800 grams of rice, 15 grams of salt. If there is no meat, it is replaced by 50 centimes in cash, which does not represent a fair replacement.

The ration is adequate as far as calories are concerned, but lacks fresh food and is not varied enough. At Kwenge 190 hectares of maize, potatoes and ground-nuts have been planted.

Wages
Imported cutters receive 1.50 francs per crate of peeled fruits (25 kilos) plus the ration. Local cutters receive 2 francs per crate, without a ration.

Leverville factory sometimes turns at night. Some men do 12 and 13 hours, and consequently get a supplementary ration in the form of cooked rice.

Accommodation
Generally good, often in fact very good, comprising detached houses made of baked bricks or adobe, with straw or corrugated iron roofs, consisting of a 4 by 4 metres room and a 4 by 2 metres covered veranda. The houses are provided with doors and windows.

The finest brick-built camps are situated along the river banks. Four of the houses have groups of individual kitchens. Some fumigation ditches are even luxurious. There are still some old and dilapidated camps, namely, at Leverville that of the coastmen, along with two camps of 80 and 36 households respectively that do not have suitable latrines . . . The camps are sufficient for the population; only the imported workers are housed by the company.

The building of camps in brick is ongoing. The type of house used is one of the best to be found in the Colony . . .

Medical service
– at Leverville: a doctor and a sanitation agent. The doctor is an excellent surgeon performing 50–60 operations a month, above all hernias.
– at Tango: a doctor, an adequate dispensary, a small and overcrowded hospital.
– at Pindi: the doctor has just arrived, and there is as yet no hospital complex.
– peripatetic service: a doctor and a sanitation agent, dealing with sleeping sickness.

Mortality
It is difficult to assess. Many ill people, above all locals, desert without notifying anyone and it is impossible to discover what has become of them.[13]

In April 1929 the position of head of the sanitation service for the Congo-Kasai was entrusted to Victor Daco, who had just entered the employ of the state after practising medicine in Liège for 16 years and running the medical service of the Kilo-Moto gold mines for five years. He was a very active man, 47 years old, who, though he considered his assumption of the role of *médecin provincial* to be just a stop-gap affair, took his duties as sanitation officer very seriously.[14] So it was that during the second half of 1929 he carried out inspections of the majority of HCB enterprises operating in Kwango district. He of course inspected Lusanga and turned his observations into a bulky report, dated 15th November 1929. His conclusions were presented as follows:

1. *The HCB's organisation of work* is flawed, in the sense that it imposes work upon the vast majority of the native population. The management itself recognises that improvements should be made to the workers' conditions, and especially in the case of those bound by

supply contracts, which are of indeterminate duration or, in other words, unlimited.

The current conception of work, the ultimate aim of which is above all to boost production, is based on the notion, in my view erroneous, of the company holding absolute property rights not only in the soil conceded to it in order to add value to it, but also in the native who used to live there freely, and who now finds himself deprived of the right to dispose of the fruits of his labour as he wishes. The heads of posts where production drops are all too often engaged in "shaking up recalcitrant cutters".

The forced and discontinuous labour to which the natives are subjected is bound to have an adverse effect on their health and to inspire hostile feelings in them towards Europeans, hostile feelings which, according to both company agents and territorial administrators, are already evident in the categorical refusal of the younger generation to enrol with the company.

A labour crisis is to be anticipated, and it would be sound policy to avert it. Work should therefore be regulated, and the number of workers restricted to a standard percentage of 25%, including those with supply contracts.

Porterage of fruit by women, and child labour, should be abolished.

2. *Accommodation.* A number of camps are magnificent and furthermore are skilfully presented, in order to elicit admiration from visitors.

However, there are manifestly too few houses. It is vital that the deplorable state of the Yanzi villages be remedied without delay.

The HCB should also consider improving the accommodation provided for local workers, in whom it has shown such a lack of interest from several points of view.

3. *Rations* in kind should replace rations in cash. The company must have its own plantations and fresh food, and local workers should be fed just as imported workers are.

4. *Medical service.* The existing hospitals are in a very good state but there are too few of them. The number of beds should be quadrupled. A hospital must be built at Kwenge and at Pindi.

The medical service ought in my opinion to try and provide more wide-ranging medical care for natives, in order to be able to treat a greater number of local workers.

Treatment centres should be operative in native areas, beyond the small dispensaries attached to posts. Sleeping sickness, syphilis, yaws, stomach complaints and worms would be usefully treated there.

The medical staff is insufficient. Aside from doctors attached to the hospitals (Leverville, Pindi, Tango, Kwenge), of whom three only are at their posts at the moment, a minimum of two peripatetic doctors and of four sanitation agents seems to me necessary to ensure the smooth running of the dispensaries to be set up in the native areas.[15]

Daco sent his report to the governor of the Congo-Kasai, who at first did nothing more than inform the HCB boss in Kinshasa of it. The latter responded with a memorandum dated 12th May 1930 in which he questioned the investigator's good faith:

We have read with surprise and some disquiet Dr. Daco's report on our services in Lusanga concession, and we would make so bold as to point out, with all due respect, that the criticisms made by him are unfair and founded in various cases on inaccurate information. The tone adopted in the report reflects a desire to criticise without reflecting with sympathy on the difficulties our company has had to face while setting up a prosperous industry, the purpose of which is to improve the living conditions of the native peoples.

Where the particular points made by Daco are concerned, the memor-andum did not have much to counter them with, save for some fairly specious arguments, among them the claim that the system of paying rations then in use reflected the African's preferred way of being paid.[16] Among the elements pointing to the existence of harmful forced labour in Lusanga, Daco might have mentioned in his report the assistance given by the territorial authorities to the HCB recruiters. The minutes from the meeting of the Regional Committee of the province of the Congo-Kasai held on 10th April 1930 prove that such assistance was in fact given. Here are a number of extracts:

The president [the governor of the province] proposes to discuss the question of government involvement in recruiting for private bodies. A telegram from the department is read out . . . The minister asks if two modes of involvement could henceforth be abolished: 1) the presence of territorial agents alongside recruiters; 2) the granting of subsidies to chiefs.
    The president also reads out chapter IV of the Report of the Consultative Committee on Labour (1928), which treated the issue of recruitment. The involvement of territorial agents alongside recruiters is specifically mentioned . . .[17]
    After a few exchanges, the president proposes to answer the minister's

telegram by pointing out that territorial agents no longer appear alongside private recruiters in the province, save in Kwango district, where as chance would have it there were still some territorial agents travelling with HCB recruiters.

The district commissioner for the Kwango specifies that all the enterprises in his district (HCB, Compagnie du Kasai, Comanco, Unatra) have recourse to the territorial authorities for the purpose of recruiting. The territorial agents, when they do not actually travel with the recruiters (an exception is made for certain HCB recruitments), are to be found in close proximity to the latter. He reckons that if this method is abolished, the enterprises will no longer stand any chance of being able to recruit the labour they need.

The president recalls that the territorial authorities have a duty to induce the natives to work, but recruitment must remain free.

The commissioner of the urban district of Kinshasa, claiming to speak for all the district commissioners, points out that it is not enough to tell the natives that they ought to work. It is to be feared that in cases where recruitment proves unsuccessful, the territorial authorities may be induced to punish refusal in one way or another . . .[18]

6

The Portuguese of Bumba
Against the HCB, Act Two (1928–1930)

Petitions and reactions

In chapter 3 I recounted the protests made by the Portuguese of Bumba, in 1924, against the obstacles placed in the way of their trade with the Africans, occurring through the imposition of the tripartite contract in the southern region of Modjamboli *territoire*. These protests did not prevent the HCB from asking the government, at the end of 1925, to arrange for the signing of a tripartite contract covering the region extending from Bumba to beyond the river Itimbiri. This region, like that of Modjamboli, was inhabited by the Budja. The Budja living to the east of Bumba, knowing of the damaging HCB monopoly imposed upon their brothers from Modjamboli, did not wish to hear a word about the contract for which their approval was sought. The merchants of Bumba had no difficulty in persuading the Budja to maintain trade relations with them.

The HCB, for their part, persisted in their efforts to implement the so-called Bumba-Est tripartite contract, which would cover the fine palm groves it had already asked to lease in 1919. It was in this context that they set up trading posts in Warsalaka (at the end of 1925) and in Yambinga (in 1926). At the beginning of 1928, the company and the administration had finally managed to assemble the chiefs and notables of the region in the notary's office in Lisala (administrative centre of the region of the Bangalas), with a view to signing a contract covering 80,000 hectares. This notary was the deputy public prosecutor Edouard Mendiaux, who took his role as protector of the Africans seriously.

Mendiaux had been delegated by the provincial governor to help the Budja at the time of signing the contract, which, like all such agreements: 1) arranged for all produce from the palm groves to be surrendered to the HCB; 2) granted the HCB the right to have their own cutters; 3) accorded the HCB the right to claim a part of the palm groves as their own, unfettered property. Mendiaux began his task by asking the Africans if they accepted the agreement and they replied in the affirmative. He then explained the main points contained in the contract to them. They immediately cried off and told him that they on no account wished to yield even the smallest plot from their palm groves, or to tolerate the presence of strangers as cutters in them. Mendiaux did not proceed any further.[1]

At this period a new management in Alberta was over-zealous against the Portuguese of Bumba. On the one hand, it was trying to end all sales to the Portuguese of oil and of palm nuts originating in the tripartite *territoire* of Modjamboli, though this had been more or less tolerated after the protests of 1924.[2] With this aim in mind the management posted company sentries along the road leading from Alberta to Bumba.[3] On the other hand, it set up trading posts in Bumba-Est, the *territoire* where the tripartite contract had failed, particularly in Lolo, Samaki, Engengele and Yalingimba.[4] At the beginning of December 1928 the director of Alberta wished to set up a trading post in Bofunga, a village situated between Yamangua and Bumba. The villagers were none too enthusiastic, given that a few days before, the people of Yamangua had likewise opposed the building of a trading post among them. The chief of Bofunga went to the territorial administrator in Bumba to tell him that the first HCB workers to venture again into his village would be attacked with knives.[5]

Faced with Alberta's attempts to expand, Bumba Chamber of Commerce lodged appeals with the higher authorities, asking them to intervene against the HCB. On 11th November 1928 it sent the following telegram to the governor-general: "We beg you to intervene to stop the arbitrary arrests by the Huileries private police, who are preventing the natives from coming to sell palm oil products at Bumba market. We presume that this state of affairs stems from the tripartite contract. Letter follows." In the letter which followed, dated 12th November, the Chamber let it be known that incidents had occurred on the Bumba–Alberta road, infringing the individual and commercial liberty of the inhabitants, and causing the utmost damage to its members' interests. Furthermore, that:

the Huileries are opening a certain number of canteens on all of the roads and not always within authorised limits, which are shielded from competition. That would be a scandal, and we are confident that it will not happen, due to the favourable consideration that you have so far shown us. I trust that you will not fail to give the relevant territorial authorities such directives as will produce the outcome we are entitled to expect.

The letter was signed "Ferreira", President of the Chamber. Five days later, on 17th November, the Chamber sent a further letter to the governor-general, containing more detailed information. It confirmed that it had questioned those African chiefs in the region who were rebelling against the implementation of the tripartite contract. The HCB police, the letter continued,

> detain the natives in order to buy their produce at the lowest possible prices, while the commercial part of the company [the SEDEC] sells them goods at inflated prices. SEDEC already boasts some thirty or so canteens installed in the villages and is still building others. These canteens are doing a roaring trade while our own sales and purchases are falling away badly. Why are commercial centres like Bumba set up, when SEDEC is only paying a paltry sum for the privilege of installing canteens? It is a question of life and death as much for Bumba as for Itimbiri, and we are confident that your intervention will lead to the suppression of the tripartite contract.

A month later, on 14th December, the Chamber sent the Colonial Minister a long letter, reiterating the grievances it had earlier addressed to the governor-general. The letter pointed out that the management in Alberta and the territorial authorities were still trying to impose tripartite contracts in Bumba *territoire*, from Molua to Itimbiri, although several chiefs in the region, namely, Ebubu, chief of the Warsalaka, Mandumba, chief of the Manga, and Bunda, chief of the Motuki, were categorically refusing them. They justified their refusal by saying that they did not wish to be slaves like their brothers on the other side of the Molua, who had signed just such a contract.

The letter went on to raise the following questions regarding the numerous stores set up by the company in the previous year:

1 Do the Huileries have the right to set up "canteens" wherever they please?
2 Do the Huileries have the right to use their "canteens" to sell whatever goods they please to whoever they please, and not only to their own workers?
3 Do the Huileries have the right to buy products in the "canteens", and even to exert pressure with this aim in mind?

On 14th December 1928, the governor of Equateur province, Charles Duchesne, wrote to tell the governor-general that he had got wind of the

November petitions from the Bumba Chamber of Commerce. He suggested that the joint ownership of land in Modjamboli *territoire* be gradually suppressed, and that the *terres indigènes* be demarcated in such a fashion that the villagers could once again send produce from that land to traders. As far as the arrest of natives by the HCB private police was concerned, he asked the district commissioner of the Bangala to look into the matter. As for the canteens engaged in general trading, he pointed out that the company had been authorised to open them by the governor-general's letter of 26th December 1923.[6] This authorisation stemmed from an order given by Minister Louis Franck dating from November 1923, stipulating that the company should pay annually a sum of 50 francs per trading post set up on the blocks it had leased. In December, Moeller, the acting governor of Orientale province, had reacted to this order as follows:

> I reckon that it would hardly be fair if the HCB, who deem themselves entitled to open trading posts outside of the commercial centres, should also be granted particularly favourable leases. Indeed in the commercial centres of the Aruwimi [the district in which Barumbu circle was located] there is no longer a single plot that can be rented at less than 200 francs per trading-post site. I propose to the governor-general that the same tariff should be applied.[7]

The governor-general had sent a telegraph rejecting this proposal, alleging that the rate of 50 francs should be maintained, in line with a prior accord between the Colonial Minister and the Huileries.[8]

Franck based the order granting these extravagant commercial advantages to the HCB on article 10 of the 1911 Convention, which had listed the rights that the leases gave to the company, among them "the right to set up on the plots rented and to install places of residence, warehouses, factories and other buildings of use to the company". The administration had up until then always quite rightly understood that these warehouses could only be storehouses stocking merchandise needed for industrial production or canteens for supplying white and black personnel. Louis Franck's entirely fanciful interpretation, according to which these warehouses were for the purpose of general trade, is a fine example of his habitually obsequious attitude towards William Lever. The warehouses for general trade set up by the HCB in the zone between Molua and Itimbiri were doubly illegal, because in 1928 the company had no lease, or tripartite contract standing in for it, in this region. In this regard the district commissioner for the Bangala, Louis Bareau, wrote on 10th January 1929 to the governor:

The HCB management in Alberta in general always presents us with a fait accompli; it builds canteens—or, strictly speaking, general trading posts—before receiving any authorisation, and without waiting for the outcome of the enquiry into the availability of plots of land. This company ought in each case: 1) to await the approval of the district; 2) to make a declaration to the effect that the trading post in question is open; 3) to provide it with registers 5 and 6. On my next journey to Ebonda I will take up these issues with the management.[9]

The final sentence is a good example of the servile attitude adopted by the local authorities towards the HCB managers. Having emphasised that the management was brazenly flouting all regulations, Bareau concluded that he would go and talk to them about it, instead of simply calling for the closure of these illegal warehouses.

In the same letter Bareau spoke of the outcome of the enquiries launched by the territorial administrators of Modjamboli and Bumba into the arbitrary arrests on the Alberta–Bumba road denounced by the Chamber of Commerce. He wrote: "As usual the Chamber has greatly over-dramatised the sole incident that took place. On the basis of a single, isolated case, it has sought to demonstrate that there was an organised police force in the HCB, harrying the natives and committing the most serious violations in liberty of trade." As far as this last allegation is concerned, I would point out that it is in flagrant contradiction with a communication made by the director of Alberta circle, Amrein (sic), to the managing director of the company in Kinshasa, a communication stating that "two or three sentries at our agricultural posts and one at the station in Alberta have extorted tips and let through women going with oil and palm nuts to Bumba, having sought at first to bar their way. These incidents occurred despite the formal instructions given to all the agricultural agents."[10] Besides, Bareau's allegation was certainly not the most logical conclusion to have drawn from the report of 10th December 1928 that the territorial administrator in Modjamboli, Gaston Paucheun, drafted on the basis of his inquiry. Yet the latter likewise sought to absolve the company's bosses of any responsibility for hindrances to trade on the Alberta–Bumba road. He wrote as follows:

The orders given by the HCB management to its sentries are as follows:
– Ask the natives going to Bumba to sell palm nuts and oil about the provenance of such products, and also about the identity of the land-owner.
– Invite the natives to come and sell the products to the HCB.

– Under no pretext whatsoever should they arrest natives refusing to reveal their identity, or force them to sell products to the company [one cannot help but smile when one reads this].

Despite this obliging attitude, Paucheun wrote in his letter of 10th December regarding the arrests on the Alberta–Bumba road:

> On 4th November last M. Costa Mariano, a trader at Bumba, brought three women before the judicial police officer [in Bumba]. They had fallen victim to sentry Palangi (alias Balanga Antoine), to whom they had had to pay a sum of 10 francs in order to go to Bumba with their palm-nuts . . .
>
> The case of sentry Palangi is certainly not an isolated one, but the natives, being in the wrong, say nothing about their treatment at the hands of the company sentries. HCB Europeans are of course unaware of such doings [this remark, too, raises a smile].

Further on in his report Paucheun writes:

> In the course of the year 1927, the police court passed 4 sentences on 18 women [who were selling to the traders in Bumba] palm-oil products originating in the HCB concession.
>
> Attracted by the high prices paid by the Bumba traders, the natives make large quantities of oil which they then sell to the traders. Transportation may even occur at night.
>
> Since a thriving trade existed between the natives in the concession and the Bumba traders, in response to a request from the company management, in August 1927 I drew up two affidavits in my role as process-server, for violation of clauses in the tripartite contract. My affidavits were sent to the public prosecutor in Lisala, but no response was forthcoming . . . During the year 1928 the police court handed down no sentences for illicit trade within the concession.

Paucheun also mentioned that he had taken down the particulars of three women, on 27th November 1928, for violation of article 5 of the tripartite contract, and that he had dispatched the three accused the same day to the public prosecutor's office in Lisala.[11] Bareau tells us in the letter mentioned above that the district court (over which he presided) condemned these women on the count of theft of palm-oil products to a 25-franc fine, but that the public prosecutor's office gave notice of an appeal. On the other hand he tells us that the deputy public prosecutor forwarded the file on the Palangi case to the chief prosecutor in Mbandaka.[12]

Public prosecutor and deputy public prosecutor were none other than Edouard Mendiaux, a man firmly opposed to judicial punishment for failure to observe the monopoly stipulated in the tripartite contracts. As for the Palangi case, I presume that Mendiaux submitted the file to the chief prosecutor because in his view something more than the extortion of 10 francs was involved. He probably saw the case as illustrating the procedures used by the company to enforce its monopoly, where the judicial authorities failed to act.

A month before he had received the petitions from the Bumba Chamber of Commerce, Governor-General Tilkens had been sent two petitions of the same kind, in October 1928, emanating from traders in Basoko. Taking all such memoranda seriously, Tilkens undertook a thorough examination of the problematic issue of tripartite contracts. Upon receiving at the beginning of 1929 the Department's correspondence surrounding this issue, he drafted a lengthy report, which he sent to the minister on 25th January. Here are some extracts, some of them in abbreviated form, from this report:

– I am convinced that no contract has been introduced against the wishes of the local inhabitants, and that preliminary explanations, given before the said contracts were concluded, were lavished upon them, but I find it hard to suppose that they could have been understood. Now that the consequences of the new dispensation have made themselves felt, and the natives by the dint of direct experience have grasped its real meaning, protests are almost unanimous.
– The traders complain about the lack of palm-oil products on the Basoko and Bumba markets. The fact is undeniable. The good palm groves are subject to the tripartite system.
   Bumba Chamber of Commerce reports arbitrary arrests made by the Huileries private police. On the other hand, the Basoko traders allude to the government police's interference in the sale of palm-oil products to the traders.
– The question as to whether withholding, or purchasing, palm-oil products in a manner detrimental to joint ownership constitutes a violation, has not been settled, and no judicial ruling has been made, so far as I know. [A manifest error on the part of Tilkens, as is proven by the convictions mentioned in the letter from Paucheun in Modjamboli quoted above.]
– The traders also complain about the lack of a native clientele for the articles traded, due to the general trading posts set up by the Huileries. Like you, I reckon that the term "warehouses" in the 1911 Convention

can only refer to warehouses used to store the substantial quantities of goods needed by a major enterprise. For my part I support the idea of closing down those trading posts that lie outside the commercial centres.

– The tripartite contracts should remain in force, but it would be desirable to limit the tiresome consequences as much as is possible. My fear is that if we do not proceed as swiftly as possible with the demarcation of the *terres indigènes*, we shall find ourselves in 1936, the date when the tripartite contracts are due to expire, in the same situation as existed in 1924. Once these demarcations have been completed, joint ownership will come to an end and, save in the case of land reserved once and for all for the Huileries, regions under the sway of the tripartite contracts would recover their economic independence.

Should you agree, it would be necessary to boost the number of surveyors, with the hiring for a three-year period of a dozen or so seconded for the job in question.

As may be seen, Tilkens was only lukewarm in his support for tripartite contracts. His report explicitly confirmed the Africans' opposition to the HCB monopoly, a fact which had been much stressed by the traders. The report made an impression upon the Colonial Minister, Henri Jaspar, who on 29th March 1929 wrote to the HCB management in Brussels:

> The information communicated to me leads me to conclude that the implementation of the tripartite contracts no longer answers to the natives' wishes, once they realise what prices are offered to them for their fruit. In these circumstances, I have decided to delay the introduction of tripartite contracts in regions where such contracts have not yet been introduced, since the natives will not give their consent to them there.

Jaspar further noted that he had asked the governor-general to take the necessary steps to set in motion the demarcations which would bring joint ownership to an end.[13] Although Jaspar, like Tilkens, was an opponent of the company's general trading posts, no measures were taken against them. On the contrary, in mid-1929 the governor of Equateur province informed Bumba Chamber of Commerce that these trading posts were legal, in the light of the interpretation of article 10 of the 1911 Convention formerly advanced by the Colonial Minister. The Chamber responded in no uncertain terms, in a letter sent to the governor on 30th July 1929:

The government shared our perspective up until just a few years ago. The sudden change in governmental opinion dates from the time when the spectre of the tripartite contract began to be discussed. Previously, the administration reckoned that the HCB could certainly set up workers' canteens in their blocks, but that they should erect their general trading posts in legally authorised commercial centres. We ask if you would be so kind as to call for a fresh examination of the question by the Department, and we wish to reiterate what we said in our letter of 14th December 1928 to the Colonial Minister.[14]

The letter was signed by De Maerschalck, President. A Belgian-sounding name beneath their new petition seemed to the Portuguese of Bumba to promise better chances of success. On 20th January 1930, Bumba Chamber of Commerce, having heard nothing more of its petitions, sent the minister a further letter, which referred again to its report of 14th December 1928. It appended to it a copy of its letter of 30th July 1929 to the governor of Equateur province. That same January, Jaspar let the HCB management in Brussels know that it would have to relinquish the privilege of paying a 50 francs rent for the plots occupied by its trading posts, and that it should thenceforth be in the same situation as everyone else and pay the rent fixed for plots of land in commercial use. He also let them know that government authorisation was needed for the setting-up of a trading post, and that this authorisation would only be given for blocks of 250 hectares minimum, which the company had reserved in accordance with article 4 of the tripartite contracts.

The HCB management acquiesced, because just then there was a serious possibility of its illegal warehouses in Bumba being shut down. On 11th February, Jaspar telegraphed the governor-general to tell him that the HCB accepted the conditions governing the setting-up of trading posts within their blocks, and that their canteens were comparable to trading posts. On 17th March the minister sent the governor-general a copy of the Chamber's above-mentioned letter, asking him to advise the latter of the agreement reached in Brussels. He added the following somewhat vague instructions: "As for the question of the siting of HCB trading posts, the authorities in Africa will consider policing and surveillance, rather than commercial competition, when addressing it."

On 20th June the Chamber telegraphed the minister to say that the governor-general had informed them of the recent arrangement agreed at Brussels with the HCB, authorising them to undertake general trade within their blocks. "If the arrangement continues", the telegram went on, "trade in Bumba is heading for certain disaster, as was indicated in the memoranda sent to you." The reasons for sending this telegram may readily be under-stood, since the arrangement reached in Brussels had in no sense resolved the Bumba traders' problem, which was only secondarily the preferential tariff for the plots of land granted to the HCB, and primarily the authorisation still given them to trade outside the commercial centres.

The Bumba Chamber of Commerce then had recourse, as in 1924, to the press, in order to mobilise public opinion in favour of its members. Thus, in the Antwerp newspaper, *Neptune (Belgian Lloyd and Daily News)*, on 8th July 1930, there featured a letter entitled "A cry of alarm". In this letter, which recapitulated its various memoranda to the authorities, the Chamber more particularly claimed that the government of the Colony had promoted the development of Bumba up until 1927, whereupon it had signed its death warrant by authorising the HCB to set up illegally, all around it, 27 general trading posts in close proximity to the villages. The letter further specified that in the Congo the setting-up of such trading posts was governed by a regulation stating that no one was entitled to set up a concern outside of the commercial centres designated by the government. With just one exception, the letter concluded, all the HCB trading posts lay outside these same centres.

On 18th July Jaspar wrote to the Chamber of Commerce to inform it that he had forwarded its telegram of 20th June to the governor-general, who alone was competent to resolve the question.[15] The ball was now in the local authorities' court, and more particularly, in that of the governor of the province. For guidance the latter only had the vague directive mentioned above regarding the siting of HCB trading posts. Yet he came up with a solution which, after their long campaign against the company, did not leave the Bumba traders empty-handed. Authorisation for the HCB to set up trading posts within its blocks was subject to the condition that trade within these same blocks should be free. The traders could set up trading posts outside the commercial centres, even on the periphery of the regions subject to tripartite contracts, and they could conduct peripatetic trading operations in the interior of these regions.[16]

The Budja of Bumba-Est robbed of their palm groves

A letter of 26th December 1928, sent by the managing director of the HCB in Kinshasa to the governor of Equateur province, gives a sense of how the company imagined the Africans' situation in the aftermath of demarcation and the leasing-out of unoccupied land:

They will be forbidden to move their villages and their cultivated fields outside the boundaries assigned to them, and they will be forbidden to gather fruit from palms on our land without rendering themselves liable to prosecution . . .

We shall set up factories in the Bumba-Est block and we shall have palm clusters on our own land harvested there by our own workers, just as we are doing in Alberta . . .

They should remain confined to their reservations . . .

We shall not allow them to take palm fruit from palms growing on our concessions, in order simply to sell them to other traders; and if they engage in acts of violence against our workers or against our European agents—as they have threatened to do—we shall invoke the protection from the state guaranteed us by article 18 of our Convention . . .

In February 1929, the process of demarcating the plots of land occupied by Africans in the Bumba-Est region began, its purpose being to allow the HCB to get their hands on the others. Several surveyors in succession undertook this task, the most ambitious work of boundary demarcation in the whole of the HCB's history, for a period of fifteen months. The HCB obviously sought to restrict the surface area of land held by Africans to a minimum, and it did so by first of all demanding that the thesis they had been defending since who knows when be respected, namely, that the villagers' property rights were limited to the land occupied by them in 1911. But how was one to distinguish between the land occupied in 1911 and that occupied nineteen years later? It was indeed an impossible task.[17] Deputy public prosecutor Mendiaux, in Lisala, realised that the company was aiming to confine the Africans to cramped reservations. He visited the surveyors engaged in the demarcation process and urged them to include in their sketches the land occupied by villagers after 1911. He drafted a tripartite contract to which the village communities assented, at the same time stipulating that the latter would surrender all fruit gathered by them to the HCB. But the company refused to accept this agreement, on the pretext that its rights had not been wholly respected.[18]

In a letter dated 25th January 1930, administrator Stubbe in Brussels took the case of the chimerical demarcation of the land occupied in 1911 to the Colonial Minister, Jaspar. He emphasised that Colonial Minister Renkin, in the "Guide for the application of the 1911 Convention", had stipulated that the natives' rights which might be set against those of the HCB were such as existed at the time of the latter first being established in the region. He added that this rule would appear to have been disregarded when demarcation took place in Bumba *territoire*. The minister replied that it was up to the authorities in Africa to assess the claims made by Africans, in accordance with the general legislation touching upon the question. To which Stubbe riposted that such claims should in the main be assessed in accordance with the 1911 Convention, and with the directives published by the government in 1917. The minister conceded the point some six weeks later, while still arguing that the directives given in the 1917 guide could only contain guidelines compatible with the general legislation. Stubbe having responded immediately, the minister wrote to the governor-general on 8th April to say that he wished to go on record as agreeing in principle with the company's position.[19]

No sooner had it arrived in the Congo than this letter became redundant, since Duchesne, having become acting governor-general, had already sent a telegram on 14th March requesting the governor in Mbandaka to remind the district commissioner in Lisala that the natives only had the right to the palm groves they were exploiting in 1911. Duchesne had acted in response to a letter from the HCB's secretary general in Africa, dated 25th February 1930, which noted that Director General Dusseljé had just written to him from Alberta, to the effect that he had seen the man in charge of boundary demarcation, the surveyor Henri Piette, and that the latter had told him that he had had precise instructions to assign to the natives all the palm groves that they were exploiting in 1930. In the same letter the secretary general claimed that Dusseljé, when in Alberta, had had in his hands a note from the district surveyor, Léon Jacobs, which recommended that villagers were to be given all the palm groves that they were working and claiming, even if that would give them more than 1.75 hectares of palm grove per inhabitant. He made the following observations in this regard:

> These directives seem to us to contain two errors. The first is to say that the natives should be assigned all the palm groves that they are actually working at the present time, when it should read "all the palm groves that they were actually working in 1911, and within the bounds worked by them at that date".
>
> The second is to imply that each native will have the right to a minimum of 1.75 hectares of palm grove, which is wholly inaccurate. This figure of 1.75 hectares is the figure that has been taken up until now to represent the average to be assigned per head of inhabitant in Alberta circle in cultivated and outlying land [that is to say, cultivated land and land lying fallow].

What this quotation clearly means is that the Africans have the right to 1.75 hectares in fields and fallow land, but not to the palm groves, since they were not exploiting them commercially in 1911. Duchesne agreed with this outrageous claim, and had therefore laid down in the above-mentioned telegram to the governor of Mbandaka that 1.75 hectares was the total average surface area granted to each inhabitant as land, be it inhabited, cultivated or lying fallow.[20]

One cannot help but be staggered by Duchesne's obsequious attitude towards the HCB bosses. I imagine that it was for form's sake that in his telegram he was revoking the application of the minister's directive of March 1917, which was anyway unenforceable. But why then stipulate that the Africans' rights in land were limited to cultivated and fallow land, thereby excluding gathering rights in the palm groves? Why follow the company in its determination to confine the Africans to meagre reservations, and why follow it in its avaricious desire to snatch fully operative palm groves from the populous Budja?

At the end of March 1930 Dusseljé, having returned from Alberta to Kinshasa, declared to Duchesne that Chief Ebubu of Warsalaka had told him that he was willing to enter into a contract to supply the company with fruit. He therefore suggested making a fresh attempt to agree a tripartite contract. One might suppose that—following the minister's decision the previous year to postpone the concluding of previously rejected tripartite contracts—Duchesne would not have acceded to the suggestion. On the contrary, he responded immediately and, in a letter dated 31st March, asked the governor of Equateur province to order the competent authorities to make one last effort to sound out the people in the *chefferie* in question.[21] The district commissioner, Bareau, set to, and found that the people were in fact willing to entertain the idea of a contract for supplying fruit to the HCB, not only in the *chefferie* of Warsalaka but also elsewhere in the Bumba-Est region. This change of heart was a natural response to the intimidation they had suffered through the tracing by the surveyors of countless demarcation lines across their palm groves in the course of the previous year. These lines, as the HCB agents certainly took care to repeat to them, foretold their future confinement in reservations. The colonial authorities explained to them that the tripartite contract represented their only way of eluding such confinement, and redoubled their efforts to convince them, having received directives from the governor-general, dated 8th May 1930, to do so.[22]

Luckily for the HCB, deputy public prosecutor Mendiaux was no longer in the area, having left for Mbandaka to perform the duties of chief prosecutor. The management in Alberta helped to ensure the success of the operation by driving up the purchase price of palm fruits to 20 centimes a kilo,[23] at a time when the company was paying 6 centimes in Lusanga. In a period of world economic crisis, 20 centimes was a price that the Portuguese traders could not match.

On 30th July several dozen chiefs, notables and *capitas*[24] in Bumba-Est region met in Lisala. They "signed" four separate tripartite contracts, the original, grand scheme for the whole of Bumba-Est having been split up into several more limited contracts. The four contracts signed on that day covered the *chefferies* of Warsalaka, Yambondjo, Manga and Yalingimba. In the case of Warsalaka, 25 *capitas* and notables, led by the invested chief Ebubu, applied their thumbprints to the document. Along with the Africans, the others who signed were: Bareau, representing the Colony; J. Barella, director of Alberta, on behalf of the company; and Jean Taquet, the new deputy public prosecutor in Lisala, but on this occasion a delegate with special responsibilities towards the Africans. The contracts stipulated that the *chefferies* would surrender all fruit present and future to the HCB, who were authorised to use their own cutters to harvest such fruit. They likewise stipulated that the company could reserve for itself as future property all the palm groves recognised as unoccupied, that is to say, not included in the surface area assigned to the villagers in accordance with the norm of 1.75 hectares of cultivated and fallow land per head. They further stated that the delegate with special responsibilities had explained to the African parties to the agreement its precise scope.

The archives only contain documents referring to the Warsalaka agreement, which served as a model for the three others. Among these documents, the report compiled by the special delegate, Jean Taquet, occupies pride of place. The latter had co-signed the contract, knowing full well that the Africans did not agree with some of its key clauses, while he himself was convinced that it was flawed. As a young deputy public prosecutor, Taquet had not dared to oppose it, but redeemed his pusillanimity by means of a lengthy restatement in his special delegate's report. In this report, Taquet first of all stated that the majority of the Africans' palm groves had not been included in the land assigned to them, which amounted to 4,692 hectares, where the land in joint ownership came to 11,713 hectares. He pointed out that it was not enough to assess the Africans' rights in land on the basis of fields that were cultivated or lay fallow; what counted here was the surface area of the palm groves they were exploiting. On this point, Taquet explained, the minutes of the enquiry attached to the file were not at all explicit. He could therefore only approve the agreement on the understanding that all the palm groves worked in 1930 should revert to the villagers as freehold property in 1936, when the agreement was due to expire. It was therefore out of the question for the HCB to take possession of the palm groves subsumed within the surface area placed under joint ownership.

Secondly, Taquet reckoned that the agreement laid down inadequate remuneration for the cutting of fruit by the villagers. The agreement thus

stipulated that the quantity of fruit garnered in a day's work would be paid
for at the same daily rate as any unskilled labourer in the region received.
Taquet had been moved by the Budjas' fondness for their palm groves, and
denounced the fact that they were to be paid only for cutting and not for the
value of the fruit of which they were the owners. As for the Africans' attitude
towards the agreement, Taquet wrote:

> The natives absolutely do not agree to foreign cutters, even if they were
> employed by the HCB, coming into their fields and harvesting alongside
> them. This is a key point and, I would go so far as to say, a sine qua non of
> the acceptance by the native communities of the tripartite contracts. Their
> representatives have several times insisted upon it and very clearly stated
> their wishes in this regard.

Taquet's report concluded as follows:

> The special delegate can only express a favourable opinion regarding the
> present tripartite contract if account is taken of the reservations formulated
> above concerning demarcation [that is to say, the non-inclusion of the
> palm groves in the fields granted to the Africans] and concerning the
> natives' refusal to tolerate foreign cutters in their *chefferie*, whoever they
> may be, coming to cut fruit.[25]

A fortnight later, on 16th August—the tripartite contracts having to be
authenticated—Taquet drew up a deed authenticated by a notary in which
he attested that all the parties that had signed the Warsalaka contract had
appeared before him, that he had had it read to them and that the contract as
it was drawn up did indeed express their wishes.[26] He made no mention of
the reservations recorded in the report he had submitted as special delegate.

Bareau sent the provincial governor copies of the four agreements signed
in Lisala on 30th July, enclosing them with a report in which he wrote that,
in order to calculate the surface areas to be reserved for the villagers, the
directives issued by the provincial government, based upon the principle of
1.75 hectares per inhabitant, had been taken into account. This, as the reader
will recognise, was the figure imposed by Duchesne, in response to the
HCB's request. On 30th September, the interim governor, François Justin
Jorissen, forwarded these same documents to the governor-general, express-
ing a favourable opinion and adding that some of the special delegate's
formulations in his report were muddled.[27]

Taquet, for his part, sent the Warsalaka file to Mendiaux, in Mbandaka.
The latter grew angry when he discovered that the Africans had refused to

surrender their palm groves and to admit foreign cutters to them, and that the deputy public prosecutor in Lisala had nevertheless first signed the contract, and then in the guise of notary certified that the contract did indeed represent the wishes of the Africans. Mendiaux severely reprimanded Taquet and, when forwarding the documents to the public prosecutor in Kinshasa, he observed that the deed could not be ratified, since it was vitiated by errors and was consequently worthless. But the deed came back to him, ratified by governor-general Tilkens. It is hard to grasp just why Tilkens should have proceeded with the ratification, given that eighteen months before he had persuaded his minister to postpone the conclusion of the tripartite contracts in those regions in which the consent of the Africans could not be won.

The Compagnie Du Kasai Proves to be Worse Than the HCB (1927–1930)

During this period the Compagnie du Kasai (CK) had several oil-producing zones in Kwango district. The conditions in which workers lived in these zones remained worse than those prevailing in Lusanga circle. This can be demonstrated by considering the reports of three doctors, who should be allowed to speak for themselves.

Dr. Mouchet's reports

In his note of 20th September 1928 on the situation in the palm oil producing region of the northern part of Kwango district, Dr. Mouchet devoted two pages to health and welfare in the CK's Mushuni circle. The information featuring in that note derives from reports supplied to him by the company doctor, Raingeard, whom Mouchet quotes:

In the whole of Mushuni circle public health is in a deplorable state. The north of the Lukula may still be the least affected, but it is nonetheless very much affected. Not a single village unscathed, to the north of the Luie, Lukula and Inzia rivers, with swamp fever as well as sleeping sickness.

There are also several leper households in Kitoye on the banks of the Inzia; the village of Makulu between Dunga and Kalunda is a natural breeding-ground for leprosy.

The wretched physical state of the natives paves the way for all these illnesses.

A good many villages, where they do not occupy a clearing, border on the edge of the forest; being beside the rivers, settlements are never far from the marshes, and may even be in the middle of them, as is the case with Kapiti.

The dwellings are falling to rack and ruin and the bush is encroaching on them. The natives are no longer cultivating their fields; villages in the environs of Tangango . . . go and buy their manioc on the other side of the Luie . . . 20 kilometres away. In the whole region, only three of the larger villages have their own cultivated fields and of course sell to their neighbours at a steep price.

Everywhere roots and the fruits of the forest go to make up the basis of the diet; sickness ravages a population so weakened by famine that it is no longer able to respond . . .

The above assertions [regarding the depopulation of the oil-mill region] have been confirmed by Doctor Raingeard, at any rate as regards Mushuni circle: the population there was 5,380 in 1923 but has fallen in 1927–1928 to 4,265.

Births stood at 444 in 1923, or 8.3%, but have fallen to 231 in 1927, or 7% (mortality in this latter year being 611, or 12.4%).

Some villages seem to have grown in size; Dr. Raingeard says, however, that this is deceptive, and that the apparent increase is due to the need to assimilate vestiges of villages that have disappeared.

There is no recruitment in this region, since the entire population works for the Compagnie du Kasai. It really is then a question of an actual and unfortunately very severe depopulation, and with a striking fall in the birth rate.

The situation is therefore very serious, and all the more so given that the region, which is really very rich in palm groves, is simply attracting a more and more intense industrial and commercial development. The companies exploiting the region do not seem to have grasped that development is itself threatened by the drop in population, which it is to be feared could cause an economic crisis.

Mouchet concluded that it was necessary to launch a major medical campaign, to intervene administratively to improve sanitation in the villages, and to eradicate transportation by canoes and by portering.[1] He sent his note to the governor of the province, who in turn forwarded it to the district commissioner in Bandundu, Léon Vandenbyvang. The latter rebuked Mouchet for his lack of objectivity and accuracy. The situation remained unchanged.

The Daco report on the Compagnie du Kasai

Daco inspected the CK's Mushuni and Mombanda circles between 20th and 30th October 1929, in the company of Dr. Raingeard. At the same period he visited the adjoining posts of the Compagnie du Congo Belge, a company founded in 1911 through the merger of the ill-famed Abir and Anversois companies. After his inspection of the CK circles, Daco wrote a long report, dated 13th November, from which lengthy extracts follow. It began with the following observation:

In order to avoid the reproach of a lack of objectivity and of inaccuracy, which was levelled in 1928 at the report compiled by the deputy chief medical officer regarding the general sanitary situation in the Kwango-Kwilu, I will simply list what I have seen, heard and verified in the course of my tour of inspection. I wish first of all to state that the situation as depicted here will be despite everything better than it is in reality, because the CK management has issued directives to all its agents to the effect that "on the occasion of the provincial doctor's visit, the camps should be in a good state of repair, and on no account should any woman or child be seen to be working" . . .

Medical facilities

The treatment centres are the key medical facilities. The proliferation of such centres is due to the initiative of Dr. Raingeard. This conscientious doctor sought to decide whether the most effort should be directed towards the workers in the posts, who number around a thousand, or towards the natives and their families, from amongst whom are recruited the cutters and the paddlers, the women who act as porters and the children who do the crushing.

It was this second category of worker that seemed to Dr. Raingeard the more deserving of attention, and that justified the setting-up of the various centres. We reckon that Dr. Raingeard's scheme was well-judged and wholly adequate for working conditions within the CK.

There exist nine treatment centres in the two circles. Each of them comprises: a large barn for the examination of the sick, a dispensary for treatment, an infirmary for hospitalisation, a house for the nurse together with the requisite outbuilding, the whole complex being securely enclosed. Manioc plantations exist in each centre and provide food for those who are hospitalised.

The various centres that we visited are well maintained.

In the various treatment centres, the local populations are surveyed for sleeping sickness, ganglionic palpation and puncture; also for the treatment of the sick.

Aside from those suffering from sleeping sickness, various conditions such as yaws, syphilis, intestinal and respiratory complaints are regularly treated. Treatment is carried out by a black nurse, overseen whenever possible by the doctor.

The various villages are from 2 to 4 hours' journey from the treatment centres. The medical records of those suffering from sleeping sickness are in good order, and the number of patients of every kind treated per month has risen to an average of 150.

Categories of worker
a) workers attached to posts (the minority), in principle housed and supplied with rations by the company; are for the most part imported workers in a pitiful state (Yaka and Suku), hired without the doctor being informed;
b) cutters of fruit (the majority), neither supplied with rations nor housed; they live at home in their villages.

Wages
a) workers attached to posts: 15 to 25 francs per month;
b) cutters: 3 francs per crate, which officially weighs 30 kilos but in reality is almost 35.

Ration
In theory, per week: 3 to 6 francs in cash + 300 grams of rice, 300 grams of oil, 1 herring, 100 grams of salt.

Whatever the ration is supposed to be in theory, in practice it is often not respected. Thus, at Mokamo and Kalunda the herrings handed out were in very poor condition. Some posts do indeed have a few hectares of manioc. Nowhere have I seen a plantation of any great size.

Percentage of the population at work
The post at Dunda employs 70 men in the factory and 500 cutters, that is to say, five times the number of able-bodied men in the region in a position to take up employment.

Where Dunda, Kimbili and Tangango regions are concerned, Dr. Raingeard has estimated that 77% of the adult population is at work, that is, 533 workers out of 687 adult, able-bodied men.

Punishments and acts of violence
Chief Lombo (Mokamo) declares that all his men are at work and that those who refuse are sent to Bulungu. He has been summoned to go to the villages of Kikongo and Kibunzi in order to administer the *chicotte*[2] to cutters whose output had fallen.

Four village chiefs have lodged a complaint against the manager of Mokamo, Péchet, regarding events which occurred in July 1929. The territorial administrator Briard had ordered the villagers to build a barn-cum-wayside rest post. Péchet turned up to ask them why they were not cutting fruit. He lined the men up and gave them ten lashes of the *chicotte*. Two chiefs lodged a complaint against him for having seized 3 and 2 goats respectively from their villages.

I have brought these charges to the attention of the district commissioner.

Use of women and children

The precise directives given by management to its sector chiefs at the time of our arrival in the region make it plain that women and children are still being employed. Near Mokamo we came across 71 women and 34 children returning from the factory in which they had worked for a whole week. In April 1929, the Colony's chief medical officer, Sulsenti, found children aged from 5 to 10 at work in Dondo, Mokamo, Saka and Ngaba.

Porterage

Porterage has been somewhat improved through the introduction of mechanical means of locomotion (motor-boats and lorries) but does nevertheless still continue. There are three lorries in Mombanda circle, two of which (those in Dondo and Fumu-Putu) are currently out of action. The distances between the villages and the CK posts vary from 3 to 15 kilometres.

Working conditions

The managers repeatedly claim that work is in general not hard. Piling up fruit the whole day long is hard work. In Dondo and Puanga we have seen this work continue past six o'clock in the evening.

As for the cutters, who are often made out to be more concerned with filling their calabashes with palm-wine than with putting in an honest day's work, their job is far from being a sinecure in the Lukula, where the palms are so far apart.

Most of the principal articles of the ordinance on workers' health and safety are not observed. The physical fitness certificate exists almost nowhere. Workers provided with a blanket are rare indeed.

Rations solely in kind are not given anywhere. The company is under an obligation to provide the workers with foodstuffs in return for the cash paid as a ration, but its reserves of fresh foodstuffs are non-existent. No camp measures up to the requisite conditions.

Ordinance on sleeping sickness

The clearing of the undergrowth from the beaches is almost everywhere inadequate.

Dr. Raingeard's latest report on sleeping sickness gives the following figures for 1929:

a) Dondo sector: population 2,474, patients treated 650, that is, 26.2%;

b) Kabanga-Katika sector: population 1,981, patients treated 597, that is, 30%.

The experiences of Dr. Raingeard

After almost four years' service in the Mushuni–Mombanda zone, Raingeard left the Congo around mid-1930. He was not re-employed by the CK, very probably because he pestered the bosses with demands concerning the well-being of the Africans, nor was he hired again by the State, despite the great esteem in which he was held by Mouchet and Daco. The latter, though very critical, as we have seen, of the HCB's medical service in Lusanga, was highly appreciative of the treatment centres set up by Raingeard in Mushuni and Mombanda circles, and of the manner in which he was running, on the State's behalf, the service for the prophylaxis of sleeping sickness.[3] While Daco was transferred to Katanga in 1930, the door to the Congo remained closed to Raingeard who, in order to unburden himself, began to write a long article describing his experience with the CK. The article was published in the January–February 1932 number of *La Revue de Médecine et d'Hygiène Tropicales*, a reputable journal published in Paris. The piece, which was 28 pages long, was entitled "Labour in the Kwango (Belgian Congo)". Here are the key passages, in abridged form:

Fruit cutters

The work done by a fruit cutter is very painful. With the help of a strap passing behind the thighs and around the tree, he climbs to the top of the palm tree, to a height of 20 to 30 metres. This work becomes very hard when it is a question of finding a crate of fruit, or in other words 30 kilos, in a natural forest in which palms are quite rare. When he is required to supply, as he usually is, 4 to 6 crates a week (9 to 12 for the HCB), he has to cover, in order to find the necessary quantity of ripe clusters, many kilometres in uneven and all but impenetrable forest. This work, which lasts from morning to night, and which is painful enough for an adult, becomes an intolerable strain for old men and for the infirm, who make up the majority of cutters.

In order to supply the required quantities, the cutter of fruits has to call upon his wife to help him. She it is who has to assume responsibility for cleaning, sorting and carrying the fruit either to the post or to the road, which may lie 5, 10 or 15 kilometres away.

In the CK oil mills the fruit is boiled, then crushed, in order to separate the kernel from the fibres; the oil is squeezed from the latter, while the stone is crushed in order to extract the kernel [the palm nut]. These diverse phases are the responsibility of the workers at the post.

Workers at the post

The condition of workers at the post is wretched; none of the recommendations contained in ordinance 47, which was promulgated to protect them [as regards clothing, diet, accommodation and medical care], are observed. They work from six in the morning to six in the evening without a moment's rest, even in the very middle of the day. In 1927 their weekly rations and monthly wages were only from 1.50 francs to 2 francs and from 6 to 8 francs respectively. In the following years the company increased the ration in cash a little and sometimes gave a semblance of a ration in kind. The ration as laid down in ordinance 47 would amount to 3.5 francs per week.

As far as the ration in kind is concerned, only salt and oil are more or less regularly distributed, while meat is only on offer very rarely and rice very irregularly.

Ordinance 47 recommends the supplying in kind of 3,500 calories a day. The employer may substitute cash for supplying in kind, on condition that foodstuffs are available and that the cash given makes it possible to buy food containing the recommended number of calories at competitive prices. If a part of the ration is given in kind, the amount of cash must make it possible to buy the remainder. As we have seen, the amount given did not make this possible.

The Suku workers [from Feshi *territoire*] spend their Sundays searching in the forest for wild yams, a few handfuls of caterpillars or other insects; in threes or fours they buy a kilo of manioc for the week and their weekly ration is thereby made up; they supplement it each day with a few handfuls of manioc leaves. Those who do not die at the trading post return to their villages as walking skeletons.

It was three years ago, although my first report on this subject was described as tendentious, that I first drew the attention of the company to its criminal methods, and I have observed in the course of my last trip that the situation was the same as before.

Accommodation

Some posts boast fine houses built of half-crumbling adobe, 4 metres by 3 or 4 metres, in which 15, 20 or 25 natives are piled on top of one another.

Other managers settle for allowing the new arrivals to build straw huts, outside work hours of course. In these huts, which are 1.50 metres high, the blacks sleep one on top of the other. In Dunda I saw five in the same bed, which was 1.20 metres long and 0.80 metres wide (sic).

Siting of the posts
Most of the posts are set up by waterways, in order to transport their produce more easily. The steep slope would require, for the convenient handling of the goods, some terracing. In order to cut back on such expenditure, the company sets up its posts in small swampy clearings whose banks are nearly at the same level as the river. There are oil mills in which during the rainy season the natives are up to their chests in water when they are loading up the boats.

Women and Children
In 1927 the barns at the posts in Kimbili and Puanga contained boys and girls indiscriminately, from the age of 4 upwards.

More generally, women, young women and girls are conscripted from the surrounding villages, either for the crushing of the nuts, where there are no mechanical crushers, or for sorting, in the more modern oil mills. In Dondo I saw kids from 8 to 12 years old, piling up fruit from morning to night, which would be hard work even for an adult. Behind the work team stands the *capita*, with a stick in his hand, always poised to revive the slackers.

At Puanga non-adults make up half of the boat crews.

At Kindinga, in 1930, kids aged from 5 to 14 made up the entire workforce at the post.

Recruitment and the role of the state
It is of course the case that when an entire population is put to work, in a manner harmful to its very existence, it cannot be a question of voluntary labour. Legally speaking, relations between native and employer are regulated by a contract. But ordinarily the black is forced to sign such a contract, to renew it for life, to abide by the relevant clauses regarding working hours and numbers of crates of fruit, whereas the employer can violate his clauses regarding food and payment with impunity, etc.

If the work were free rather than forced, a good number of natives, tempted by European goods, would come and sell their fruit.

Entering into the agreement, and then honouring the contract are enforced by means of prison and the *chicotte*, which are generously administered by government officers, who have been reduced to acting as labour recruiters and as guards supervising convicts on behalf of the companies.

I have frequently had to intervene on behalf of sufferers from sleeping sickness, who are summoned because they do not work regularly. I have seen a territorial agent install himself at a trading post, assemble the fruit cutters, among them a good many old and infirm, and have them dealt as many lashes of the *chicotte* as there are crates short.

When a native, remarkably enough, managed to resist the threats and blows of the merchants, I have seen government officers offering him the choice between signing a contract and prison.

I had to intervene officially in order to stop the porterage of palm nuts from Kimbolo to Mushuni, a distance of 25 kilometres. In order to guarantee that porterage, the territorial agent in Ngaba, being on the best of terms with the manager, was perpetually conscripting women from the neighbouring village, whether they were young, old or pregnant. These forced labour methods require not only the complicity but also the active help of the state, which is no more sparing of it in the recruitment of men than it is in the grabbing of land.

In breach of all the laws and circulars on landed property, nine-tenths of the blocks conceded in the Kwango contain cultivated fields, which are necessary to village life. Their transfer was granted on the basis of fraudulent enquiries by the administrator and the circle head. Furthermore, government officers are liable to commit just as many abuses in the exercise of their own duties, and first and foremost in the collection of taxes.

Suppose we leave to one side the legitimacy of a tax which benefits only the Europeans and which presents the blacks with no compensatory advantages. This tax, which is sometimes equivalent to two or three months' work, ought to replace *corvées* in kind, it used to be said; in reality, the two co-exist, and the natives have now to bear the burden of both a tax in money and a tax in kind.

By law old men and adolescents of less than sixteen years old are exempt from taxation. In practice, as I have many times observed in Mushuni and Mombanda circles, 80% of old men and 40% of children pay. A sizeable tax levy is equated with a big population, a flourishing *territoire* and an agent in favour with the higher authorities!

The colonial administration is responsible for public works, roads, bridges and state posts. It is the women who make up the labour force needed for such tasks, since all the men are employed in industry. Most of the roads were built to ensure the movement of oil-mill products from the interior. For weeks, and even for months, the women—when they are not crushing palm nuts—work on the roads.

The territorial administration
While merchants rob the natives on their own account, it is only fair to point out that generally speaking government officers do much the same. They consider it very generous when they pay 50 or even 30 centimes for a chicken for which the natives among themselves will pay fifteen francs. They are generous indeed when compared to those who give nothing at all, and yet demand two chickens a day for themselves and two for their dogs. They readily justify this elegant solution to the problem of the high cost of living by declaring that the prestige of officials, and the authority of the state, must be maintained.

The territorial administrator in Bulungu set up a chicken market for Europeans. His messengers rounded up all the chickens in the *territoire*, paying 1.50 francs for each of them. He then re-sold them in Bulungu at 9 to 12 francs each. A manager, when the champagne was flowing, confided to him that he needed a hundred or so natives to move his produce. Two days later the porters asked for paraded in front of him, old men, invalids and women, with ropes around their necks.

Honest officials and territorial administrators do exist. Of the eight administrators who served in Lukula *territoire* over a four year period, I knew two who had a clear notion of what their duties were. Alas, no sooner did such a just man try to restrict the extortion perpetrated by the companies than he would immediately be reined in by his immediate superior, the district commissioner.

I know one administrator who used to beg the district to reduce the demand for labour to which a miserable and crushed population was subjected. The district's response was to instruct him to harry those rare natives who had up until then managed to avoid work, and to compel the others to produce more. One of its letters, which had delivered a stern rebuke, had been forwarded by the district commissioner to the CK manager before the administrator had even received it. A copy of this same letter was pinned up in all the trading posts in the *territoire*.

It goes without saying that, after granting such favours, and after submitting so many reports to the province in which the allegations of the doctors were depicted as lies and the condition of the region depicted as flourishing indeed, the CK could not do other than offer a directorship to this brave commissioner.

The methods employed by the province were not so different from those used by the district. I know of a report on a tour of inspection in the

Kwango made by a senior civil servant [Daco] which, though submitted at the beginning of December 1929 to the provincial government, had not yet reached the offices of the governor-general in June 1930, although these offices were no more than half-an-hour away.

It was not the only report to suffer such a fate for, generally speaking, the state medical corps is clear-headed and independent.

Unfortunately, its opinions count for nothing. For some, the doctors are Utopians, while others complain about a medical dictatorship and make it their business to have those whose attitudes do not suit them moved to the other end of the Colony. [This is an allusion to the transfer of Daco to Lubumbashi. However, a transfer to that spot, with its pleasant climate, was generally seen as a promotion.]

Personalities are not the issue here, for the agency responsible for the current labour crisis is the state as state. It is the state, a major shareholder in the companies, that has always left them free to act as they saw fit.

The results

Everyone works for the oil mills, men, women, children. Only the old, the weak and the sick stay in their villages. The men only return to the village once or twice a month, hence the rapid fall in birth rates. We have seen that 95% of able-bodied, adult males—a good many of the chronically ill but non-cachectic being counted as able-bodied—are estranged from family and social life.

Formerly, the men would clear the forest so that the women might cultivate it, and by hunting every day they would provide a regular supply of meat.

It would be an error to imagine that in equatorial regions everything simply grows without being tended. The women now are simply workers; the children, dirty and covered in vermin, wander listlessly among the ruined huts. There are no cultivated fields, no large livestock, because the tsetse fly reigns supreme; no smaller domestic animals, the natives reckoning that there is no point in tempting the whites any further; and there is no meat to be had from hunting, for there are no hunters. In short, famine has reigned for years in the whole of the Kwango industrial zone.

Sanitary conditions are lamentable. Sleeping sickness ravages the local population. How could it be otherwise? The natives, whether they work in posts from which the undergrowth has not been cleared, or traverse the swampy forest in search of palm trees, live all the time in the haunts of the tsetse fly. In the zone between Luie and Inzia, for example, at the time of my last tour of inspection in 1930, out of 4,482 inhabitants 54% had been treated for sleeping sickness, 29% of whom were new cases, since my previous examination a year and a half before.

Demographic tables, covering virtually the whole region, show that from 1927 to 1930 the total population fell from 5,677 to 4,544, in other words by approximately one-fifth.

In the zone between Lukula and Gobari, the population fell from 4,535 to 4,222.

The fact of depopulation hardly needs spelling out, in the face of such eloquent statistics.

The state is certainly trying to fight against depopulation, but its medical service is not equipped to deal with so grave a situation. As for the efforts made by the companies, sometimes it is simply that their procedures are inadequate, as is the case with the HCB, which has set up dispensaries and a model hospital on the banks of the Kwilu, within range of European visitors, but whose workers in the interior are subject to the harshest slavery and are decimated by sickness. In the case of the CK, when I first arrived in Africa its director said to me: "You must remember that we are a commercial company not a philanthropic enterprise, and that our share-holders will not ask us if we have taken good care of the natives but what dividends we have earned them."

If these men, who have been so badly affected, so gravely stricken, by the oil mills, are not allowed to rest, the disappearance of the population, if not total at any rate sufficient to prevent any economic activity, is certain to occur within a few years. Before their industrialisation the natives enjoyed a state of equilibrium appropriate to their resources and to their needs, and a stable familial and social organisation.

These populations, which once knew only a form of domestic slavery, have been subjected to the harshest industrial slavery. These calm and tranquil natives have been condemned in perpetuity to forced labour. These regions have been raided by the slave-traders of modern times, who snatch the blacks from their families and villages and dispatch them to distant work sites.

These men no doubt had their troubles and their illnesses, but they ate and they died in the normal fashion; we have decimated them, sometimes we have exterminated them, by bringing famine, syphilis, tuberculosis and sleeping sickness. What are the few thousand lives saved by our serums and vaccines when compared to the millions of deaths for which we are responsible?

What is one to say of the natives' moral state?

Robbed, ill-treated, condemned in perpetuity to forced labour, they relapse into utter apathy and come to loathe us.

When I got back to Europe, in order to compensate for the fall in prices in the metropolis, the already derisory wages were being cut still further, and harsher work discipline was imposed so as to produce a higher yield; taxes remained the same.

The response to the doctors' reports

At the beginning of December 1929, Daco submitted the reports on his diverse inspections of the oil-producing enterprises in the Kwango to the governor of the Congo-Kasai, in the form of a single report consisting of several notes, the report on Lusaka being note 6 and that on the CK note 5. Consequently later correspondence concerning these notes tends to refer to a single "Daco report". As Raingeard had noted, the report was blocked at province level for five whole months. On 18th May 1930, the interim governor-general, Charles Duchesne, having got wind of the report, asked the provincial authorities if he might see it. Governor Beernaert sent it to him, together with a letter dated 26th May.[4] The titular governor-general, Tilkens, having taken up his post at just this moment, paid no attention to the report, and did not forward it to Brussels. He may perhaps have concluded from the Ministry's muted responses to previous reports that criticisms of the HCB were not taken seriously. Moreover, this same Ministry regularly used to send him copies of Horn's reports which so flattered the company that the minister was prompted to offer his congratulations.[5]

The Daco report remained buried in the general government's filing cabinets in Boma for two and a half years, emerging then on Raingeard's initiative. The latter, at the time of his article's publication in *La Revue de Médecine et d'Hygiène Tropicales*, had informed the leader of the Belgian socialists, Emile Vandervelde, by now a government minister, of the identity of the provincial doctor mentioned by him. He had also spoken to him of Daco's report, of its general tenor and of its being locked away in government filing cabinets in the Congo.

On 14th June 1932, during an interpellation on the Congo, Vandervelde informed the Chamber of the existence of the Daco report and asked Colonial Minister Tschoffen what use had been made of it. The latter, flabbergasted, instructed his civil service to seek out the document in question. In the course of this same interpellation, Vandervelde also spoke of Raingeard's article, which, according to him, had been sent to the government in the form of a report. He stressed that the article contained some truly terrible things, and he read out a number of extracts.

The former Colonial Minister, Henri Jaspar, pointed out that it was not within a CK doctor's remit to submit a report to the authorities. Minister Tschoffen, for his part, declared that he had no knowledge of the report and that, furthermore, it should not have been forwarded to him, given that it emanated from a doctor employed by a private company. He added that he knew of Raingeard's article published in a review, but breathed not a word about it. Tschoffen might however have said that the article had been taken very seriously within his own department, which was preparing a rebuttal. He in fact understood the gravity of the charges that had been made. The director general of the department of public health, Albert Duren, had summarised the report for Tschoffen as follows:

> Dr. Raingeard unleashes a very violent attack on the Compagnie du Kasai and the Government with regard to the brutal and rapid industrialisation occurring among populations who are not prepared for it; he depicts the populations of the Kwango as having fallen below the level of slaves, and as being held ransom by the Compagnie du Kasai, with the complicity, and often with the assistance, of the governmental authorities. The ordinances on workers' health and safety are mere facades, behind which lurk the base spirit of lucre, extortion from the natives, and the oppression of women and children. The inevitable result must be the moral and physical degeneration of the natives, a terrifying increase in the death rate and an alarming fall in the birth rate.
>
> Precise observations are quoted, and a name could be put to a particular district commissioner whose lax complicity earned him a post as director with the Compagnie du Kasai. Spiteful allusions are also made to the Huileries du Congo Belge. If the truth be known . . . the Compagnie du Kasai has never been noted for treating its native workers well, nor for paying its European agents enough.

The above reflections feature in a note addressed to the minister, dated 3rd May 1932, in which Duren pointed out that the department should urgently request the governor-general to prepare notes refuting Raingeard's article.[6] On 24th May, the department asked the governor-general for a well-documented response to the article, which was wired on 29th June. The response consisted of three notes, the first by Maron, acting governor of the Congo-Kasai, the second by his deputy, Wauters, and the third by Mouchet.

The lengthy notes by Maron and Wauters claimed to refute virtually all Raingeard's allegations. With this end in view, they were stuffed with pages and pages of statistics and extracts from official reports supposedly proving that Raingeard was mistaken and prone to exaggerate wildly. Wauters' note presented statistics for output per cutter and per day's work, in order to prove that it was unjust to claim that the work required of the cutters was excessive, and that the latter did not have enough free time to tend their fields, to go hunting or fishing, or to rest. The vast majority of cutters did not work for more than two days out of six.

Maron's note was likewise full to bursting with materials designed to prove that Raingeard had greatly exaggerated the figures regarding the percentage of villagers at work, and it juxtaposed his figures and the far lower ones recorded by the administration. The note reproduced an extract from a letter of April 1930 from the civil servant (district commissioner René Preys) who had been sent to the scene in order to check Daco's findings recorded when accompanying Raingeard. According to the extract, abuses were punished: in Lukula *territoire* alone in the course of the previous few months, 23 lawsuits had been filed against Europeans, chiefly for violations of health and safety legislation and for maltreatment of natives. More particularly, the abuses identified at Mokamo—the Péchet lawsuits mentioned by Daco—were the object of proceedings against the manager. In other respects, Maron acknowledged in his note that there was truth in two of Raingeard's assertions, regarding the trading in chickens by the government officer in Bulungu, one Dewilliamort, now suspended, Maron added, and the traders' theft from Africans. Where this theft was concerned, Maron quoted an extract from the 1931 annual report for Kwango district, which stated that the suppliers of fruit had more than once been cheated of a certain quantity of fruit, and that others had not been paid regularly. All these misdemeanours had, however, been punished by law, according to the extract from the report. (I ought to point out that I have my doubts about these punishments, since no further details are supplied, and about the 23 lawsuits filed in Lukula *territoire*.)

While the notes written by Wauters and Maron should be treated with caution, the one submitted by Mouchet, and dated 26th June 1932, should not. Here it is:

During his stay of over three years in the Colony, Dr. Raingeard has always been regarded as a conscientious doctor, mindful of the health of the natives placed in his care.

I knew at the time that his relations with the Compagnie du Kasai, which had employed him, were frosty. This was owing to the interest, which the company no doubt deemed excessive, taken by this doctor in his medical mission. I have never heard any criticism of his ability or of his work.

As regards the article in question, it would be hard to contradict it. I would willingly admit that Dr. Raingeard, in order to highlight the situation he depicts, has accentuated the main lines of the picture, by bringing the darker features to the fore. It is nevertheless true that, generally speaking, the article is accurate . . .

As to the situation of the workers and the work imposed upon them, I would remind you that as early as 1928 I had written a note relating to an inspection in which I recorded analogous facts, based not only upon what I had heard, but also upon what I had been able to see in the course of a fairly rapid visit. [He is referring here to the note of 20th September 1928, extracts from which are reproduced above.]

There should be no need to remind you that district commissioner Vandenbyvang, who claimed that this note was neither objective nor accurate, shortly afterwards became director general of the CK.

In 1929, Daco himself visited the Kwango, in the guise of *médecin provincial*, and spent more time there than I did. His reports, which are more detailed than mine, confirm my findings and lend credence to my opinion regarding a wide range of facts and observations. I do not know what effect his reports had.

This is too often the fate of doctors' reports. Once they are forwarded to company bosses, the latter defend themselves like the very devil, deny the evidence and make endless promises. They have even invented for the purpose a term, medical dictatorship, which is proving a hit in Brussels and in the Congo, but which would be very hard to justify.

Local officials generally attach too little importance to the health of the natives, being too much preoccupied with economic matters. As for the doctors, many tire of compiling reports which cause them only anxiety, and grow indifferent.[7]

When the notes by Maron, Wauters and Mouchet arrived in Brussels, Duren wrote to the administrator general, Paul Charles, on 29th July, to say that, though they did not answer every accusation, they did rebut some of them; that some of the facts asserted by Raingeard could not be denied; and that a note from the chief medical officer tended rather to confirm the CK doctor's claims. Duren added:

> Raingeard's article was not unrelated to Minister of State Vandervelde's interpellation in the Chamber, to which . . . the Colonial Minister had replied. The directorate of the public health department deems it inopportune to re-open the question and, by giving a belated response, to rekindle a polemic which the minister's response has already closed.

Charles was of the same opinion, and wrote on Duren's note "to be filed".

The Colonial Minister had indeed answered Vandervelde, but the reader knows that he refrained from saying a word about the actual content of

Raingeard's article. The article, which had been deliberately left unrefuted, and which had been corroborated by the Daco report, proves that the situation of workers was even worse with the CK than with the HCB.[8]

As for the "Daco report" itself, it did not appear on the minister's desk until the end of February 1933.[9]

8

Pierre Ryckmans' Report on Lusanga (1931)

Before Governor-General Tilkens buried the Daco report on Lusanga in the filing cabinets of his administration, the general HCB management in Kinshasa had responded to it on 12th May 1930. I presume that their response was drafted or inspired by Charles Dupont, who at this date was serving as director general in Lusanga.[1] The management in Kinshasa then forwarded the Daco report to Lever Brothers Ltd., the parent company of the HCB in Europe. The latter responded in a letter of 20th October 1930, signed by its vice-president, Harold Robert Greenhalgh, and addressed to the secretary general of the Colonial Ministry, Charles. I give here some extracts from this letter:

> In a recent report drafted by a senior agent in the Congo of the S.A. of the Huileries du Congo Belge, it was pointed out that the natives in Lusanga concession are induced to bring to this company's posts supplies of palm fruit exceeding the local population's normal capacity for work, and that, in this concession, recourse is still too frequently had to portering . . .
>
> The undersigned has recently made a journey to the Congo, accompanied by the managing director of the Huileries du Congo Belge in Brussels, and in the course of this visit, they have been given every assurance, not only from the heads of the religious missions, but also from the Colony's civil servants, including the author of the report referred to below, that the policy adopted towards the native workforce, was wholly satisfactory. The surprise caused by the report in question was therefore all the greater . . .
>
> Given the conflicting opinions that have come to our attention, my colleagues and myself are very keen that there should be an inquiry into working conditions in Lusanga concession . . . We take the liberty of asking you kindly to propose to Monsieur the Governor-General to stage an enquiry to be conducted by one or two impartial persons . . .

It is hardly necessary to assure you that we are profoundly convinced that an enlightened policy aiming at the general improvement of the living conditions of the workforce and protecting the natives from unwarranted excesses or from ill treatment, is the sole policy offering any hopes of lasting success.

Charles passed this letter on to the Colonial Minister, Henri Jaspar, who without delay asked Tilkens to entrust the investigation to Pierre Ryckmans, a former governor in Burundi (1925–28) and a future governor-general of the Belgian Congo.[2] Ryckmans was in the Congo during this period, as a member of a commission consisting of four specialists, which had been instructed by the minister to examine the effects of measures designed to curb the excessive recruitment of workers, and thereby to ensure the preservation of the African population. There were four such specialists, one to each province, and Ryckmans himself had in fact been responsible for the province of Congo-Kasai.[3] This had been his first job in the Belgian Congo.

Ryckmans encounters recruits headed for the Offitra and Brabanta

Ryckmans received the order to conduct an investigation into the HCB towards the end of November 1930. Before embarking upon it, he went to the Sankuru in order to complete a part of the task for which he had originally come to the Congo at the beginning of October. During his journey he happened upon two wretched groups of recruits—one headed for the Office du Travail, the other for Brabanta—described by him in his letters to his wife, who had stayed behind in Belgium. The group destined for the Office du Travail, and who were originally from Lusambo, was composed of one of the last batches of forcibly enrolled workers rebuilding the Matadi-Kinshasa railway. In my book *Travail forcé pour le rail* I have described the terrible conditions suffered by such men en route. In order to give a further illustration of such conditions, I will transcribe here what Ryckmans wrote of the group that he encountered at Kwamouth around 25th November 1930:

On my arrival here, I am told that there is a barge in the port. I go there to see it dock. A disgrace. 80 men. I ask to see the register for the journey. It was in the hands of the captain of the steamer. Who was absent. I ask to see the convoying officer. I am presented with a native who is certainly more stupid than the most stupid of those in the convoy.—I ask to see the nurse, and he's not there. I summon the sick: 15 or so. Have they received any medication?—No.—Are there provisions? Yes, *chickwangues*.—Is that all?—That's all.—No fish, oil or rice?—No.—How long have you been on the road?—A long, long time.—Has no one at the post looked after you?—No one . . . The nurse turns up. Where are the medicaments?—In the ship's chest.—Show me.—That's impossible. The *capita* has the key.—Where's the *capita*?—He stayed in Dima.—Why?—I don't know, he did not come back on board when the siren sounded, and the boat left without him.—And what then do you give the sick?—I give those with headaches ammonia to inhale, but the others, nothing.—Besides the ship's chest you should have a medicine chest. Show me it. I am shown it: a huge great box with an impressive red cross. Inside, a flask of Dover powder, and a flask of ammonia. That was all.—At Kwamouth, there was no official, and therefore no one to restock it [there was only a military officer].

The captain of the tug-boat had gone to load up with wood from a post on the opposite bank. I run across him there this evening. He did not know that the barge's *capita* was not on board! Or that the medicine chest was locked! Or that the workers had not been fed! Or how long they had been travelling. He did not know a thing. He left Ilebo on the 12th, ran a barge loaded with 700 tonnes of copper on to the rocks, and spent 8 days attempting to refloat it. That had simply been an accident. The workers helped with the pumping; in exchange he bought them *chickwangues*. They helped transport the wood (I do not know if this is authorised by the regulations). But the captain did not trouble to ensure that they had a full ration. I had them given what they needed and telegraphed to Maron [acting provincial governor], in order to ask him to instigate an enquiry once the detachment arrived. Since I was unable to see the register for the journey, I do not know when these people left Lusambo. If they are to be believed, they spent three weeks in Ilebo! I will check later. If that is the case, these people must have left Lusambo around the time I arrived in Africa. Some of them may have already been on the road for several weeks, even before their arrival in Lusambo . . . It is hardly surprising if they arrive at their destination in a bad state!

At the beginning of December 1930, Ryckmans visited the Offitra camp in Ilebo, from where the people he had seen in Kwamouth had come. He wrote to his wife as follows:

Hard to believe. The recruits spend varying amounts of time here, ranging from 1 to 10 days [to three weeks, as we have just read]. The local authorities are not responsible for this. It is the fault of Unatra [a shipping company], which has failed to synchronise its runs on the Lusambo–Ilebo stretch and on the Ilebo–Kinshasa stretch. But during their stay, the recruits are left to starve. For example, the agreed ration for a woman would be 750 grams of manioc, 105 grams of fish, 57 grams of oil, 13 grams of salt. Or else, it would consist of the same amount of oil, salt and fish but, instead of manioc, 375 grams of rice! When I ask these imbeciles, L., the administrator, and P. [?], the police commissioner, why they do not give the legal ration, they tell me that that is the ration they have always given! To people exhausted by their journey and housed in the manner that you'll discover below! I ask if I may visit the camp. They tell me that they have asked for credits to extend it, that for the time being they are engaged in spending a supplementary credit of 21,000 francs, after 14,000 francs, for a smoking ditch. These things "under construction" or "which we are going to do" always seem to me suspect. Finally, five houses with four rooms in each, in adobe; the roofs are leaking, and are being redone. But for how long were they leaking before they were redone? Neither doors nor windows. No beds, just bare earth, and not even a mat. In each of the 20 rooms one can accommodate, given the legal amount of air-space per person, 3 single persons or one household. Normal convoys consist of 125 men, but sometimes there are as many as 240. What then? Then, they are a little cramped for space . . . It is harrowing and foolish. It costs so much: 27% of the recruits, as I have already told you, never even get to see the work-sites. The best is yet to come. I ask where the latrines are. I'm shown the foundations of a fumigation ditch. I insist upon seeing current facilities, and the police commissioner, with an airy wave of the hand, points towards the forest!

It was at Ilebo, on 6th December, that Ryckmans happened upon the group of recruits in transit to Brabanta. He described it as follows:

What are these *basendji* [savages] crouching on the sand, waiting for I know not what? They are a hundred or so, dressed in raffia *pagnes*, with funny little straw caps fixed to their mops of hair with a pin. Some workforce!—And yet that is what it is: they are recruits for the oil mills, come from Mweka (Kasai) and going to Brabanta.—For how long?—They have no idea.—To do what?—They have no idea.—To receive what wages?—They have no idea.—Where are their papers?—They don't have any . . . The *capita* from the oil mills insists that they have been hired as fruit cutters, for a year; if they pretend not to know this, it is because they are playing the *mayele* [the innocent]. The only thing they have not been told is the size of their wage (a small and unimportant detail, obviously).

The contingent contains a number of skeletons with a Pignet of 45 at least. One old man, with lips turned in on his gums and with hollow cheeks, has just one tooth in his mouth. When all is said and done, these are typical "volunteers" sold by their chief, resigned in the way that one may well resign oneself to the blows of fortune, and setting out like the most wretched of livestock. The white who had recruited them was M.G., the director of Brabanta in person. He was at the hotel. I went upstairs. I have rarely seen a man so bored . . . I ask him to come downstairs with me, he was wearing his slippers.—Is that a man you'd have climbing palm trees? I ask, pointing out the old man.—No, I can't have seen that one.—It is easy enough to make sure: ask him what his name is.—The name was indeed written on the list. The recruiter may perhaps not have looked at the man but he certainly saw him (unless of course, and this is also very possible, he saw none of them, and simply wrote down the names of those handed over to him, without taking the trouble to see them). I ask him what he plans to do. He answers that it is basically not of great importance, since the doctor at the oil mills will see them tomorrow. I counter with the text of the decree, which states categorically that no recruit may leave his *territoire* without a physical fitness certificate. No certificate of physical fitness can be issued if an individual's Pignet is above 35. There's no way round it.—Besides, Monsieur, do you really suppose that the doctor could pass that one, and that one, and that one. Do you suppose that this one has a Pignet lower than 45? (The man had a Pignet of perhaps 60.) . . . It is distressing isn't it, that one of the largest employers in the Colony should have come to this? Note that what I object to is not primarily the forced nature of the recruitment. I am prepared to accept that in new regions one may force a few single men to fall in with a new experience—as has been done in the Urundi for the Union Minière. But what troubles me are all the other illegalities surrounding recruitment. To tear from their village old men who are not up to doing anything at all, to seize people without even telling them why, nor what they will earn . . . and this after some years have gone by! I can live with the fact of there being some abuses, given the efforts that are made to curb them. But here there is no possibility of progress. So long as the employers can have people by such means, they will obviously make no effort to obtain them in some other way . . .[4]

Ryckmans' report on Lusanga

The published parts of Ryckmans' correspondence with his wife regarding the enquiry in Leverville are meagre indeed. The key passages read as follows:

> My initial impressions have been confirmed. Overall the outlook is fine; an encouraging future—but with some shadows in the picture, and very well-defined shadows at that. Now we are in a position to grasp that the shadows are very black—villages in a ruinous state owing to the excessive workforce [owing to excessive recruitments], excessive workloads, arbitrary methods, arrests of chiefs, *chicotte* etc.[5]

The reader will be interested to learn that these "very black shadows" also feature in the official report on the enquiry, from which lengthy extracts are given below. It was signed at Kikwit on 29th January 1931 by Ryckmans and the two others appointed by the minister to take part in the enquiry, namely, the district commissioner for the Kwango, Jules Vanderhallen, and Father Fernand Allard, representing Sylvain Van Hee, who had become apostolic vicar for the Kwango.[6] Here, to begin with, are a number of extracts shedding a harsh light upon the exploitation of the palm groves by the fruit cutters, forced to practice an occupation they detested, and for good reason. I have stripped the quotations of the flowery phrases used to adorn them, and to mask abuses:

> Fruit cutters are better paid than ordinary workers; the rate of remuneration, 2.40 to 2.60 francs per crate of fruit (25 kilos) delivered to the reception centre, is much higher than in the surrounding areas [worked by CK, CCB and others]. The HCB have until now stuck to the earlier rate, despite the crisis . . . Nevertheless, the occupation is not valued. The young people in general, above all the *évolués*,[7] and more particularly the Christians, feel a genuine aversion for the healthy and remunerative work of picking. One of our interlocutors has thus spoken of "an extraordinary repugnance, and the term is really not excessive". [The Daco report on Lusanga likewise speaks of the categorical refusal on the part of the younger generation to enrol with the company.]
>
> And, strange to tell, local residents, who would benefit from the most favourable circumstances for such work, display more reluctance, and are more determined to refuse, than are peoples from further away . . .
>
> The free purchase of fruit does not occur in Lusanga circle. As a general rule, the purchase of fruit from the cutters is done by means of a contract to supply precisely defined quantities; sometimes a monthly quota is involved, sometimes a specific number of crates have to be delivered within a given period of time. Almost all the imported workers have the latter type of contract: 200 crates in 6 months [5,000 kilos].
>
> The contract recommended by the company bosses—a three-year contract with the obligation to deliver a minimum daily quantity of 40 kilos

of shelled fruit—is one that no native could ever freely and knowingly accept, because in most cases it would be impossible for him to honour it . . .

Production from the palms in Leverville circle, an area with sharply defined seasons, is clearly seasonal. The natural yield of the palm groves varies from season to season and from month to month, in the proportion of 1 to 3. In order to grasp just how great such seasonal variations are, one merely has to consult the statistics for the test palm grove in Leverville, where all the clusters reaching maturity are harvested with care. The greatest extremes occurred in 1930, with 156 kilos in December [rainy season] and 536 kilos in August [dry season].

A more or less constant output can only be achieved . . . by imposing an effort upon the natives that is in inverse proportion to the natural production of the palm groves. Hence . . . the grievances of the state officials "harassed" by complaints, to borrow a phrase used by one of them, invariably during the rainy season, hence the excessive pressure put upon the cutters by some company agents, who fear being in the company's bad books if production should fall; hence, finally, the bitterness and disgust for the occupation of cutter felt by the workers, who are accused of laziness and of ill will, and who are sometimes even prosecuted . . .

I have in front of me some directives issued by company headquarters at Leverville for Kwenge sector, dated 23rd March 1930, in which the following passages feature [in English in Ryckmans' report]:

". . . It is your responsibility to organise the cutters' deliveries so as to obtain on a regular basis an average production of 40 crates per month.

"I agree with you about delaying authorisations to go on leave to the villages until such a time as the cutters' production has regained its normal level. Leave is obviously more or less a reward and, in any case, it must not be granted to cutters failing to give satisfaction. Furthermore, I plan to approach those government officers who arrange contracts for our cutters, in order to see if the state might actively assist us in dealing with the more recalcitrant among them. You may rest assured that well-deserved punishment will not shade into ill treatment. However, by punishment we do not necessarily mean physical chastisement, but first of all assignment to another kind of work, transfer to headquarters or to another sector, the imposition of fines and, finally, recourse to the state. [This way of phrasing things, for which Dupont was probably responsible, would seem to confirm Daco's claim that almost everyone in Lusanga circle was regarded as being in the service of the HCB.]"

What is an agent to do upon receiving such directives, except abide by them? He will harass the natives, pester them, set *capitas* and sentries on their heels, punish them for having failed to harvest non-existent fruit, while waiting until such a time that, through the above-mentioned labour contract, he may have recourse to the state to apply still more effective sanctions to the "recalcitrant" . . . Is it any wonder that the occupation [of fruit cutter] has a bad reputation?

When their sectors in the Kwilu opened, one by one, the HCB used authoritarian methods in hiring their workforce, the only ones possible with the highly primitive races inhabiting their concession. In order to hire cutters, the chiefs were approached. The chiefs supplied slaves. The slaves, once designated, were resigned to their fate. They were given a work-book, a blanket and a machete. They were told what work was expected of them, and in general they do it fairly willingly. When treated well and paid well, they are satisfied with their lot . . .

As a general rule, it is not a question of re-enlistment. When the three years of the labour contract have expired, it is automatically renewed by giving the cutter, as had been done at the end of the first two years, a new blanket and a new machete. In practice, a cutter is never set free but cuts fruit until he dies, or until his manager lays him off because of old age . . .

But conditions are changing fast. If one seeks to extend recruitment to other classes of the population, authoritarian methods are no longer applicable . . . As a general rule, recent contracts have been voluntary, and cutters enlisting nowadays do it of their own free will . . .

My informants are virtually all agreed that one could not, without irremediably compromising the development of the country, insist today upon freely undertaken agreements in the case of the renewal of contracts of former cutters recruited through chiefs . . .

At the outset . . . recruitment [of "imported" workers] entailed the direct intervention of government agents and chiefs. As a matter of fact, state involvement is dwindling, and now only occurs in exceptional cases. It generally takes the form of a reminder to the chief responsible for the relief of hired men nearing the end of their term. In some regions, replacement occurs automatically, with no outside intervention; this replacement is now customary, and is only too readily accepted.

As is clear from the paragraphs on enrolment and recruitment, Ryckmans is making three basic claims: first, that the company is using three-year contracts; second, that current recruitments have become virtually automatic; third, that in the past recruitment involved authoritarian methods, in particular, the supplying of slaves by the chiefs. These claims do not tally with the reality, as described in the earlier chapters of the present book. As far as the first point is concerned, the company may well have wished to introduce a three-year contract but it had failed to do so. Moreover, we have just read, at the beginning of the extracts reproduced above, that "imported" workers had contracts to supply 200 crates in 6 months. As far as the second point is concerned, and as we saw earlier, in 1930 recruitments were not always free, since they were carried out by labour recruiters escorted by territorial agents. As far as the third point is concerned, the earlier chapters estimate the number of workers at Lusanga to be, roughly speaking, 2,000 in 1918, 6,000 in 1923 and 10,000 in 1927. These workers would serve for terms of three months. Which plainly means that during these three years 18,000 x 4, or 72,000 men, were recruited. For the entire period extending from the beginning up until 1927, that would give a much higher figure, even if one takes into account the fact that the same man could have completed several terms of service. I am quite ready to admit that among these recruits there were some slaves, but the notion that the bulk of cutters in 1930 consisted of former slaves whose enlistment had been extended for life is nothing but a fairy tale. Had that been true, there would have been no need to be constantly recruiting.

Let me stress in passing the shocking nature of Ryckmans' claim that the government could not insist upon the laying-off of cutters hired for life. Furthermore, earlier chapters have taught us that those in the past who had re-enlisted, like the new recruits, were neither well treated nor well paid. Numerous, repeated official re-enlistments occurred, without the question of slavery or otherwise ever being an issue. Ryckmans speaks of slaves in order to condone the practice. Daco had been forthright in denouncing contracts with no time limit in Lusanga. Raingeard likewise did not mince words in the article he published on his experiences in the Kwango. The main reason for Africans holding the occupation of cutter in such horror, and for recruitments in 1930 being no freer than they had been at the outset, was the excessive workload imposed upon the cutters, and the means used to enforce its execution. This is plainly stated in later sections of Ryckmans' report, which read as follows:

The company has to be able to count upon a full complement of workers. For this reason it normally tries to tie cutters by means of a compulsory contract. It is generally agreed that 400 crates per year [10,000 kilos] is a maximum. But how should this output be distributed across the different months of the year? The only reasonable answer must be to correlate it with the rate at which clusters ripen. If January gives 4% of the annual production, and August 12%, a satisfactory quota would be 16 crates in January and 48 in August.

[And yet] the directives issued by the board recognise only one quota, namely, 40 kilos a day, whatever the season, "the daily amount that can easily be picked in five or six hours". One sector [Kwango] has gone even further and imposed in December 1930 a quota of 2 crates a day, and 50 to 54 crates a month, adding that this is the requisite quota "at this season". How much then is required at other seasons? . . .

When a cutter fails to meet his quota, various measures may be taken, involving the company's black officials ("sentries" and *capitas*), native chiefs, the HCB's agricultural agents or even the directors of the sector, the territorial administrators acting through messengers, in person or finally, as a last resort, as magistrates.

Sentries and *capitas* are, for their part, a real nuisance. They are veritable busybodies, whose zeal generally takes the form of yells, insults, chicanery and daily harassment, and who continually molest, pester and enrage the cutters. I will give some typical figures. For 298 cutters on the books at Kisia in February 1930, there were 40 sentries; at Kimbinga, in April 1930, there were 32 sentries for 260 cutters. One sentry to harass 7 to 8 cutters.

The involvement of chiefs is harmful, and that of the messengers an outright abuse. A chief receiving a bonus for increases in production is faced with a conflict between self-interest and duty.

As for the messengers, the territorial administration has for long periods done the great wrong of employing in some sectors messengers who are plainly on the company's pay-roll . . . We reckon that the employment of state messengers ought generally to be condemned. They understand just one thing, namely, that they are responsible for getting people to work, and they are ready to use any means possible to carry out this mission.

These paragraphs demonstrate quite clearly that the exploitation of palm groves in Lusanga circle was a system of forced labour pure and simple, bearing a strong resemblance to rubber production in the epoch of the Congo Free State. Despite these paragraphs, Ryckmans wrote in his report that where local workers were concerned the high levels of recruitment, exceeding the percentages stipulated, were not all in all a cause for concern. The cutter of fruit was in principle still able to play a part in village life and to participate in all of the community's activities, at any rate if his quota was reduced. In the case of workers coming from a distance, there was no need to worry about exceeding the percentages, Ryckmans said, since recruiting only affected the numbers defined by civil servants as available for work. Ryckmans spoke here as if the ordinary routines of village life, once held in the vice of HCB coercion, had not been profoundly disturbed, and as if recruiting at a distance did not consist of capturing workers for forced labour. We shall see in the next chapter how one such operation left a trail of misfortunes in its wake.

In his report Ryckmans also backed the colonial administration's implementation of something the company had long desired, namely, the moving of villages to its palm groves, a scheme rejected outright, as we saw in chapter 2, by the acting governor-general, Léon Bureau. The HCB bosses in Brussels again alluded to this scheme in a memorandum dated 17th May 1926, in which they thought to entice the Colonial Minister with the glittering vision of creating garden cities out of the relocated villages.[8] (I will return to this question in chapter 10.) The lack of any response to this memorandum had not prevented the director in Lusanga from promoting the settlement in the vicinity of the palm groves of as many as possible of the cutters who came from far away. This settlement took the form of what were known as "stand-in villages", the idea being that, to begin with, these cutters' families would come and join them, and that later on the rest of the village would follow. Ryckmans wrote of the stand-in villages and of the transfer of population to the palm groves in the following terms:

The imported workers coming from just a small distance away are treated in the same fashion as the local workers, and are responsible for their own food supplies. They are not subject to any preliminary medical inspection. They settle, generally speaking, in "stand-in villages", which, being poorly supervised, all too easily become centres of disorder and prostitution . . .

Since Ryckmans was not troubled by the disruption of African communities and of their habitat, done to boost the profits of their despoiler, he was hardly likely to be disturbed by female and child labour. He wrote as follows in his report:

As in all Africa, so among the people of the Kwilu, porterage is a burden shouldered by the women. The same is true of the cutters. It is a regrettable situation, but one for which the company is not responsible. By making women take part in economic activity on behalf of European enterprises, there is a strong risk of overburdening them. But, given the native mentality, it does not seem to be possible to prevent most of the porterage imposed upon the cutters from being transferred by the latter on to their wives' shoulders. One cannot ask the company to reject fruit simply because it is the women who bring them to the reception centres.

The company is investing large sums in the development of mechanical means of transportation by water and by land. There are now no posts at which the transport of fruit by the cutter, or rather by his wife, involves distances of more than 5 kilometres.

But even 5 kilometres is asking much of a woman who is pregnant or burdened with children. She has to go and find the fruit in the forest, shell it, carry it from the early morning onwards to the reception centre, and return home exhausted to perform her domestic duties.

Alongside porterage by women there is porterage by children. A monogamous man, being obliged to deliver two crates per day, will have his wife carry one and the children of the family, even though they are sometimes very small, the other.

Such were Ryckmans' arguments in justification of female and child labour. He could have argued for better rates of pay for cutters working without a wife, such as those workers "imported" without their wives into the palm groves. He could have demanded the immediate implementation of a measure, namely, that of entrusting teams of ordinary workers with the sole responsibility for shelling and transportation, but he merely recommended a study to see if it were feasible. He could not see that female and child labour were simply further aspects of the system of slavery in force in Lusanga, where a lump sum was paid for porterage irrespective of the distance covered.

There is one important point glossed over by the report, namely, the involvement of territorials, sworn in as magistrates, in maintaining the cutters' output by handing down prison sentences, implying the use of the *chicotte* against those found guilty. Ryckmans would have us believe that recourse to such sentences was very rare, and yet he himself tells us that for half the year the territorials were inundated with complaints. These complaints were of the kind mentioned by him in his report: a letter, dated 19th December 1930, from the chief of Kwango sector to Territorial Agent Emile Jochmans of Kongila-Kikongo, requesting a heavy punishment for five cutters from Yoko village and for three from Bosongo village, the reason being that their poor output was greatly hindering the work of post 4a, which went by the name of Kolonie. The sector chief added that, along with the letter, he was dispatching four of the eight malefactors, I imagine with a rope around their necks, with an escort composed of sentries. There is no doubt that territorial officers countenanced prison and the *chicotte* as responses to the complaints with which they were plagued. The use of the *chicotte* was the sole means available in the Congo to ensure the smooth running of a system hated by the Africans.

Being myself a former territorial officer, I speak from experience. It often happened that a magistrate could not be bothered to hold a hearing and to draft a judgment in due form, but had the *chicotte* administered without any other form of trial. This was true of the case recounted by Raingeard, quoted in the previous chapter under the heading "Recruitment and the role of the state", in which an official had the number of lashes with the *chicotte* tally with the number of missing crates.

As one reflects on this report, one is forced to acknowledge that Ryckmans, who already had his eye on the post of governor-general, sacrificed the best interests of Africans to the material success of the HCB. The reader cannot help but be astonished by:

1 The frivolity with which he handles serious questions regarding the relocation of villages or female and child labour.
2 His conviction that it was too soon to think of introducing the free purchase of fruit, a method which, if recourse had not been had to the system of monopolies and forced labour, would have succeeded.
3 His mistaken conviction that Lever's workers were well paid. He should not have compared their remuneration to that paid by the CK, which was a pittance, nor to that paid by Forminière, which was somewhat more appropriate, but to that dispensed in the neighbouring colonies, which was as much as eight times that offered in the Congo.
4 His failure to condemn the use of labour contracts to exact excessive quotas from cutters. It is to this that Charles Dupont was referring when he insisted so vehemently at the beginning of January 1924 upon the need to obtain government endorsement for piecework contracts.

One also cannot help but be astonished by Ryckmans observing in his report, and reckoning it to be in the HCB's favour, that he had received no complaints from the workers. He had forestalled any such complaints since, as he tells us in the introduction to the report, he had conducted his questioning of the Africans in a discreet fashion, "so as to prevent the enquiry from undermining the impression one has of the harmony which should prevail, and does in fact prevail, between the powerful concessionary company and the populations whose collaboration it seeks". The report contains scarcely any details on some of the darker aspects of the HCB's work, as identified by Ryckmans in his correspondence with his wife, namely, villages ruined by excessive recruitment, arrests by chiefs, use of the *chicotte*, etc. Yet praise there is in plenty. Here is one example, taken from Ryckmans' preface:

The wages exceed the average paid in neighbouring regions. Accommodation is in general excellent. Rations are regular and first-rate. Where they are paid in cash, the nearby canteen is always supplied with high-quality goods, sold to workers at lower prices than those charged by local traders. The workers' families are not forgotten; *pagnes* are dispensed free of charge to the women, and blankets for new-born infants boost the birth-rate. Old workers are pensioned off, and the victims of accidents at work are paid compensation. Finally, the company medical service, while being especially concerned with the fight against sleeping sickness in the whole sector, opens the doors of its hospitals and dispensaries to anyone who turns up, whether they are workers or no.

These fine words in no way square with the system of exploitation described in the main body of the report, which calls to mind that of the Congo Free State. Besides, they defy belief. The wages may have exceeded those paid in neighbouring areas, but they were still wretchedly low; and the majority of workers, the so-called locals, were not housed. Did Ryckmans even set eyes on the Yanzi camps? I doubt very much that the rationing system was as perfect as his description suggests, and the report anyway gives no details. The praise lavished on the ration in cash is surprising, given Daco's recommendation that it be replaced by a ration in kind. Was the company supplying the workers with fresh food? The fields planted with food crops in Kwenge, which year after year had been announced for the following year, were certainly not yet yielding anything, since the large *chefferie* of Yongo (in Kandale *territoire*) was forced to grow food crops for the company.

As for the company's purported concern for the well-being of mothers and new-born children, it would have done better to address the role of women and children in porterage and shelling. The claims, never previously made, regarding pensioned workers and compensation paid for accidents need to be buttressed by solid facts. We need to be told just what the schedule of compensations, assuming there was one, amounted to. The "pensions" consisted of a yearly payment of 100 francs to cutters boasting over 10 years' service (there were 230 such men in 1932).[9] As we know from Daco's account, a medical service welcoming one and all, and struggling everywhere against sleeping sickness, had not existed 14 months earlier. This service had certainly not undergone a miraculous transformation, at a time when the proposal was made to cut the European staff to two doctors and the sanitation agents to zero, thereby reducing the staff by one half.[10]

The report concludes with yet more words of praise:

In the space of a few years, the HCB have achieved a great deal in the Kwilu, in the midst of countless difficulties, among tribes which, barely 15 years ago, were still plunged in utter savagery. Older residents still recall a time when it was dangerous to go from one village to another. Sleeping sickness threatened to exterminate the race.

Today, thanks to the economic activity fostered by the HCB, the country enjoys a remarkable degree of prosperity. Sleeping sickness, which is still rife in neighbouring regions, has almost disappeared from the circle. The population, and the areas under cultivation, are increasing . . .

These are nothing but empty phrases, copied from the introduction to the 1905 report of the Commission d'Enquête,[11] which stated that: "In these territories which, 25 years ago, were still plunged in the most terrible barbarism, which only a few white men, through their own superhuman efforts, had traversed . . . [etc.] Today, security reigns in this vast territory . . . [etc.]". Just as such praise lavished upon the Congo Free State in 1905 was undeserved, so too were the praises heaped upon the HCB by Ryckmans. His vacuous admiration for the HCB prevented him from grasping the sheer extent of the system of implacable coercion prevailing in the Kwilu for well nigh 20 years.

Ryckmans could have recommended the study of the palm-oil industry in Africa's biggest producer, Nigeria, where there had never been any desire to force the Africans to supply fruit, nor likewise to adopt the system of coercion and monopoly created by William Lever in the Congo.[12] Ryckmans might have asked himself just why this Englishman had set up business in the Belgian Congo and not in British Nigeria.

As he travelled from Kikwit to Tshikapa, Ryckmans passed through the country of the Pende, a people whom he admired. He took pleasure in winning over the children during the long waits beside his bogged-down vehicle. "It is perhaps the most sympathetic population", he wrote to his wife, "that I have encountered in the course of this journey."[13]

My next chapter is concerned with the Pende, who lived in the country to the south of Kikwit, between the river Loange and the river Kwenge, which later became Gungu *territoire*.

9

The Revolt of the Pende (1931)

The revolt

The origins of the revolt may be traced back to a recruitment on behalf of the HCB, launched on 14th May 1931 by the territorial agent Edouard Burnotte in the village of Kilamba, situated in the far north of Kandale *territoire*, on the borders of Kikwit *territoire*. Burnotte was accompanied by a company recruiter, Alphonse Vanhombeek. Burnotte and Vanhombeek at first had no success at all, since all the men took to the bush. Burnotte then ordered the messengers, who accompanied him, to arrest the women and to shut them up in a barn.

That same day, Bandu, the "decorated" chief of the Yongo *chefferie*, had 47 men in Kilamba lashed for having failed to deliver their quota of fruit to the (hand-powered) CK oil mill in the village of Bangi. The latter lay in Kikwit *territoire*, 20 minutes away from Kilamba.[1] Like all the "decorated" chiefs, Bandu was an usurper, the genuine chief of Yongo being called Katshinga.[2] Birching with the *chicotte* was probably carried out in the presence of Collignon, who was in charge of the CK post at Bangi. At this moment two other CK agents were in the area, namely, R. Polet from Lutshima and Khoudiacoff, from Indele. The latter had come to ask for Burnotte's support in ensuring a supply of palm fruit for their hand presses.

On the evening of 14th May, the labour recruiter Vanhombeek regaled Burnotte and his three CK agents with a case of drink. The five began to drink and carouse, and then had some of the women shut up in the barn brought to them. There followed one of those extended orgies legendary among white single men in the interior of the Congo. Three days later, Burnotte and Vanhombeek, having managed to round up and dispatch a contingent of recruits towards Lusanga, set out, after a detour by way of Kandale, to recruit on the left bank of the Lutshima, in Kasanza region. On 27th May, as they approached the village of Kasandji, they were met with volleys of arrows. The following day Burnotte took the Kikwit road in order to go on leave in Europe.

Around this same date Collignon went to Kilamba, where he was jostled by Africans because he had taken chickens from them without paying and because he had not paid a woman by the name of Kafushi, having dallied with her on the night of the orgy. The husband of this woman, Matemo, alias Mundele Funji, then went to Bangi oil mill to claim the payment owed him by Collignon, in accordance with African custom, for having slept with his wife. Collignon ordered him to clear off, and slapped him about the face. Matemo was then beaten by the servants and workers in the oil mill. He fled naked, his *pagne* in his hand, and returned in an enraged state to Kilamba.

For his part, Collignon had the gall to lodge a complaint in Kandale against Matemo, without breathing a word about what had taken place at Kilamba, be it the business with the chickens or the orgy. The territorial administrator, Léonard Vaninthout, ordered the territorial agent Maximilien Balot, a former sergeant in the Force publique, to hold an investigation on the spot.[3] In the meantime, on 25th May, the territorial agent for Kikwit, Michiels (being at Pukusu, 15 or so kilometres from Kilamba) had written to his superior, administrator Gustave Weekx, alerting him to an anti-white movement raging thereabouts and spreading towards Bangi. A sect by the name of *satana* had just formed, which sought to have nothing more to do with the white man, to stop working for him, and which was instructing people to throw away tax counters, order books, work-books and any money received from the white man. Michiels had added that there was a large gathering of armed men at the former depot of Valle et Valle in Kisenzele, and that it represented a real danger to the Europeans in Lutshima region. He had begged his superior to come as soon as he could and, given the great urgency of the situation, to send him soldiers and ammunition.

Weekx went immediately to Pukusu, having forwarded Michiels' message to the district commissioner in Bandundu, Jules Vanderhallen. On 30th May, he wrote to the latter, from Pukusu:

The openly anti-European movement is characterised by a total cessation of economic activity. For several days now, not a single crate of fruit has been delivered to the [Portuguese] firm of Madail de Banza.

The sect is known as "the devil's" ("the shades' "), and it originated in Kandale *territoire*; to join, one has to get rid of all objects of European provenance; special paths are prepared behind the villages, which the shades are supposed to use; in the forest small barns are erected, and offerings are left there.

I was myself subject to armed attack yesterday in Kisenzele, to which I had come in a lorry driven by M. Quadrio of Madail and co . . .

I went to the end of the village, accompanied by four soldiers and by M. Quadrio. I noticed a large group of around 200 men, armed with rifles and arrows, intoning their battle cries as I approached them. When I had come within 75 metres, we were assailed by arrows from all sides. I then ordered my troop to open fire . . . seeing some of its number wounded, the whole group fled.

Weekx concluded his letter by calling for the whole of the southern region of the Lutshima to be placed under military occupation, as a matter of the utmost urgency. Once such an occupation had been effected, the administration could, by virtue of the decree of 31st July 1920, station soldiers in those villages where public order had not been breached, in order to set their inhabitants to work, while compelling them to shelter and feed the troops free of charge, failure to meet this obligation resulting in a three-month prison sentence.

On 3rd June, District Commissioner Vanderhallen decided to proceed with the requested occupation and therefore dispatched to the region two platoons (75 men) from Bandundu company, under the command of Warrant Officer Zéphir Faucon.[4] At this time Congo-Kasai province was intermittently in the charge of Commissioner General Constant Wauters, during those periods when the titular governor, Beernaert, replaced Governor-General Tilkens, when he was travelling or otherwise prevented from carrying out his official duties. On 6th June, Wauters sent a telegraph to Vanderhallen requesting him to turn the military occupation into a police operation. At the same time he instructed him to go to the places in question, to take vigorous action and, where necessary, to send for reinforcements.[5] Wauters reckoned that a police operation was more appropriate to the situation in Lutshima, since law and order were under threat there. A police operation, of the kind stipulated in the ministerial decree of 25th October 1920, allowed for the circulation of detachments, with a view to forestalling or dispersing any large gatherings of Africans. Yet such operations were supposed not to involve the use of arms, save in self-defence. On the very same day that Wauters transmitted this order to Bandundu, he also asked the district commissioner in the Kasai to take whatever steps were necessary to prevent the rebels' movement from encroaching into his district.

In the meantime the anti-European movement had gained a solid foothold in Kilamba thanks to the initiative of none other than Matemo. In this locality the forcible recruitment perpetrated by Burnotte for the

HCB, and the mass use of the *chicotte* on behalf of the CK, had caused this population's cup of bitterness, after suffering 10 years' brutality at the hands of both companies, to overflow. When Balot, accompanied by a soldier and four messengers, arrived there on 8th June to investigate Collignon's complaint, he encountered a hostile crowd led by Matemo. In order to disperse the crowd, Balot had shots fired into the air, and then, when the Africans failed to disperse, he took up his hunting rifle and shot someone in the forearm. It was then that Matemo hurled himself at him, struck him on the head with his double-bladed knife, chased after him when he fled into the bush, and finished him off.[6]

Collignon, who was in the area at the time, wrote the following day from Mbushi to the his company headquarters: "On the 7th inst. M. Balot, territorial agent at Kandale, summoned me to Kilamba for the 8th. On this same date, hearing shots, I ran to the aid of M. Balot, but too late, for M. Balot, being wounded, had been forced to flee. Fearing for my own safety, the natives having cried that they would subject me to the same fate, I took flight, placing everything under lock and key."[7] Collignon thus pretended not to know what had happened to Balot, and the outside world would long remain ignorant of his fate.

In a letter dated 9th June, the administrator of Kandale, Vaninthout, en route for Kasanza, where Burnotte and Vanhombeek had been showered with arrows, transmitted the following, recently acquired information on the devil's sect to Vanderhallen:

1 A certain Sangu, a Pende of the Bakwa Kangu, from Mapungu village, Tianza *chefferie*, has declared that he had a dream in which the devil . . . had instructed that all blacks should:

2 . . .

3 build beside each village and close to the river a *sombolo* (hut), make a path between this *sombolo* and the river, on the one hand, between the *sombolo* and the village on the other.

4 dress themselves solely in *pagnes* of native provenance . . .

5 abstain from eating manioc leaves, fish, groundnuts; abstain from drinking palm wine . . .

6 round up all goats, dogs and chickens that are black in colour, kill them and preserve only animals that are white in colour.

7 no longer work for whites in general in any shape or form; no longer honour fiscal obligations or prestations [for the HCB, the CK and the State]; refuse food crops, porters, etc.; no longer let messengers pass; seize messages and destroy them . . .

Vaninthout went on to speak of the benefits that the adepts of the sect would enjoy:

1 In the *sombolo* the devil would come and fill receptacles left there by people with gunpowder (for rifles), salt, money, white cloth, etc.
2 *Bula Matari* will be powerless, and the whites will anyway not dare to do anything to the adepts. Where necessary, the devil will kill the whites . . .
3 Providing you remain in the village, do nothing at all and simply follow orders given, the devil will send beer instead of palm wine, cattle in place of the small black-coloured livestock that has been killed . . .

Vaninthout further added:

All the villages are laying claim to Sangu, who now has himself called Muluba, and want him to come and build a model *sombolo* and spread the word. Muluba has himself transported in a *tipoye* and declares himself to be chief of all the Pende. From Kobo onwards all the blacks take flight when I approach; they are armed with bows and shoot arrows at any messengers sent to summon them. Today catechists from the two missions came to find me, saying that people are preventing their children from following religious instruction. Other catechists have been attacked, and the blacks have torn their clothes . . . telling them to follow the whites, who will soon be forced by the adepts of the sect to go back to Europe.

Vaninthout ended his letter by asking Vanderhallen to call for a military occupation to be imposed upon the Kandale *chefferies*, which had been assailed by the evil just as the Kikwit *chefferies* had been, so that, through vigorous and concerted action, the rebellion in both *territoires* might be put down.[8]

At this time the CK managers in Indele, Lutshima and Mbushi took flight. Their posts were looted, just as that at Bangi had been.[9]

The defining features of the repression

Upon his arrival in Pukusu region, on 12th June, with the soldiers from Bandundu, Warrant Officer Faucon sent Sergeant Milongo and 28 men to reconnoitre in Kisenzele, where Weekx had been attacked with arrows. The platoon killed seven rebels.[10] On 18th June (10 days after Balot's death), the district commissioner for the Kasai in Luebo telegraphed Bandundu and Kinshasa, after having learned of a revolt in Kandale *territoire* that had led to the murder of Europeans. On the following day, the governor of the Congo-Kasai placed Kikwit and Kandale *territoires* under military rule and requisitioned troops from the commander of the province's Force publique. According to the terms of the above-mentioned ministerial decree of 1920, a military operation of this sort entailed the dispatch of units charged with quelling the rebellion by armed force. During such missions it was standard practice to shoot at virtually everything that moved.

On the next day, June 20th, the commander of the Force publique in the Congo-Kasai appointed the following troops to the operation: a) the platoons of Bandundu company, which were already on the spot; b) two platoons from Luebo company; c) the machine-gunners' company (three platoons) from Djoko Punda (Charlesville); d) a platoon of cyclists from Djoko Punda. One of the Luebo platoons was not available, being at this time in Idiofa *territoire*. On 21st June Governor Beernaert sent his deputy, Wauters, by airplane to Luebo, with orders to proceed by way of Kilembe to Kandale, from where there had been no news for some time, because communications with Pukusu had been cut by the rebels, and because the Lufuku ferry beside the Kandale–Kikwit automobile road had been destroyed. Furthermore, the rebels had blockaded Administrator Vaninthout in Kasanza.

On 23rd June Wauters telegraphed from Luebo with news of Balot's death. In the same telegram he mentioned agitation among the Pende in Idiofa and Kilembe *territoires*; he asked if the troops from Luebo might stay where they were, and their part in the operation be played by a company from Kinshasa. Consequently, the following day, in accordance with the governor-general's orders, a company of fusiliers (infantry) from Kinshasa was appointed to the military operation in the Kwango.[11]

In the meantime Vanderhallen had arrived in Pukusu, accompanied by Commandant François Vissers, who was provisionally in charge of operations. He learned there of Balot's violent death, and in turn informed the governor of the province, in a letter dated 24th June. In that same letter he stated that his deputy, Omer Dewilliamort, who was about to go on leave in Europe, would be passing through Kinshasa, and would therefore be able to explain in detail the scale and gravity of the situation. Dewilliamort had prepared a report prior to his briefing in Kinshasa. In this document he repeated the information that the administrators Weekx and Vaninthout had supplied regarding the insurrection. But he accounted for its success not only in terms of magic but also in terms of real causes, such as:

- The enforced lowering of the price for a crate of fruit: 30 kilos of fruit now fetched a franc (3.3. centimes a kilo), whereas previously the average price had been 2.50 francs (8.3 centimes a kilo).

- The significant increase in the head tax (to be paid by adult, able-bodied men) and above all in the supplementary tax (85 francs for a man having two wives), despite the crisis; the enormous difficulties involved in paying them. One had to cut 2.5 tonnes of fruit to get 85 francs.
- The difficulties often faced by the blacks in getting paid their due when they delivered fruit (especially by the Portuguese palm-oil firms).
- The abuses and thefts committed by the industrialists' representatives.
- The suppression of the perks which labour recruiters had customarily accorded to chiefs of both *chefferies* and villages.
- In Yongo *chefferie*, the failure of the HCB to buy up the bulk of the food crops which, according to the State, it was supposed to produce.

Dewilliamort also noted in his report that during the two engagements in Kisenzele village (involving Weekx and Milongo), the women had been mixed up with the rebels, and had cried out that the soldiers' shells, being nothing but "*meya*" (water), were not hitting them. He added that the rebels were convinced that their seven comrades, who had been killed by the Milongo platoon, had died because they had broken one of the sect's rules.[12]

On 25th June Vanderhallen and Vissers left Pukusu with the troops from Bandundu, and headed for Bangi. The following day, in Kitengo, they advanced boldly towards a large group of rebels who, gathered beside the *sombolo* of *satana*, were awaiting the troops. When the latter had come within 30 metres, they launched an assault. Those in the front rank tried to break through the soldiers' square, while those in the rear fired a great many arrows over the heads of the combatants. Some kept their backs turned to the troops, threw sand in the air and uttered the cry "*meya*" in order to ward off the bullets and render them harmless. Some women, carrying machetes for their husbands, were to be seen in the assailants' ranks. The soldiers very nearly yielded, but the outcome of the fight remained undecided. Vanderhallen and Vissers abandoned their plan to reach Bangi and set out for Pukusu, to wait there for reinforcements from the Kasai.[13]

On the July 1st they headed with their men towards Kakobola, situated at the crossing of the Lufuku river on the automobile road to Kandale. There they encountered the cycle platoon from Djoko Punda commanded by Lieutenant Boniface Robin. This platoon had reached Kakobola by way of Kilembe, Kandale and a detour through Kasanza. In Kandale it had come across Madame Balot, and had arranged for her to be evacuated to Belgium by way of Kilembe; in Kasanza it had relieved Vaninthout. The latter had then followed the platoon in the direction of Kakobola.

On 2nd July, the other reinforcements from the Kasai arrived at Kakobola, namely, the machine-gunners' company from Djoko Punda, a second cycle platoon from the same locality and the platoon from Luebo company, on leave at the time it had been designated for the Kwango. Consequently, Vanderhallen and Vissers had 250 men at their disposal. With the latter, and five other Europeans, they set out on 3rd July, before daybreak, in order to conduct a major operation in Kilamba. Vanderhallen gave two different accounts of the operation, and Faucon a third. Vanderhallen's first account, taken from a journal kept while on the road, is from 3rd July:

> At 11 o'clock arrived near to the village, take up our positions. Sudden attack by the rebels, engagement, capture of village, occupation. Duration of the engagement about 1 hour. The blacks were put to flight towards the Kwilu. The blacks tried to encircle us, and launched an attack on our rearguard. Villagers seen to have been killed 66, wounded 3, soldiers killed 0, lightly wounded 28, more seriously 2 . . . We camp at Kilamba and spend the night there.[14]

Vanderhallen's second account, taken from his general report on the revolt, is dated 31st December 1931:

> The engagement took place around 11 o'clock. Fierce attack, of a startlingly fanatical kind, impressing the troops and forcing them into a retreat that might have proved disastrous. I should mention the dashing conduct of Lieutenant Robin and of Administrator Vaninthout who, at risk to their own lives, showed great bravery in making a breach in our assailants' ranks, and thereby turned into a victory an engagement which, had it been lost, could well have resulted in disaster.[15]

Warrant Officer Faucon's account read as follows:

> Our forces were drawn up in a square which came to a halt about 70 metres from the rebels . . . The rebels, who had probably advanced by crawling through the tall grasses that covered the space separating us from them, hurled themselves upon our formation [the square] in a frontal attack, and the latter gave ground only to reform afterwards, 3 or 4 kilometres further back, it seems to me . . .[16]

The three versions agree that the rebels' initial assault was victorious, but they differ radically as to what happened next, with Faucon suggesting that the Force publique suffered a defeat in Kilamba. One may suppose that Faucon was a coward, and had fled that day, and that this explains why he was sent back to Europe. According to Vanderhallen, on the other hand, the heroic conduct of the two whites turned defeat into victory and allowed the troops to spend the night in Kilamba. I should add that I do not myself believe in this heroic conduct, just as the commander-in-chief of the Force publique, Léopold Dekoninck, did not believe in the part played in it by Vaninthout.[17] I presume that the change in the fortunes of battle was due to the machine-gunners' company going into action, and that the large number of dead in the rebel camp may be explained by their involvement. The fact that Vanderhallen does not speak of the company does not of itself mean anything. The machine-gunners, under the command of Lieutenant Maurice Van Ceulebroeck, took part in the military operations in the Kwango up until the month of October. I presume that whenever there was an encounter with the rebels which resulted in the massacre of the latter, as discussed below, the machine-gunners were involved. Why was the use of their weapons never mentioned in the official reports? This was simply because the machine-gunning of villagers armed only with harmless bows and arrows was incompatible with the "civilizing mission" that Belgium claimed to be undertaking in the Congo.

The press, however, did speak of the massacre perpetrated by the machine-gunners in Kilamba. Thus, on 14th July 1931 a daily newspaper, *Le Soir*, published the following information, which had reached it from Kinshasa that same day:

> The military operations undertaken in Kandale region to put an end to the troubles are making rapid progress. Rebels who had taken refuge around a barn intended to receive the gifts of Satan have been ordered by the troops to surrender. Inside this barn *"lupele-pele"* fetish-worshippers have continued to stir up the natives by beating with all their might on tom-toms and have refused to give in. The troop has opened fire with machine-guns on the insurgents. According to the information telegraphed to us by our correspondent in Luebo, the troops have had two wounded, whom it has been possible to bring to Luebo. The rebels have suffered a hundred or so deaths.[18]

The following year, the fact of the massacre was acknowledged by the Colonial Minister, who made a declaration to the Chamber:

> At a given moment, a serious engagement occurred between a small detachment of soldiers from the colonial army and several thousand natives who hurled themselves at them. These young soldiers were out of their depth, some machine-guns were wrested from them. They were a hair's breadth from disaster. By great good fortune, the officers

managed to rally their troops and issued orders for a fusillade which, at that moment, was inevitable. The use of murderous, perfected weapons, against people who were not protected by any trench and who, in a fanatical frame of mind, were rushing headlong, rather, towards danger, and who had to be kept at a distance, led to this battle producing numerous victims.[19]

Vanderhallen spent the evening of 3rd July and the following night in Kilamba. The next day he brought to Pukusu a woman prisoner, named Kazinga, who would tell him three days later that Matemo had given orders for Balot to be cut up while still alive, and for the pieces of his body to be distributed among the chiefs and notables of several different Pende villages.[20] According to oral tradition, Balot had been caught as he fled by the man called Shakindungu, who finished him off. His head had been offered to the "decorated" Chief Bandu, who turned it down, on the pretext that, as game, it reverted by rights to Katshinga, the land chief of the *chefferie*.[21] Towards the end of August, Vanderhallen had received the following directives by telegram from Wauters, who was then acting governor:

> I lay particular store by the return of Balot's skull, crucial evidence, a trophy of the Pende chiefs. They will claim not to know where it is. The other remains are of less importance, but do as best as you can . . .
>
> You must make a show of authority in order to forestall further disaffection and to assert the government's prestige over the surrounding populations, who are watching our actions with interest.[22]

This telegram clarified earlier orders urging Vanderhallen to refuse all offers to submit until Balot's remains had been handed back. The district commissioner's show of authority was successful, as the following sequence of events makes plain:

- 2nd September: An emissary from Bundu, invested chief of Yongo, arrived, announcing his readiness to submit. He was told that the submission would only be accepted on condition that Balot's head, along with other parts of his body, was handed back. The chief of Bangi came forward, but his submission would only be accepted if similar conditions were met.
- 4th September: Bundu surrendered, while a significant number of his subjects waged a struggle against the whites on the Lufuku river. His submission was refused, because Balot's body parts had not been handed back.

- 6th September: Kilamba village handed over those responsible for mutilating Balot, together with their main accomplices. Four hundred villagers are arrested, but the pieces of Balot's body had not yet been returned.
- 9th September: Balot's head was recovered at Kilamba, a foot at Kisandale [Kisenzele?] and a finger at Kasandji. Fourteen villagers were killed during a reconnaissance in Indele region.
- 16th September: Sangu, the founder of the *satana* sect, surrendered at Kasanza. Balot's left leg and foot, right hand and forearm were recovered in Kilamba region.

On 14th September 1931, the governor-general telegraphed the minister, informing him that the military operation was to become a military occupation, that the troops sent as a reinforcement from Kinshasa and elsewhere would rejoin their garrisons in the course of that month, and that, judging the Kwango revolt to be over, he would cease sending special communications forthwith.[23] But it was only the bulk of the Kinshasa company that left the theatre of operations; the other troops remained and went on patrolling the country in all directions, even though, according to the terms of the military occupation, they could no longer shoot on sight.

In Brussels, Colonial Minister Paul Crokaert—who had taken up his post on 5th June just as the military operation against the Pende was launched—was questioned in Parliament by Deputy Jacquemotte, on 15th July. The latter made much of the article which had appeared in *Le Soir* the previous day, quoted above, and which brought to light the massacre perpetrated by the machine-gunners in Kilamba. He declared:

As the price of palm nuts has fallen, the blacks are at present obliged to work for several months in order to pay their taxes. On the other hand, no one is unaware that this region, in which the revolt broke out, is essentially under the control of the HCB, whose recruiting operations have made it impossible for families to cultivate their fields as they would wish. An attempt has been made to depict this revolt as exclusively religious in nature. This is wholly false. In rebelling the blacks naturally rally around their religious organisations, since they have no others. *Le Soir*'s claim that this revolt is essentially due to the practices of such-and-such a sect has no bearing whatsoever on reality.

Le Soir and other newspapers seem to attach considerable significance to the fact, for example, that the Congolese rebels were invoking the spirit of the ancestors. This formula is employed by negroes in much the same fashion as in Europe, in order to instil soldiers with confidence, we say "God is with us". That does not mean that revolts broke out in the Congo for religious reasons. The reasons are economic in nature. The oppression weighing upon the tribes of the Congo is growing heavier by the day, and the exploitation of the blacks is every day more intense and more inhumane. The revolt is simply the logical and inevitable consequence of this oppression. It is the outcome towards which all those who, preferring anything, even death itself, to continuing their existence under present conditions, now willingly run.[24]

Jacquemotte called on Crokaert to give him the official version of the Kilamba massacre. The latter declared that he did not have it, at the same time implying that he did not know very much about the revolt of the Pende. The next day, 16th July, he sent the following telegram to the governor-general: "I am without any information on Kwango events while every day the press publishes comment on this subject. It is quite impossible for me to furnish Parliament with official information. This is an intolerable situation, and one wholly unacceptable to me. I desire to be kept informed by daily telegrams."[25] From this moment onwards, Crokaert regularly received news by telegraph, although it was not always too easily understood. The telegrams referred not only to the revolt in the Kwango but also to a simultaneous revolt in the district of the Mai Ndombe (Equateur province).

Towards mid-September, the minister received a long report from Wauters, dated 20th August 1931, on the causes of the Pende revolt. It was closer to being an ethnological account of the Pende people, in which Wauters insisted that Dewilliamort was mistaken in supposing that there were economic reasons for the revolt. To his mind, the cause lay rather in "the violent reaction of conservative elements (the *lemba*) seeking to win back their independence and to maintain their authority over the mass of the people". A further cause of the revolt was, he said, the intrusive propaganda of the missionaries, which was designed to destroy African social organisation. The report also reproached the public prosecutor's office with having undermined the authority of the territorial authorities, thereby undermining the authority of the state and fostering hopes of a victorious revolt.[26] Being wholly unconvinced by Wauters' report, Crokaert cabled to the governor-general:

Crucial to order in-depth enquiry into the immediate and long-term causes of the Kwango and Equateur revolts. I deem it necessary, given the scale of the events and the disquiet within Belgian public opinion, to entrust a magistrate with this mission. I propose to appoint Jungers. Kindly advise by telegraph and immediately sound out the party concerned.[27]

Eugène Jungers, who at this time was President of the Court of Appeal in Kinshasa, accepted, and by the beginning of October he was already in Kandale *territoire*, having travelled there by way of Kilembe.

Eugène Jungers on the spot

The arrival of Jungers caused consternation among government officials, since they were busy both consolidating repression by means of forced marches across the country with many occupying troops still on the spot, and recruiting for the HCB while compelling the ravaged populations to supply palm fruit for the CK and other oil mills. Jungers' arrival was also a source of embarrassment for Governor Beernaert, who had retained the majority of the troops used in the military operation in the Kwango for the occupation of the same, despite the assurances he had given the minister that the troops used as reinforcements were to be sent back to their garrisons in September. On 9th October he gave orders for the reinforcements, save for one company and one platoon, to be disbanded.[28] The machine-gunners from Djoko Punda left the Kwango at the end of October, while the cyclists, for their part, had already left.

On 20th October, Jungers telegraphed the governor-general from the Kasai:

My enquiry conducted in Kilamba establishes beyond all doubt that three Europeans committed serious abuses in this village on 14th May and on the following days, causing Balot's murder three weeks later. I propose the immediate lifting of all military occupation in Kikwit *territoire*, on account of the abuses that soldiers, being inadequately supervised by European officers, commit in the villages. This occupation, coming in the wake of military repression, constitutes a further unjust punishment. It serves absolutely no purpose at present and is on the contrary prejudicial to the establishment of a normal situation. It can have no other outcome than that of directly forcing the blacks to work for the European oil mills.

Beernaert, once again the acting governor-general, forwarded this telegram to the minister, observing that the dispersal of the troops had been effected, and that he was inclined to lift the military occupation, but that he deemed it necessary to keep one company in the region in order to maintain pressure on the blacks, and to make effective armed intervention possible should the territorial authorities need to undertake requisitioning.[29] In a second telegram, sent from Tshikapa on 13th November 1931, Jungers responded to a letter sent to him by the governor-general, which mentioned the Wauters report of 20th August. Jungers' cable to the governor-general began as follows:

> I think it best to forewarn you regarding the report mentioned in your letter. Its author, in the course of a fruitless journey, saw no blacks and no villages in the region when it was in rebellion or even in turmoil. His account of the revolt, which ascribes such weight to the activities of the public prosecutor's office and of the religious missions, is phantastical and inaccurate.

Then Jungers came to his main point:

> I wish to draw your attention to the key findings of my investigation into the Kwango.
> Firstly, as regards the causes of the revolt; secondly and above all, as regards the nature and outcome of the military repression; thirdly, as regards cruelties involving the use of the *chicotte* on prisoners taken during the military operation. Bandundu public prosecutor's office has been apprised of these cruelties. The main person accused is the district commissioner himself. . . . Since my term of office expires on 3rd January, I propose to return home to Belgium, bringing the report, on the steamer leaving Matadi on 10th December.[30]

I have not seen the Jungers report. It does not feature in any of the archives I have been able to consult. But crucial pieces of information drawn from it were presented by Deputy Vandervelde in the course of his interpellation[31] to the Chamber on 14th June 1932.

One of these pieces of information concerns the cruelties inflicted by Vanderhallen on prisoners, using the *chicotte*, in order to get them to hand back Balot's remains. Vandervelde spoke as follows in his interpellation:

> I will not speak of the judicial investigation now under way concerning the district commissioner . . . I will not speak of it, first of all because justice must be allowed to run its course. Next, because one should not, in order to cover up the abuses—I would as readily speak of atrocities—perpetrated by the regime, look for scapegoats and, at various levels of the hierarchy, for admissions of responsibility which should perhaps be sought at a still higher level. But in order for you to be able to gain some idea of the

state of affairs existing in this miserable region, I would like to read out to you some of the explanations and causes invoked by the district commissioner accused, in order to justify his conduct.

Here is what he says in a report which is in my possession . . . [Vandervelde quotes here from the above-mentioned orders given by Wauters to Vanderhallen regarding the giving back of Balot's remains. Then he continues with his reading out of the explanations.]

"In abiding by the directives given, I was obliged to continue the military operations until such time as the remains were handed back . . . I was obliged to maintain the wretched situation produced by the operations, to attack people who had no part in this murder, consequently, who were innocents.

"On the other hand, I was informed that many people were dying in the bush, most of them old men, women and children . . . Balot's head had to be recovered, whatever the cost. In order to get it, I was obliged to resort to actions other than those already mentioned . . . Having exhausted all the legal means at my disposal, including the military operation, what means were still open to me? Should I have persisted with military operations and had the people hiding in the forest driven out? This would not have been a good solution, since those holding Balot's remains had already been arrested . . . Have the guilty parties shot or hung? Such means were to be avoided, since a legal judgment was needed, and a solution of this sort would have elicited angry responses from my superiors and from the public prosecutor's office.

"There therefore remained only one way of forcing the guilty to confess to their crime and to say where the remains were hidden, namely, the lash."

Vandervelde himself concluded as follows: "Now, several of the blacks lashed in this fashion died. Was their death caused by illness or by the ill treatment they suffered? It is for justice to inquire into the matter. I shall say no more."[32]

During the suppression of the revolt, the *chicotte* was wielded not only in order to secure the surrender of Balot's remains, as the following confidential document serves to show:

For want of a timely intervention on the part of the Council of War, which was supposed to meet on the spot, Vanderhallen, being obliged to fulfil multiple duties on his own, was minded to look into and adopt an irregular but expeditious procedure, the first applications of which, having produced the expected outcome, have prompted him to use it more often and to extend it.

There was, however, the aggravating circumstance that the ineluctable consequences of the example set by him were such that—although he had expressly neither tolerated nor permitted it—other civil servants and agents, his subordinates, thought themselves entitled to employ the same illegal means and to extend, indiscriminately and immoderately, the use of the lash to every kind of native.[33]

As may plainly be seen, the repression of the revolt entailed more police raids and more massacres, with the unrestrained use of the *chicotte*, although there was no word of this in the official accounts, just as there was no word of machine-guns. Among those colleagues of Vanderhallen who used the *chicotte*, mention should be made of Lieutenant Robin, who had used it on some people from Bondo, according to a declaration made by the territorial agent, Xavier Mons, to Pinet.[34] This declaration was, however, not likely to cause Robin any problems; indeed, he was later awarded a decoration for bravery in the "fight against the rebels". He owed this honour to the praises lavished upon him by Madame Balot in August 1931, in the course of an interview published in the newspaper, *La Meuse*.[35] Here are a number of passages drawn from her narrative:

> The natives killed my husband in the most horrible fashion. Yet, in spite of everything, I understand their revolt . . . The agents of the private companies—it is fair to say—have mistreated the blacks, and exploited them. The facts need to be known, what's going on down there must be put a stop to, for otherwise there will be revolt everywhere. M. Crokaert has asked me to give him all the details known to me. [The latter had just presented her with the croix de chevalier de la couronne, which had been awarded posthumously to her husband.]
>
> Some company agents have assumed powers that belong to the administration alone; there are not enough territorial agents. There are also territorial agents who have not conducted themselves as they should have done. My husband has paid for the misdeeds of others.
>
> We had only been in Kandale a fortnight. My husband had never had any difficulties with the blacks before, for they are sweet-natured when treated well . . . I have spent my entire married life in Africa. I used sometimes to remain for an entire fortnight, alone, in the midst of blacks. I used to go and visit them, and look after their children; I never had any fear . . . My husband was accompanied by just one soldier . . . He was betrayed by his messenger . . .

In a letter dated 8th September 1931, the minister asked the governor-general to clarify certain matters to which reference had been made in this interview. On 24th October, Wauters came up with the following explanation:

> Madame Balot must have known . . . of the activities of territorial administrator Cryns and of his deputy Moritz, in the *territoire* of Haut-Kwango. In Kandale her husband no doubt spoke to her about the brutality of territorial agent Gaspard, who died in November 1930, in the vicinity of Lusemfu.
>
> But these were local incidents, which cannot have had any influence upon the Pende rebellion . . . The natives complained and justice was done. In the Kwango the natives know very well that there is a public prosecutor's office in Bandundu . . . As to the lack of an armed escort, it was common enough in *territoires* that were lightly garrisoned to set out without any soldiers, or perhaps with one or two of them.

This specious claim regarding the administering of justice tallied with Wauters' overall position on the purported undermining of the territorial authorities by the public prosecutor's office, but it is belied by archival documents. Where escorts are concerned, whilst it is quite true that the territorials used to travel in the Kwango during this period with very few soldiers, they were always surrounded by a throng of "messengers", policemen in the pay of the *chefferies* or the companies.

Along with information on Vanderhallen's use of the *chicotte*, Vandervelde, in his interpellation of June 1932, provides us with the gist of the Jungers report on the causes of the revolt. Vandervelde summarises and comments upon the causes as follows:

The indirect causes

1 The unjust exploitation to which the natives living in palm-grove regions were subjected by the CK and by Portuguese traders, along with the abuses and acts of violence to which such exploitation gave rise.

2 The unjust administrative regime to which these same populations, residing in the south of Kikwit and of Kandale *territoire*, were subjected by the authorities, entailing excessively onerous taxation, compulsory labour on automobile roads, and the obligation to "produce" despite the too-low prices paid.

3 The recruiting operations, involving moral and physical violence, by the HCB in Kandale *territoire*, to which one should add the violent and illegal acts committed by certain government agents, and their violent methods, together with the violent abuses committed by the messengers

attached to posts and *chefferies* and in the pay of territorial administrators and agents, above all in Kandale and particularly in Kasanza . . .

The primary cause of the revolt

Unfortunately there can be little doubt that the activities of CK agents have
long caused trouble in the regions which they are "working", and provoked
reprisals on the part of individuals driven to extremes by the ill treatment to
which they have been subjected. [Vandervelde is referring here to events
occurring prior to 1929.] Where the last two years before the revolt are
concerned, there would seem unfortunately to be little doubt that the
economic crisis caused the situation to deteriorate still further by placing
the commercial agents under an obligation to go on "producing" as much
oil or palm nuts as before, although with means reduced by at least half.

The prices paid to the natives for the palm fruit are so low that, if they
continue to supply the European oil mills with them, this is solely because
of the force used against them:

a) directly by the managers of these oil mills (blows, threats, arbitrary
arrests, etc.) and by the agents of the colony (orders, threats), "produce"
being the order of the day.

b) indirectly by means of excessive taxation . . . In order to earn enough to
pay taxes which, in the region in which the revolt broke out, amounted to
as much as 85 francs, while the sale of the palm fruit would earn them only
3 centimes a kilo, the natives of these regions would need to work not a
few days, but three or four months a year . . .

At the end of 1931, that is to say, after the revolt, the Department of
Colonies received the following information, from an official source:

Since the revolt, the prices paid the natives for their fruits have not
increased anywhere, neither in the CK areas nor in zones dominated by the
Portuguese traders. Exploitation continues, indeed, it is more intense than
ever, military repression having served to boost oil production in all the
trading posts . . .

. . . Having come to this point in an exposition which is intended to be
strictly and rigorously objective, I will not try to disguise the painful sense
of astonishment I felt at discovering that the Huileries du Congo Belge had
some responsibility for the tragic events which, in 1931, culminated in
bloodshed in the Kwango. In earlier years I had known Lever, later Lord
Leverhulme, a great businessman and philanthropist, quite well. I know
that his traditions of philanthropy outlived him, in his European enterprises
at any rate. I had been wholly convinced, when he acquired a vast territorial
concession in the Kwango, that this would be for the greater good of the

colony and of its native peoples. I was anyway influenced by the praises lavished upon Lever by all, or almost all, those who have visited Leverville . . .

Nevertheless, as things now stand, we are faced with the weighty question as to whether, behind the proud facade of Leverville, there are not, in that vast and little-visited zone known as the Lusanga area, living and working conditions for imported workers or wages for the natives employed in the cutting of fruits and in porterage, so deplorable that by themselves they serve to explain the overwhelming repugnance felt by local peoples at the thought of going to this region.

One thing, at any rate, is sure, namely, that the colonial administration possesses documents which reveal, in these *territoires*, the existence of a system of forcible recruitment, which in the long run could not fail to drive the natives to open revolt.

Already, prior even to carrying out a full investigation, the following facts should be regarded as well established:

During the first eight months of 1929, Kandale *territoire* has supplied the HCB with 356 cutters of fruit. During 1930, it has supplied 987 of them. During the five months of 1931 preceding the revolt, it has supplied around 300 of them.

Now, who would dispute the extreme seriousness of the following declaration, made by the most senior of the magistrates who have been in a position to see things close to and on the ground [Jungers]:

"It can be said that virtually all these cutters of fruit were compelled and forced to set out for Leverville, either by their own 'decorated' chiefs or directly by the civil servants and agents of the territorial service. How could it be otherwise? No 'bushman' knowing something of the tastes and habits of the natives would admit that the latter, when very few things were lacking in their own village, would go and work five or six days' journey away, abandoning for a six-month term their wives and children, in order to live in conditions which are still for all too many of them quite abominable."

It should not be forgotten, indeed, that out of 20,000 workers in the service of the HCB, scarcely 4,000 live in the magnificent camps set up on the river banks and that, according to a witness quoted by President Jungers, a great number of others, living in wretched huts, are simply kept "like animals".

One can thus readily understand how the obligation to submit to such recruitments should have played a large part in driving the natives of Kandale to open revolt. All the more so given that it was in large part an attempt at violent recruitment by an agent of the colony, acting on behalf of the HCB, which lit the powder.[36]

Balance sheet and aftermath

Vandervelde's interpellation was based on the Jungers report, although it is not known who gave him access to this secret document. In this same address, he spoke of a terrible repression which caused 500 blacks to lose their lives, among them women and children who died of hunger in the bush. Eight days later, he came up with an exact figure: 550 dead.[37] We shall see in a moment that Crokaert himself spoke of the death of 500 Africans, without counting women and children. How anyway could one hope to estimate the numbers of the latter, since they had died in the bush?

On the other hand, death did not cease to strike just because the rebels had surrendered. 1,356 persons were arrested, 400 of them in Kilamba and the surrounding area on 6th September. The greater number of these detainees were mustered first of all at the base in Kakobola, where Vanderhallen set the *chicotte* working for as long as was necessary (40 lashes per session) in order to recover a good part of Balot's remains.[38]

On 31st October the number of detainees stood at 637, 372 of them in Kandale, 195 in Kikwit, 40 in Feshi and 30 in Kahemba.[39] I presume that all these detainees had been tortured with the *chicotte*. They died in great numbers, some "decorated" chiefs among them, according to Vanderhallen, whose supplementary note refers to five such deaths. He also tells us that these chiefs were the last to surrender, itself a good reason for subjecting them to the *chicotte*. Their death was due to a dishonourable torture inflicted upon them by their masters, who formerly had awarded them subsidies for supplying forced labour to the palm groves. Other Pende chiefs died honourably with their subjects in military engagements, among them, Matemo, the chief of Indele and the chief of Mukuku.

From the information in the archives regarding figures for Africans thought to have perished in the revolt itself and in the ensuing repression, it seems reasonable to conclude that their number greatly exceeds the 550 quoted by Jungers. A more satisfactory assessment would give us twice the number.

As for the troops in the Force publique, they would seem to have suffered minor casualties, with just one soldier killed and three badly wounded in the course of their engagements. Two soldiers died in accidents.[40] The troops had all too easy a time of it, save during the initial engagements, those of Kitengo and Kilamba, which were real battles. On 26th June, in Kitengo, they did not yet have machine-guns, and had to retreat towards Pukusu.[41] On 3rd July, in Kilamba, the rebels launched wave after wave of attacks, encircled their adversaries and would perhaps have crushed them, had the latter not managed to set up their machine-guns.

To my knowledge, the archives contain no information on the manner in which the later engagements were fought. They make it plain that soldiers were harried on several occasions, but do not go into any detail. The villagers often used their bows and arrows, without however doing much damage, and they lacked powder for their muzzle-loaders. They did not set any ambushes. Yet they resisted bravely for long weeks despite a series of merciless police raids.

One further consequence of the Jungers report was the investigation conducted by chief prosecutor Pinet into the use by Europeans of the *chicotte* in quelling the revolt. However, at the beginning of October 1932, the public prosecutor took the decision, very probably under pressure from the governor-general, to classify the investigations into the acts of violence perpetrated during the suppression of the revolt as discontinued. One non-commissioned officer was subject to disciplinary action, in May 1932, following the complaint contained in the telegram from Jungers mentioned above, denouncing the abuses committed in the villages by soldiers inadequately supervised by European officers. The non-commissioned officer in question went by the name of Eloy; he was sent to gaol for six days without access.[42]

It only remains for me now to speak of District Commissioner Vanderhallen. No sooner had Jungers returned from the Kwilu to Kinshasa at the beginning of December 1931 than he called for Vanderhallen to be suspended; but the province's interim governor, Amour Maron, was against, and argued that the affair should be classified "for reasons of political expediency", reckoning that a district commissioner could not be prosecuted for charges of the kind made. Having arrived in Brussels, in January 1932, Jungers had no difficulty in convincing the minister that a suspension was indeed necessary, since new judicial investigations could not help but be impeded if the senior civil servant called into question by them was still in overall charge of the region where they were to be prosecuted. In a telegram dated 19th January Crokaert instructed the governor-general to proceed with an immediate suspension in the interests of public order. The governor was in no hurry to take such a step, but after a month of procrastination, he had to yield. Vanderhallen was suspended from his duties on 27th February 1932.[43]

It was a unique circumstance in the history of the Belgian Congo for a senior civil servant to be punished for having successfully quelled a revolt against the whites. There were many such revolts, but never before had the methods used to break them been penalised. On 25th February 1932, Crokaert had written to the governor-general:

Vanderhallen is charged with having acted with unusual cruelty while searching for the limbs of the murdered agent Balot . . . He had the *chicotte* administered to fifty or so detainees, some of whom died as a result of such cruel treatment. The party in question has confessed . . .

I would urge you, Your Honour, to be so kind as to make some observations to M. Maron regarding his proposal to classify the affair. It is unacceptable for hateful actions to be treated with impunity, simply because they were perpetrated by high-ranking officials . . .

I have read the report by His Honour Commissioner General Wauters, who was entrusted with the task of conducting a preliminary investigation. I regret to note that this report contained no detailed facts and restricted itself to generalities of a historical nature. Thus I would be obliged if you were to address a severe rebuke to M. Wauters, and tell him that in my opinion he has failed in his mission.[44]

In the meantime, Crokaert had had Jungers appointed vice-governor-general and governor of Rwanda-Burundi. Jungers would remain there for 14 years, before becoming governor-general of the Belgian Congo in 1946.[45] On 23rd May 1932, Crokaert was transferred from the Ministry of Colonies to the Ministry of Defence. He was too sincere a man to be minister for the Congo. He used to avoid the bosses of the Union Minière, and, where they were concerned, would complain of running up against a "wall of money".[46] There is no doubt at all that the offence he caused in the Congo, by way of the Jungers mission, played some part in his transfer.

As for Vanderhallen, he left for Belgium on 7th October 1932, after having hung around in Kinshasa for seven full months at the disposal of the law, while awaiting the above-mentioned ruling regarding the classification of the cases having to do with use of the *chicotte* as discontinued. On 18th September he was punished administratively, for form's sake, by the governor of the Congo-Kasai, with 21 days' suspension from his duties. Crokaert's successor modified this punishment, turning it into 3 months' absence for disciplinary reasons, suspended without pay. On 2nd April 1933, Vanderhallen re-embarked for the Congo, where he was appointed district commissioner for the Tshuapa in Boende. He would remain there for the rest of his career, until the end of 1939.[47]

The Lusanga HCB Transformed into a "Model Employer" (1931–1932)

The relocation of villages—third phase

The HCB considered the land containing the palm groves to be their property, just as they considered the inhabitants of that land to be their serfs. They therefore believed themselves to be wholly justified in moving villages nearer to their industrial enterprises, and had been attempting to do so since 1918. A memorandum dated 17th May 1926, submitted by the company to the Colonial Ministry, inaugurated a second phase. Phrased in the company's usual bragging style, the memorandum held out the dazzling possibility that the villages to be installed on the HCB's own land might become garden cities. The Department of Colonies raised a number of objections to the settling of whole groups on the aforementioned land, the risk being that they would become something like serfs depending entirely on the company.

In a letter of 19th July 1926, the HCB bosses answered that, in the majority of cases one had to do with land which, upon the liquidation of the joint ownership created by the tripartite contracts, would be "native land". "It is very probable", they added, "that these natives will be dependent from an economic point of view upon our company. But is this not also true of populations settled in the vicinity of a major enterprise in Europe, be it Port Sunlight, Krupp's, or the collieries of la Campine?" Alfred Moeller, the governor of Orientale province, when asked to give his opinion on the garden cities project, which would have impinged on Barumbu circle, wrote on 28th November 1926:

> I do not see what advantages the HCB policy would have, save that of reducing the natives to a state of genuine serfdom, not so much through their being settled on land belonging to the HCB, since the latter have

renounced any such settlement, but through the rights that the HCB would claim in preparing the land to be put at the natives' disposal, and in the construction they would undertake, etc. All the objections raised by the Department of Colonies to the HCB programme are sound, namely, that it would bring about the destruction of a social organisation based upon custom, that it would undermine communities and unsettle the individual members of such communities and their authorities, that it would uproot the native from land that he still regarded as his own, and that it would destroy the native's sense of solidarity with the social organism to which he belonged, so that he would cease to be a member, and would instead become an individuality lost in an inorganic mass.[1]

The fact that there was no positive response to the memorandum of 17th May 1926 does not mean that the second phase in the proposed relocation was stifled at birth. On the contrary, this memorandum masked the surreptitious introduction of the stand-in villages first mentioned in Ryckmans' report. The reader will recall that the term "stand-in village" referred to places in which cutters might stay for short periods if they came from a "short distance" away, which could be several dozen kilometres, and which made it impossible for them to return home each day. Precisely in order to force these people to settle in these villages, they were likened to local workers without accommodation. Since they were also not given rations in kind, these men would be tempted to have their wives follow on after them, in order to cultivate food crops and thereby to consolidate the temporary settlement. From the HCB's perspective, the stand-in village was designed to attract inhabitants from their village of origin and thereby to cause it to be gradually moved.

Finding that this process was not being realised, the HCB management in Lusanga put it on the agenda for their interviews with Ryckmans, during his investigation of January 1931. In his report Ryckmans recommended the replacement of stand-in villages by ordinary villages and, in addition, the complete relocation of entire villages to palm groves that lacked a population able to work them. Dusseljé, the managing director of the HCB in Kinshasa, happened to read a copy of the report, sent to him by the governor of the Congo-Kasai, and therefore came upon these recommendations. In a letter of 25th March 1931, he asked the governor whether he approved of the recommendations. This was the beginning of the third phase in the attempts made to move villages into Lusanga circle.

The task of answering Dusseljé's letter fell to Commissioner General Constant Wauters, who, through his appointment to the provincial government of the Congo-Kasai in April 1931, assumed the role of interlocutor for the administration with the local HCB management. In his reply, which was dated 23rd May 1931, Wauters explained the various circumstances under which stand-in villages might be turned into legally constituted customary settlements, or under which entire villages might be moved. Each circumstance required a different solution, depending upon the customary land rights vested in the land to be occupied by the immigrants. Wauters ended his letter with a promise to examine each project submitted to him.

In the meantime the Colonial Minister had forwarded Ryckmans' report, on 29th April, to the HCB management in Brussels, requesting it to spell out the measures the company planned to take in order to remedy the flaws indicated in its labour relations. He had added that, for his own part, he was asking the governor-general to examine, with the representatives of the company in the Congo, "how the native communities could be brought closer, while at the same time respecting the recommendations that had been made". This addition plainly amounted to a judgment in favour of moving the villages, and Managing Director Edkins made prompt use of it in his reply, sent on 1st June, to the above-mentioned letter by Wauters. He wrote to say that he had been very interested to learn of the various ways in which the problem might be resolved, but that he nonetheless thought the only satisfactory solution would be to move the entire population closer to major roads and to navigable rivers, as had been done in the case of the Forminière roads in the Kasai and elsewhere in the Colony. Edkins continued:

> For our part, we too have taken steps to respond to the main criticism made by the commission presided over by M. Ryckmans, to the effect that we have not taken sufficiently into account the seasonal nature of palm-tree production, when requiring 1,000 kilos (40 crates weighing 25 kilos each) of fruit per month, and therefore 12,000 kilos per year. Henceforth we shall only require 10,000 kilos per year, divided up as follows: 2,250 kilos for the months between December and March, 3,500 kilos for the months between April and July, and 4,250 kilos for the period between August and November. The cutters in Elisabetha and in Alberta supply 1,200 kilos per month, that is, 14,400 kilos per year. We are making great strides with our road-building programme, which will allow us month by month to reduce porterage on the heads of men, and likewise the number of messengers who liaise between the local populations and our factories.

This letter proves that the messenger system was still in full swing in Lusanga, while the overall yearly quota had not been cut there, since Ryckmans informed us in January 1931 that the usual quota was 200 crates in 6 months, that is, 5,000 kilos, and therefore 10,000 kilos per year. Two days later, on 3rd June, Edkins sent the governor-general a copy of his correspondence with the provincial governor, and at the same time reiterated his opinion that the only effective way of countering the fall in production resulting from the lowering of the quota would be to move the whole population nearer to the major roads and the navigable rivers. He added that the extremely low prices on the European market made it more urgent than ever for the government to use its local agents to exert as much influence as possible upon the population, in order to encourage it to boost production, so that its purchasing power was not lessened and customs revenues were not badly hit.[2]

Edkins had enclosed with his original letter some statistical tables which served to show that in 1930 the company's exports accounted for 25% of the total exports for the three provinces combined, namely, Orientale, Equateur and Congo-Kasai. He pointed out that this had been achieved with 26,811 men working for the company in its five circles, that is to say, with only one two hundred and seventieth of the population of the three provinces concerned. The workforce of 26,811 was broken down in the following way: Lusanga 13,841, Basongo 1,113, Ingende 1,800, Ebonda 4,289, and Barumbu 5,768. These figures demonstrate that Lusanga still accounted for more than half the economic weight of the five circles. Aside from the circles, the company employed, according to the same tables, 2,865 men in Congo-Kasai province, on its steamers and in its warehouses at Kinshasa and Matadi. This high figure strikes me as improbable. Where the workforce ascribed to Lusanga is concerned, I would point out that Daco estimated the number working in this circle alone as around 24–25,000, not counting a mass of women and children.

The correspondence regarding the relocation of villages was interrupted by the Pende revolt. Once the latter was brought under control, however, Secretary General Decoster, of the HCB in Kinshasa, returned to the attack. On 29th September he wrote as follows to the governor:

We are ready to facilitate all the compromises to which these relocations might give rise, for example, by paying a fee to the *chefferies* which had had to abandon their land or simply their hunting grounds . . .

We are not in a position in Kinshasa to give you precise details regarding the relocations which should be made. But, generally speaking, our preference would be for shifting, first of all, the peoples of the Gobari to the Luniungu palm groves, secondly, the peoples of the Pai Kongila region to the Kwenge and, thirdly, the populations of the south to the palm groves on the river Nko . . .

M. Barella [the director general in Lusanga] will certainly provide you with more information on the spot . . .

J. Barella had been a signatory to the tripartite contracts in Bumba-Est the previous year. I presume that it was he who, as director of Alberta, was making life difficult for the Portuguese in Bumba. In a letter dated 2nd October, Barella proposed to district commissioner Vanderhallen, "with a view to pacifying the Pende region", "the importation" of three *groupements*, or sub-groups, of this ethnic group, to be settled as follows:

1 750 cutters on the river Muebe (to the south-east of Kikwit);
2 250 cutters on the river Ntete (between Lusanga and the river Nko);
3 200 cutters on the river Nko.

Barella followed up this proposal with a discussion of the company's plans to compensate the people who would have to leave the plots of land reserved for the immigrants, to build villages for the latter and to provide food for them, all according to procedures to be agreed upon between the HCB and the government.[3] Vanderhallen left it to Wauters to respond to this letter, and he in fact went to Lusanga circle in order to study on the spot the question of relocating villages to the palm groves. He spent the whole of the second fortnight in December there, in close touch with Barella. The latter, in a letter dated 31st December 1931 and sent from Bonga-Kakese, let Wauters know that the Board had confirmed that the company would relinquish its property rights in the fields reserved for the immigrants. In the same letter, Barella described five regions which would, he thought, be suitable for sub-groups coming from far away:

1 The valley of the Muebe, which was to be for Pende immigrants.
2 The left bank of the Kwenge, which would be well-suited to a *chefferie* from the Feshi *territoire*, a settlement that the territorial administrator of Feshi would have to initiate by forcing the cutters, together with their wives, to go and work there.
3 The valley of the Nko, between Kunga and Gandangala, an area which might accommodate a Gobari *chefferie*.
4 The valley of the Ntete (a tributary of the Nko), which could, in the area to the north of Kikamba, accommodate another Gobari *chefferie*.

5 The right bank of the Kwilu, between Mosango and Lusanga, which would be well-suited to the settlement of cutters, either from Niadi *territoire* or from Idiofa *territoire*. (As is apparent, Barella restricted the migration of the Pende to the Muebe region, and allocated the Nko and Ntete regions to the Gobari.)

Barella ended his letter by asking whether a senior civil servant might be deputed to consider the issue in depth, and to coordinate the action to be taken by both territorial administrators and the HCB. Apparently Barella visited Bonga-Kakese in person in order to hand over his letter to Wauters. The latter wrote a reply the same day, from the same place, explaining that he would submit a report to the provincial governor, which would decide in favour of the above proposals. He summarised their conversations by emphasising that, where the stand-in villages were concerned, one would have to begin by launching a propaganda campaign to persuade the cutters to go with their wives and families to the plantations. On 10th January 1932, Wauters signed his report to the governor. Here are the key passages:

The native has a deep-rooted notion that once a cutter always a cutter. Even if the occupation were ten times better paid, it would continue to be despised, so long as this notion maintains its hold on the younger generation. All future recruitment of local cutters is therefore jeopardised.

The bosses of the HCB are aware of the danger that threatens them. Their methods are changing, and the Ryckmans commission has already noted that recent enlistments have been voluntary.

The initiative recently taken by the company to introduce material advantages [the provision of goods at low prices] in order to improve the living conditions of the cutters, has proved propitious. But far more radical measures would have to be adopted for the natives' deep-rooted opinions to be destroyed.

The losses that the company will incur in proceeding resolutely with the granting of liberty of contract to one and all, and in progressively relinquishing the involvement of chiefs, should be compensated for by the recruitment of labour both near at hand and further afield.

This recruitment, seen in the future as an enduring way of guaranteeing manpower, has, aside from being costly, the further drawback of obliging the company to adopt a policy which is authoritarian and which entails individual control of production, in short, a piecework policy of the kind condemned by the Ryckmans commission.

Thus, the only means of guaranteeing the future is to adopt the measures recommended by the aforesaid commission, namely, replacing stand-in villages with permanent villages and organising migration to major and as yet unexploited palm groves.

Is it possible to satisfy both the company's claims and the suggestions made by the Ryckmans commission? I believe so. The gradual transfer of the Mbala populations to the stand-in villages can be achieved without any great difficulty. Sub-groups from this ethnic group have indeed resettled without any problem all over the region.

Where the relocation of entire sub-groups is concerned, I would recommend the following migrations:

1. those dwelling on the banks of the Gobari to the available zones of the river Nko and the river Ntete;
2. all the Yaka villages, scattered throughout the region, to a zone reserved by the HCB in the valley of the river Kwenge to the south of Mbelo;
3. the Pende, both from Kandale and from Kilembe, to the basin of the river Muebe;
4. the Mbunda of Niadi to the right bank of the Kwilu.
[These migrations evidently tally with those proposed by Barella on 31st December, save for the substitution of a Yaka sub-group on the left bank of the Kwenge for the suggested relocation of the Feshi.]

Establishing a concentration of Yaka in the zone reserved for them should not pose any great difficulties. In the case of the Pende and the Mbunda, success will depend upon propaganda, by the company and the colonial administration alike. As for the immigrants' land rights, they are guaranteed by the company undertaking to grant the arable land to them along with additional land by genuine deed of transfer. The granting by the company of hunting and fishing rights should not occasion any difficulties.

It is obvious that if these proposals meet with the approval of the authorities, their implementation should be entrusted to a civil servant who is well-informed about native affairs.[4]

I would draw the reader's attention to the fact that nowhere in the company correspondence from this period is there any mention of a change in its methods, despite what Wauters says to this effect, or of voluntary enlistments, although the Ryckmans report refers to them. The company correspondence does no more than 1) assert that the company has stopped using state messengers, and 2) put the abolition of contracts for the supplying of fruit in fixed quotas into some sort of perspective, since it occurred when the gradual relocation of villages would anyway have provided enough cutters to guarantee the exploitation of the palm groves. The correspondence makes no mention at all of the enlisting of volunteers. Enlistment of this kind would seem anyway to be ruled out, since no new factor had emerged which might serve to explain why anyone would be willing to climb palms for the greater profit of the HCB.

Wauters wished to temper the element of coercion in the cutters' work routine, and Barella was prepared to reduce their strict quota—200 crates every six months—on condition that he obtained a sizeable new workforce through the gradual moving of entire villages. On this point the two men could agree. While Barella reduced the number of crates required and was prepared to be flexible about delays, Wauters' report, from which I have just quoted, advocated a major disruption of the habitat throughout a vast territory, and the surrender of Africans bound hand and foot to the employer, with whose rapacity the reader will now be sufficiently familiar.

It is quite true, nonetheless, that the HCB was generally regarded as a model employer at this time, simply through the fact of paying their cutters a wage that was double that paid by the other oil mills in the region.

Labour contracts and supply contracts

As soon as the insurgent Pende *chefferies* had submitted, Vanderhallen set the villagers to work again, as we have seen. He did this at the behest of Beernaert, who was acting on Tilkens' orders. The territorial personnel and the agents of firms operating in the region—namely, the Belgian CK and SIEFAC companies, Madail and Co. and Alves Egrejas and Co., which were associations of Portuguese colonists—applied themselves to the task with some vigour, all the more so given that they were having to combat the notion introduced by the Jungers enquiry, and now widely held by Africans, that work for the oil mills was not compulsory.

Acting Governor Maron, deeming it appropriate to curb this vigour, sent a telegram on 2nd December 1931 to Vanderhallen and to Wauters, who was then on a tour of inspection in the Kwango: "I have learned of illegal acts committed by purchasers of fruit, of female labour going unpaid and of payments that do not reflect the weight of the crates. I urge you to ensure that the law is obeyed by all. Persuading the natives to work does not mean letting them be coerced."[5] Wauters cabled a reply on 7th December, stating that he had noted among junior territorial personnel and among private persons a frame of mind very little concerned with legality, and the use of some very vicious administrative methods.[6]

Earlier still, in September 1931, Wauters had allowed some complaints regarding the irregular payment of cutters and suppliers employed by Madail and Alves Egrejas, and regarding payment in cloth. At the same period he had learned of grievances over the rationing (rice and fish plus a franc per crate supplied) of imported HCB cutters, who "had to seek foodstuffs in their own villages, either because they were holding on to the money paid them, or because they had not filled a sufficient number of crates of fruit to obtain an adequate ration".[7] In spite of this double explanation, Vanderhallen judged the grievances to be justified, and called upon the HCB to provide the aforesaid cutters with a fuller ration. On 4th January 1932, Governor Beernaert wrote to the commissioner for Kwango district:

> It is incumbent upon you to solve as quickly as possible the problems relating to supply, purchase and payment for fruit and porterage . . . You should see to it that the purchasers of fruit pay cash, since this is the usual practice in the other parts of the province. As for the unjust use of varied and variable measures by the purchaser assessing batches of fruit, I would have you clamp down upon it.[8]

Wauters, for his part, wrote a note dated 6th January on the economic situation in Kandale, Kikwit, Bulungu and Niadi *territoires*:

> It must be admitted that the CK's approach is open to serious criticism. At its post in Bangi, crates said in writing to hold 38 kilos of fruit in fact contain 42 kilos. The porters are forced to carry such loads on excessively long journeys without any payment. Such porterage should not exceed 10 kilometres there and back. (The actual distance is from 14 to 25 kilometres there and back.) It must be admitted that, aside from the HCB, no company or no private individual takes into account the seasonal variation in the yield of the palm tree, which can triple from one season to the next . . . Whereas the HCB have renounced the use of all forms of disguised coercion, involving the use of sentries or procurers, and endeavour by every means possible to enhance the prestige of the occupation of cutter, the CK still has recourse to less tolerant methods and, when production dips, immediately calls upon the colonial authorities to intervene.
>
> Within the HCB, production levels for 1931 are 7,000 tonnes of fruit below those for 1930. This small, temporary drop is due to the reforms introduced in the wake of the Ryckmans commission. The efforts required of porters within the HCB circle are reasonable, since the maximal distances involved do not exceed 10 kilometres there and back. Beyond that distance, porterage is paid.[9]

On 20th January 1932, the governor wrote to the district commissioner:

There is a good case for warning CK agents against acts of violence or threats against the natives designed to secure the return of looted and stolen goods. It is not up to them to enforce the law, and if they reckon that there is receiving of stolen goods, they can anyway lodge a complaint. (They do not have the right to lay into the relatives of thieves). Relatives cannot be held responsible either in criminal or in civil law.

That same day, the governor wrote a second time to the district commissioner: "I would be grateful if you could provide me with a more detailed account of the conditions under which HCB recruits work. Territorial Administrator Vanderhallen says too much about this for me to be entirely satisfied with the two lines he has written on this topic."[10] This fragment of an enigmatic letter is highly significant. It is a pity that the archives do not contain the answer to it. I am convinced that such an answer, if it were to be found, would establish the falsity of Wauters' claim that the company had completely renounced methods involving disguised coercion. All the good things about the HCB that Wauters said in the letter quoted above derived from interviews in December with Barella.

One way of masking coercion was to speak of a "contract for the supply of fruit" when referring to the labour contract imposed upon the cutters. The supply contract, a term derived from civil law, by contrast with the term "labour contract", did not bring with it the connotation of penal sanctions, namely, prison and the *chicotte*. The reactions to a circular of 14th December 1931 show that the supply contract was simply a disguised form of labour contract. The circular was sent by the territorial administrator of Bagata, Marcel Wilsens, to the traders and industrialists in his *territoire* (Bas-Kwilu). Here is how it began:

> The chief prosecutor in Luebo, M. Pinet, during his recent visit, has drawn my attention to the application of the decree of 16th March 1922 and to the fact that a good number of labour contracts are worthless, even those stamped by the state, because they fail to respect article 15 of the aforesaid decree: "Every stipulation delaying payment of any part whatsoever of a wage for more than a week is deemed null and void, if the person hired is not fed and accommodated by his master." The chief prosecutor has instructed me to see that this description is strictly observed in every case, even where that would seem on first consideration to be very difficult, forbidding me from pronouncing a sentence without my being wholly reassured as to the strict observation of the statutory payments.

Wilsens went on to emphasise the difference between the labour contract of the fruit cutters in the concessions, which was covered by the decree of 16th March 1922, and the contract for supplying fruit entered into with cutters working on their own land. Against the latter there was no recourse possible in criminal law, he pointed out, because their contracts belonged to the domain of civil law.

In the rest of his letter, Wilsens calculated that proficient cutters in the concessions, who managed 16 crates a month, would get 16 x 2 francs = 32 francs, which would correspond, where rations, wage and bonuses were concerned, to 12 francs (3 francs x 4 weeks), 10 francs and 10 francs respectively. These were the sums that ought to have been laid down in the contracts, and then paid. There was nothing to stop the employer, Wilsens added, from lodging a complaint, or to stop the judge from sentencing a cutter who failed to deliver 10 crates a month for dishonesty.[11]

I would point out that this circular did not directly concern the HCB, since they did not have any cutters in the *territoire* of Bas-Kwilu. It did, however, affect the CK. The military promenades conducted during this period in Bulungu, Niadi and Bagata *territoires* were primarily designed to stimulate the supply of fruit to CK posts. Consequently, the CK manager in Dima, Vandenbyvang, wrote on 19th January 1932 to Vanderhallen asking him to have the circular revoked. The average quantity of fruit supplied each month being no more than 7 crates, the imposed rate would come to 12.6 centimes a kilo, whereas the company was paying only 5 centimes, which would enable it to cover its costs, nothing more. He added: "if such a measure were to be maintained, we would have no choice but to shut down our factories and to await an upturn in the market".

Vanderhallen forwarded this letter to the governor of the province, noting at the same time that the contracts in question were piecework contracts, in other words, contracts requiring the delivery of such-and-such a number of crates of fruit in a given year or season. Thus, in the case of the HCB, and in that of other companies too, natives were committed to supplying 200 crates of fruit without any specific time limit being set for the fulfilment of the contract. Some cutters would complete their delivery within three months, others within six months, depending upon how assiduously they had worked or upon the abundance or otherwise of the fruit. In the case of the CK in Bas-Kwilu *territoire*, Vanderhallen continued,

> we have to do with cutters living at home. The delivery of 4 crates a week is regarded as a good return; to settle upon a regular wage for all workers and to impose a fixed payment irrespective of output, is tantamount to forcing the company to pay too high a rate for its fruit. On the other hand,

it is difficult for magistrates, when a complaint arises, to rule that there has been dishonesty, given the problem of there being different outputs from palm grove to palm grove. In addition, the proposed solution would force all the companies to alter contracts and methods of production that had become habitual to them.

Given the difficulties occasioned by the market, it was not the right time to introduce a complete upheaval, Vanderhallen concluded.

Beernaert settled the issue in a letter addressed to the district commissioner, dated 1st February 1932. Having confirmed that, with cutters working on their own land, one could only conclude commercial supply contracts, without any penal sanctions, he wrote that it was permissible for the industrialist to offer cutters in the concessions a labour contract in which payment of the wage was linked to work done. One simply had to stipulate:

> Native x undertakes to lend his services as cutter of fruit for a term of . . . From . . . until . . . The employer commits himself to paying weekly to the man hired a wage calculated on the basis of . . . francs per crate of . . . kilograms. Native x undertakes to supply weekly a minimum of . . . crates of fruit.

A contract of this kind, Beernaert continued, can be stamped and is sanctioned by the decree of 16th March 1922. An employer might thus invoke penal sanctions where, despite contractual obligations, work was not carried out.[12] Beernaert concluded his letter by further emphasising the advantages of this type of labour contract: "when output is not forthcoming, no wage is owed; no ration is involved, since the wage is paid at the end of the week; the native is obliged to work". In fact, the model proposed by the governor was in no way original, since, as we saw earlier, the HCB had been imposing such contracts since 1924, and the head of the general government's legal department had ruled at the time that piecework contracts could be regarded as labour contracts.

As far as the remainder of the present narrative is concerned, it should be borne in mind that whenever it is a question of supply contracts for HCB cutters, labour contracts, sanctioned by prison and the *chicotte*, are indeed involved.

11

Coercion and Consolidated Monopolies (1933–1935)

Reign of terror in Kamtsha-Lubue

On 1st June 1932 the river Loange became the eastern boundary of Kwango district, and the vast region between the Loange and the Kamtsha was thereby detached from Kasai district and annexed to Kwango district. At the same time Kilembe *territoire* had been merged with Kandale and Kikwit *territoires*. This vast, newly created *territoire* was called "*territoire* of the Pende". At the same date, Bulungu and Niadi *territoires* had been merged with Moyen-Kwilu *territoire*, where, furthermore, there would be a platoon conducting a military promenade between April and July 1933.[1]

The revolt of the Pende had had some repercussions in the zone between the Loange and the Kamtsha, and military occupations occurred there between 1931 and 1932. Towards the beginning of May 1933, the territorial administrator, Georges Frings, was attacked in Bakwa Puku *chefferie*, which lay to the north-east of Kilembe. The district commissioner of the Kwango immediately requisitioned three infantry platoons and a machine-gunners' section from the Luluagare batallion (Kananga). A platoon and a machine-gunners' section set out for Kilembe on 12th May. The two other platoons were set to leave the next day.[2] On 1st June 1933 Minister Tschoffen telegraphed the governor-general: "Am informed by several sources of a recrudescence of activity in the snake sect in Kwango district, especially in Kilembe, where such events are much to be feared. Request information as to the well-foundedness of such rumours and urge you to take all necessary measures to forestall the return of the events we have had such cause to deplore." The interim governor-general, Postiaux, answered the following day by telegraph, to the effect that:

- the villagers had sought to avoid all contact with the authorities;
- the *féticheurs'* medicines had continued to circulate;
- as a precautionary measure, the district commissioner had requisitioned troops from Luluagare and two platoons from Kwango company, stationed in Kakobola;
- the dispatch of troops on military promenade would be as follows: one platoon to the north of Kilembe, one platoon to the south of this same post, two platoons and the machine-gunners' section in Kamtsha-Lubue (Idiofa *territoire*);
- the arrival of the troops had had some impact, in that several chiefs had surrendered their war fetishes.[3]

Troop activities were not restricted to military promenades. Thus, a cycle platoon was sent by way of reinforcement in August. In Bakwa Puku the promenade became an occupation, which was lifted in November. The promenade was then reintroduced, because the villagers were still taking flight at the sight of Europeans, refusing to work and still supporting the *"lukusu"*[4] sect. In Kamtsha-Lubue, military occupation was imposed upon the tribal sub-groups living in the vicinity of Idiofa, which were taking flight and thereby systematically reneging upon "their obligations", namely, the repair of roads and the payment of taxes. This occupation continued until the end of the year, at which time the company from Kakobola installed itself in Bienge. The troops from Kananga, commanded by Captain Ivan Boelaert, had left at some point between the end of September and the end of December.[5]

The military occupation of the Kamtsha-Lubue was primarily concerned not with the *"lukusu"* sect, but with the exploitation of the palm groves. One can deduce as much from a report dated 8th May 1934, submitted by the deputy public prosecutor in Bandundu, Georges Beckers. Although I have not found the actual text in the archives, I know that this report was deeply critical of the cutting of palm fruit in the above-mentioned *territoire*. I happened by chance upon some comments on this question, which make it possible to reconstitute the principal lines of argument in the report. The comments are in the hand of the chief district commissioner, Marcel Maquet, who had been entrusted by the provincial governor with the task of responding to a report sent to him by the governor-general. Here are some extracts from these commentaries, which feature in a note of 27th July 1934, entitled "Opinions and reflections arising from the report of Deputy Public Prosecutor Beckers", a note plainly designed to trivialise the latter's observations:

After Beckers' lengthy and painstaking investigations, one chief has finally been charged with injustices committed against five natives: two blacks received four lashes of the whip each, and three others were imprisoned on the pretext that they were not working enough. Other charges were brought, but going back two years or more.

Taxes for Kamtsha-Lubue *territoire* have been hard to collect: by 30th June 1934 only 16,000 of the 28,120 taxpayers had paid their taxes for 1933, and 2,300 those for 1934. Despite this considerable delay, only a very modest use has been made of coercion: 248 natives were subjected to it in 1933, and 176 in 1934 [coercion in this context meant two months in prison].

The deputy public prosecutor notes that scrutiny of sentences has not brought to light the use of any direct or indirect coercion in the bringing of legal proceedings. When viewed in the light of this fact, and in the light of the difficulties involved in collecting taxes and in the limited number of injustices recorded, the report must be deemed tendentious. [Legal proceedings were out of the question anyway, since the Charte Coloniale stipulated the freedom to work.]

Monkene, who was held responsible for the above injustices, is the only invested chief in the Kamtsha-Lubue to have been moved by a desire to aid the colonial administration. Had it not been for the involvement of two Europeans employed by the CK, very probably no reproaches regarding recent events would have been levelled at him.

Among the large number of people failing to pay their taxes, there are many who have committed the most barbarous crimes on an almost daily basis in the villages occupied by troops. [The reference here is very probably to the continuation of the military occupation, at the end of 1933, mentioned above.] If there really was a regime of terror and general coercion of the kind alluded to in the report, we would not have to deplore so disturbing a situation.

The duty of the territorial authorities is to "make the natives understand that they must cut short their leisure, produce more, and direct their activities towards remunerative work; they have a duty to produce propaganda of a general kind in favour of work, in order to induce the blacks to enter the service of the European firms" . . . Since the natives have at present no other options but that of selling fruit or leaving the *territoire*, they are necessarily driven to accepting the supply contracts offered them by European enterprise. The clauses in such contracts are anyway entirely reasonable. Although it cannot be said that, generally speaking, the cutter of fruit works altogether of his own free will, the same could be said of any work not fitting precisely with his traditional way of life. This is particularly the case with such primitive and hostile populations, which have a greater need than others for the stimulating influence of taxation and of political authority . . . The territorial agents are on a never-ending round of tax-collecting, and yet the unbelievably small number of natives subject to coercion testifies to the unusual leniency shown by the local authorities.

Anyone who knows the Mbunda will not be surprised at their lack of trust in judicial police and magistrates. This is due to their hostility towards Europeans, and not to the reasons adduced in the report [the reign of terror mentioned above and below, I assume].

"In the village of Ingundu", the report says, "the natives who claim that they have to go and cut fruit, are exempt from the ordinary work duties imposed on the mass of inhabitants." The contrary would be out of the question, since this village has a centre for the purchase of fruit which supplies the CCB factory in Idiofa.

There is no doubt whatsoever that the cutting of fruit, like porterage and work on the roads, is repugnant to free men.

I do not share the view that, at current prices, the cutting of fruit no longer earns the native a good wage. On the contrary, the fruit-cutter's situation is to be envied as things now stand, since he can easily earn 1.50 to 2 francs in a single morning, whereas an ordinary worker receives just 1 franc for 8 hours' work.

During my recent tour of inspection, no case of any "hat" [the filling of crates well beyond the weight of 35 kilos] was observed; if this practice is still in favour, as the report states, it would have been helpful if more details had been given.

The system of payment at specified dates, using tokens, certainly has its drawbacks, but it reflects the wishes of the two parties involved. The native knows perfectly well that these counters are worth 1.50 francs or 2 francs to him, and, as he has never done any arithmetic, one cannot reasonably expect him to be able to tell the deputy public prosecutor the total amount that he receives. Admittedly, these tokens can cause confusion.

Those who are familiar with the natives in these regions, and with local circumstances, cannot help but be surprised by the tendency of this report to conclude so rashly that there has been a reign of terror, widespread coercion and systematic injustice.

When forwarding Maquet's commentaries to the governor-general, the provincial governor wrote, on 31st July 1934:

The systematic injustices do not amount to much, although the deputy public prosecutors seek them out and do their utmost to encourage the natives to lodge complaints.

There can also be no doubt that the fiscal coercion employed, according to the bench, "as an everyday method of indirect pressure", was applied in an *unduly mild fashion* in the Kamtsha-Lubue. If this mildness had continued, the principle underlying the payment of tribute, namely, recognition by the natives of governmental authority, would have been seriously undermined. Since this situation cannot be allowed to continue, I am now instructing the territorial service of the Kamtsha-Lubue to accelerate the collection of taxes and to apply coercion in conformity with the law.

Where supply contracts are concerned, the pay is sufficiently good *if the native works* . . .

M. Beckers reckons that "the presence of a platoon in the *territoire* amounts to indirect pressure". I would simply answer that it is fortunate that, aside from the company under the orders of the territorial service, we have two other companies in the Kwango at our disposal, and that these forces are not in the slightest supposed to increase production but rather to keep the peace, and that work under such conditions is the surest guarantee of law and order.[6]

On the basis of Maquet's commentaries, together with those of his immediate superior, we may conclude that Beckers' report had denounced:

- a regime of terror, general coercion and systematic injustice;
- forced labour as regards the cutting of fruit;
- the use of fiscal coercion as an everyday method of indirect pressure;
- the use of occupying troops as a further means of exerting pressure;
- the use by chiefs of the *chicotte* against cutters, at the bidding of CK agents;
- the payment of derisory prices for fruit by traders in the Kwilu, with the price reduced at the beginning of 1934 to 1 franc, or perhaps to 1.25 francs a crate;
- the existence of the "hat" system;
- difficulties with the cutters arising out of the exchange of tokens received on delivery for money.

One should also take note of the wretched daily wage of the ordinary worker (1 franc), the provincial commissioner's jibe, reminiscent of those made by Wauters, against the deputy public prosecutors, and his satisfaction at the presence in the Kwango of two additional companies of soldiers (around 300 men). It is not easy to believe that the presence of these troops had nothing at all to do with the boosting of production.

The sidelining of the Daco report—the protection of the oil mills

I noted at the end of chapter 7 that the Daco report only arrived in Brussels in February 1933. Three years had therefore passed since it had been drafted, during which time Ryckmans had conducted his enquiry in Lusanga, the Pende revolt had broken out, and the HCB had acquired a reputation for being model employers. The Daco report made a deep impression upon the Colonial Ministry, because it contrasted so much with the other documents received in Brussels, for example, the Ryckmans report, which had lavished praise on the HCB, and Maron and Wauters' notes against Raingeard, which had defended the CK.

In a long letter to the governor-general, dated 8th March 1933, Minister Tschoffen regretted the failure of the colonial government in the Congo to forward a document containing accusations the gravity of which his department could never even have suspected. He pointed out that decisions taken by mutual agreement and at an opportune moment in Brussels and in the Congo could have forestalled the revolt of the Pende. He then quoted at length from the conclusions drawn by Daco on the basis of his enquiries into the HCB and the CK. He ended his letter with the following observations:

> We should not pretend that the administration is not answerable for the serious charges made by Doctor Daco.
>
> It is of the utmost importance that the various issues raised be vigorously addressed. The native population must be protected and defended, and injustices suppressed.
>
> An inspector of the Department of Industry and Trade could be sent to the places in question in order to check that labour legislation is being properly applied.
>
> I would be most grateful if you would inform me of the changes that have already been made, and of what remains to be done in order to complete the necessary programme of reforms.

Asked on the 15th April by the governor-general to supply the information required by the minister, Governor Ermens answered by return of post on 18th April, sending a report in which he indicated his firm intention to sideline the Daco document. In the report Ermens observed that the province had already, in the course of the previous year, answered the allegations made by Raingeard and adopted by Daco, and that there was no longer any need to be concerned with the charges levelled personally by the latter at the CK. These same charges, Ermens stated, had been dealt with by the provincial authorities. The Daco report had in fact been forwarded to the district commissioner of the Kwango, who had then had to launch an enquiry. Ermens continued as follows:

> I am not in a position to claim that the measures recommended [by Daco] have been enacted, since the relevant file is stored in the provincial archives. [However, a letter from the district commissioner] proves that the *médecin provincial's* grievances were addressed and that steps were taken to curb the irregularities observed. Although this letter does not spell out the directives issued by the district head, it does nonetheless specify "that it be ensured, with a view to sustaining the measures adopted, that a stricter supervision be introduced in order to protect workers, proof of which is supplied by the 23 indictments filed against Europeans, and by the resulting investigations". It is therefore fair to say that reforms were implemented as a consequence of Doctor Daco's report.

This conclusion is unfounded, since nothing here is said about the outcome of the various indictments and investigations. Ermens also noted that Daco, basing his findings on a document drafted by Raingeard, had reckoned the proportion of the population within the CK circles suffering from sleeping sickness to be 30%. In order to refute this figure, Ermens quoted from a letter by the *médecin provincial*, Ferdinando Tavernari, Daco's successor. According to this letter, the government's medical mission in the Kwango had registered only 0.40% of new cases in 1932, and one was therefore forced to conclude that Raingeard, in speaking of 30% suffering from sleeping sickness, had viewed persons as sufferers when they were not. This conclusion, too, is more than a little lame, since Tavernari makes no mention of old cases. Where the situation in the HCB was concerned, Ermens declared:

> During a recent tour of inspection in the Kwango, I visited some 30 or so workers' camps, all of which were in good order; the workers' diet was acceptable.
>
> Recruitment is nowadays effected without difficulties, and without the intervention of the territorial authorities being requested.
>
> Increasingly flexible civil supply contracts *are tending to* replace labour contracts; an undertaking to supply 100 or 200 crates is no doubt still the general rule, but the latter *is beginning* to be bent a little, so that packages of 50 crates or even less are accepted.

Fruit markets introduced and already welcomed in more than one place *will help*, as they proliferate, to convince the natives of the freedom to work. [My emphases.]

Ermens then made some observations on the current situation within the CK. The progress achieved had been real enough, he asserted, and the idea of replacing labour contracts with supply contracts had *begun* to gain ground in the company, "no matter how attached it may be to labour contracts". The only reproach one could make was that the CK had not yet adopted the standard, demi-hectolitre (35 kilo) crate. Ermens concluded by offering the assurance that he would ensure that everyone adopted the standard crate, and that the territorial authorities would see to it that illegalities did not recur. He added that it would be difficult for him to send an inspector to the Kwango, since the inspection service in the Colony had been cut to a minimum (from a staff of 27 in 1930 to a staff of 6 in 1933).[7]

"The era of illegalities is over in the palm groves of the Kwango." Such was the red thread running through Ermens' report, and a slogan to be repeated henceforth by every echelon of the colonial administration. The time for criticising the oil mills was past, and besides, Ermens was a man of substance, whose opinions had real weight. Having retired in 1930 from the post of commandant-in-chief of the Force publique, after a dispute with Tilkens, he returned to the Congo two years later as vice governor-general, and took on the running of the Congo-Kasai during Tilkens' period of office. When the province of the Congo-Kasai was divided, on 1st October 1933, Ermens was appointed inspector of state, before becoming deputy to Ryckmans, Tilkens' successor.

I do not myself believe that the era of illegalities had ended. Indeed, when one scrutinises the Ermens report, and reads between the lines, one sees that nothing had changed in the HCB. Supply contracts were merely tending to replace labour contracts, and an undertaking to supply 100 or 200 crates was still the general rule. As for the claims that the territorial authorities were not involved in recruitment, and in the creation of free markets in fruit, there are signs that this was far from being the case. As for saying "no matter how attached the CK may be to labour contracts", this sounds a little grotesque given the prevailing situation in the company as revealed in the present book.

The oil-producing firms paid a price fixed by themselves for the fruit, and did not have to fear any competition. Indeed, during this period they were, like the HCB, all monopolists. Either they had old concessions of their own, as the CK did, or else they acquired their own monopoly by taking advantage of the decree of 20th May 1933 on the oil mills. This decree bore the revealing title of "Regulations for the protection of oil mills". It laid down the conditions to be observed if a company were to become the sole concessionary of an oil–mill zone, which could be as much as 30 kilometres across at its widest point. Since the decree was valid for the whole of the Congo, it suppressed free trade in palm-oil products in all the natural palm groves in the country, which were so much coveted by the oil mills.

I presume that during the Great Depression, throughout the Congo the government hounded the Africans to comply with the order of the day, which was, come what may, to cut fruit. The government did this for budgetary reasons, on the one hand to safeguard tax revenues levied on the Africans, on the other hand to maintain the level of export duty paid on oil. In 1935, the amount produced through the so-called *impôt indigène*, or native tax, still constituted 26% of the Colony's own revenues.

In the Kwango, the decree of 20th May 1933 precipitated a rush on the natural palm groves of the Kamtsha-Lubue on the part of the CK (which was already present in Mangai), the HCB, the Compagnie du Congo Belge and a fair number of small firms and of individual colonists,[8] all of whom would receive their share of the cake. This was the origin of the reign of terror denounced by Deputy Public Prosecutor Beckers and defended by Maquet and by his superior, Albert de Beauffort. Further military occupations ensued in Idiofa *territoire*, in places to which Africans had fled in large numbers from the Europeans. The villages of Luembe and Modjembila were occupied from June 1935 to January 1936, and the region of the Banguli from January to June 1936. The aim of such operations was to promote the cutting of fruit through the collecting of two years' tax, the building of roads and road-posts, and the planting of palm trees, a topic discussed below.

A major new HCB project

At the beginning of the 1930s, Arthur Ringoet, the administrator of the Colony's Plantations Authority (formerly known as Plantations de Barumbu), put the finishing touches to a plan to force Africans to plant perennial crops, chiefly palm trees and cocoa. The precedent here was the earlier plan for the enforced growing of cotton, which had been launched by Ringoet's former boss, Edmond Leplae, the director general of the Department of Agriculture within the Ministry of Colonies. The plan in fact derived from an idea formulated by the latter as early as 1924.

Ringoet promoted the plan under the heading of "collaboration between Africans and Europeans", a phrase that Leplae had himself used in 1924. For Africans, this collaboration entailed creating the plantations and ensuring that they were harvested; for Europeans, it amounted to providing selected seed and to taking delivery of the harvested crop. The government's assistance with the "collaboration" was crucial, in putting the Africans to work and guaranteeing an appropriate purchase price, while at the same time protecting the buyer from competition. According to Ringoet, it was a question of "inducing the populations to overcome their fatalism and their indifference as regards evolution towards a higher civilization".[9]

At the beginning of January 1934, the governor-general, who was then passing through the region, urged the interim district commissioner in Bandundu, Henry Vandevenne, to devise a method for developing the riparian zones of the Kwilu, using selected palm trees, with the cooperation of the HCB. The main features of the plan, as presented by Vandevenne in Kikwit on 27 January, were as follows:

a) Demarcation of the plots of land held by those living on the river banks, who would nowhere be invited to leave their settlements.

b) Once these plots had been demarcated, the unoccupied land would be allotted to families and sub-groups wishing to settle there. The latter would continue to be the owners of the developed plots of land.

c) Settlement of around 20,000 families along the river banks. It is an acknowledged fact that one quarter of the current workforce, if working the good riparian palm groves, would match the output achieved at present.

d) In order to recruit the number of families indicated above, one could issue an appeal in the neighbouring regions.

e) Having enquired into the wishes of the parties concerned, we will do all we can to facilitate ethnic reunification, although we will act prudently. The natives' interests would seem to tally with those of the company, given the suppression of porterage and the granting of other material benefits.

f) M. Pinet thinks the HCB should provide figures for the production levels it hopes to achieve.

g) The process of developing 5 hectare plots given by the HCB to particular families should not be extended any further, until the overall plan has been implemented.

On 5th February 1934, when forwarding his version of the plan to the provincial commissioner, Vandevenne wrote to say that he had asked the administrator of Moyen-Kwilu to proceed immediately with a study of the feasibility of reunifying the 130 *chefferies* in the *territoire*. The fragmentation of the *chefferies*, he went on, was advancing day by day, owing to the small clusters of men supplying fruit who were settling in a great many camps more or less everywhere, depending upon how conveniently located the work sites were. Such men came from far afield (Kilembe, Kandale, the country of the Mbunda). At the same time, the villages in the immediate vicinity were dispatching groups towards the oil-mill zone, and thus forming stand-in villages. Vandevenne went on to say that he had alerted Barella to the risks involved in allotting 5 hectares to each family, without any preliminary investigation, but the latter invoked the Convention with the State designed to secure its "rights".

On 21st February, Albert de Beauffort replied to the district commissioner that article 51 of the new decree (5th December 1933) on the *circonscriptions indigènes*,[10] or native areas, expressly stated that the relocation of villages could only be decreed for hygienic reasons. Ethnic reunifications in the *territoire* of the Moyen-Kwilu could therefore only be done with the consent of the natives involved. On 27th February, Albert de Beauffort sent the governor-general the broad outline of the programme agreed at the meeting of 27th January in Kikwit. That very same day, he added, he had received a visit from Dusseljé, who had told him that the HCB were considering two proposals for individual contracts which might be agreed with the Africans. The first such contract would be for people planting palm trees on their own land, while the second would be concluded with people developing land acknowledged to be unoccupied, and which would be assigned to them by the company after the demarcation of land specified in the programme. He asked if the authorities looked favourably upon a) this official demarcation of *terres indigènes*, and b) the relocation of villages proposed in the same programme. Dusseljé's visit to Albert de Beauffort was apparently intended to advance the implementation of the company's ambitious new plan.

In a letter of 2nd March 1934, Barella supplied Vandevenne with the information concerning production levels that Pinet had asked for. The aim of the plan, he wrote, was to produce 144,000 tonnes of fruit, that is to say, the capacity of the factories in Lusanga circle working on a double shift, as in Nigeria. This output was to be supplied entirely by the plantations, about 36,000 hectares, and it could be achieved by just 10,000 families (instead of 20,000, the figure quoted in the plan). One family could in fact easily work 5 hectares, which, according to Barella, only required 240 days of work for upkeep, harvesting and shelling.[11] This was sheer bluster, since the Lever group had no factory or plantation in Nigeria. Barella clearly sought to make old dreams come true, through the relocation of villages and the creation of "garden cities" on company land.

The type of contract the company proposed to have the Africans sign when settling on its land was phrased as follows:

The person named undertakes:
1. To plant, on a plot which will be made available to him by the company, some palm trees up to 5 hectares, and at least a demi-hectare per year; 100 palm trees will be planted per hectare; the latter will be supplied by the company;
2. To ensure that the plantation is kept up, so that passage along the lines of palm trees is unimpeded, and so that the latter are well sunned;
3. To sell to the company, at a price approved by the State, the fruit obtained; he will nevertheless be allowed to keep enough to satisfy his needs.

He will be able:
1. To install his hut on the plot made available to him, and live there with his family and his small livestock;
2. To plant a food crop other than manioc before planting out the palm trees;
3. To plant sweet potatoes, ground nuts and beans in the gaps between the rows of palm trees; the food deriving from such plantings will be his own, unrestricted property;
4. To sell his rights to another native of his own choosing; if he dies, his rights will revert to one of his heirs.

The company will pay:
– for the planting of palm trees: 25 francs for 100 palms;
– for maintenance as described above, per year: 10 francs for 100 palms.

Should the planter not abide by the clauses in this contract, the company reserves the right to assume responsibility for maintaining the plot and harvesting the fruit; the planter will have no rights over the fruit if it has been abandoned in this fashion. This sanction will only be applied with the approval of the territorial administrator who has signed the present contract as witness.

As regards this standard contract, the province's agricultural service observed that 5 hectares greatly exceeded what was feasible for a villager, who, while waiting for his palm grove to become productive, would have to undertake other work in order to live.

The Department for Native Affairs, for its part, pointed out that the territorial administrator was not supposed to act as witness or arbiter in contracts, and that it was first of all necessary to await the governor-general's answer to the letter in which Albert de Beauffort had asked him to agree to the demarcation of land and to the moving of villages specified in the programme agreed at Kikwit.[12] The answer, dated 19th March, was not long in coming. The governor-general wrote as follows:

> The question of demarcation of land does not arise at the moment. When the plan to reunify the *chefferies* is finalised, I will let you know where I stand.
>
> As regards the relocation of villages, you must abide by the directives contained in the ministerial dispatch of the 23rd June 1932, along with the following recommendation, likewise made by the minister: "There is nothing to stop you encouraging and facilitating moves which are judged to be to the advantage to the natives, and which the latter desire. But it is anyway out of the question to authorise moves which would only be justified by the best interests of the company."

In a letter of 16th April, de Beauffort forwarded a copy of these directives from the governor-general to Vandevenne, and, in order to avoid any challenge regarding the population's consent to its being moved, said that it would be necessary to put that consent in writing, once a start was made to the actual process of relocating villages.

In the same letter, de Beauffort pointed out that that the allocation to the HCB of the 10,000 hectares which it had just reserved for itself would enable it, once this area had been divided up into several blocks located at intervals along the banks of the Kwilu, to implement their programme for collaborating with the natives in the planting of selected palm trees. He added that the communities located within the riparian *chefferies* could without further delay establish plantations on their own land, on condition that the company undertook not to subsume them within blocks which it would subsequently reserve for itself.

Before he had even received the above letter, Vandevenne telegraphed the provincial commissioner, on 15th April, informing him that the HCB were persisting with their policy of installing families on plots situated on company land, which, according to Barella, would continue to be company property. Vandevenne asked what the administration should reply to people enquiring as to whether they should not be disquieted by this. De Beauffort responded by cable on 16th April, and said that his letter sent on the same day contained an answer to the question raised.[13] This was not the case, since the answer, a fairly muddled one at that, appeared to lump together the plantations to be created on land owned by Africans and those which would be on company land.

Truth to tell, de Beauffort did not have a clear view of the problem at this time. Indeed, when responding on 5th May 1934 to further entreaties from

Dusseljé, he stressed the need to settle the issue of land rights for Africans, before the relocation of populations to HCB plantations went any further. He made it clear that, given the complexity of the problem, Barella had been wrong to display "a degree of impatience". One had to devise a formula compatible with the Huilever plan, and resolve, once and for all, all questions to do with the ownership of land. "In the meantime," de Beauffort continued, "and in return for some guarantees regarding plantations created by the natives—for example, an undertaking by the company to compensate them if they were later dispossessed of them—I am quite ready to back, on a necessarily limited scale, the application of the Huilever plan to the region of Lusanga."[14] De Beauffort thus gave a cautious green light to the creation by villagers of plantations on HCB land.

On 23rd April 1934, Léon Génon, the new boss of Huilever in Brussels, had sent the minister two standard individual contracts for the HCB to conclude with the Africans.[15] Type A was a simple sale–purchase contract, while the text of type B is reproduced above. The company plainly preferred the latter. The minister did not respond for six months, probably because he had previously let it be known that it was up to the local authorities to deal with the practical organisation of plantations set up collaboratively. Génon did not insist upon a response, presumably because the authorities in the Congo had no problem with type B, once stripped of the clause providing for the involvement of the territorial administrator.

Finally, on 30th November, the minister wrote to Génon informing him that he had sent the two standard contracts to the governor-general, who would have to decide how feasible it was to implement them.[16] This answer was less than wholly frank. Indeed, three days before, in his letter forwarding the contracts, the minister had rejected type B, recommending that the Africans grow crops on land which was their own, and that consequently contracts entailing the moving of ethnic groups on to land which was neither native nor domainal should be ruled out. He had repeated that such matters lay within the competence of the local authorities.[17]

This time the authorities in the Congo took due note of the minister's order, and notified the managers of the company in Africa. The latter brought Max Horn back into the ring, and six months later he returned to the attack with a fresh proposal. In a report sent on 31st May 1935 to the minister, he wrote that the company would refrain from evicting villagers from occupied land and especially from their plantations. Even when the latter had been created with the company's technical and financial assistance, Horn specified, "it would only be able to assume or re-assume control if the natives should abandon them".[18] The Department waited three months before commenting on Horn's proposal. It decided that there was no good cause to go back over the question and that it would be better to let this matter of plantations be handled on the spot, according to the programme of the governor-general, who was keen to install the peasants on land which was their own, and wished to avoid any sort of servitude in relation to the companies.[19]

This whole affair represents a striking example of the attempts made by the HCB to play off two different planes of governance, namely, the Colonial Ministry in Brussels and the general government in Boma, against each other. It also represents an example of their impertinence in wishing to obtain something wholly unreasonable, such as the forcible moving of villages and the limiting of the Africans' land rights to what they had been in 1911.

The prolongation of the tripartite contracts

In chapter 3 we saw how the tripartite contracts, through which the HCB had been granted a monopoly over the purchase of palm fruit in their five circles, were due to expire in 1936. In order to preserve this monopoly for the future, the company urged the Colonial Ministry to grant an automatic prolongation of these contracts, on the grounds that that the demarcation of its plots of land had hardly advanced at all since the latter had been "concluded". Camille Camus, the director general of the Department of Industry and Trade who handled the HCB file at the Ministry, was only too pleased. He agreed with the company bosses that the cut-off date for the definitive demarcation should be deferred to 1st January 1945, the date specified in the 1911 Convention for declaring the company to be owner of the lands it had originally leased. He also agreed that this deferment implicitly entailed the prolongation of the tripartite contracts until the same date. Camus even acceded to the company's request for a further prolongation of 20 years, up until 1st January 1965, should it be the case that on 31st December 1944 the sum total of land to which the company had rights had not been demarcated.

The accord was cast in the form of a convention signed in Brussels on 27th April 1934 by Minister Tschoffen and by the representatives of Huilever. Tschoffen was willing to maintain the sickening hypocrisy of the tripartite contracts. He lacked the courage openly to establish HCB monopolies by applying the decree of 20th May 1933 on the protection of the oil mills. To be enforceable in law, the convention had to be ratified by a decree deliberated by the Colonial Council in Brussels. This council, a consultative body which did not usually challenge texts submitted to it by the minister, subjected the agreement to highly critical scrutiny, during its sessions of 14th December 1934 and 18th January 1935. Councillor Alexis Bertrand set the tone of the debate. He pointed out that the bill under review did not speak of provisional demarcation, which, according to the Convention of 1911, should have been implemented ten years before the definitive demarcation of the land. He denounced the fact that the text made no mention of the tripartite contracts, which had established the company's monopoly within its circles. He managed to convince his colleagues that they should oppose the putative prolongation of this monopoly for 20 years beyond 31st December 1944.

The minister, as president of the Colonial Council, acted upon this opposition, and declared that he would reopen negotiations with the HCB. At the beginning of the summer of 1935, he submitted the renegotiated convention to the Council, recommending an additional delay of 5 years, instead of 20 years, for the process of demarcation. The Council examined the new version of the convention in its session of 5th July 1935. Bertrand again lashed out against any additional delay, basing his argument on the model of the tripartite contract, a copy of which he had circulated to each of his colleagues. The text of this model contract, which proved beyond all doubt that a monopoly had been granted to the company, could not fail to encourage Bertrand's colleagues to join him in opposing the additional delay.

The new minister, Edmond Rubbens, sided with the Council and on the 18th July signed the convention, which had been stripped of the additional delay. He forwarded it to the HCB boss to sign, making it clear to him that he would have to be satisfied with the deferment of the cut-off date for a definitive demarcation to 1st January 1945, which was not so bad, since it extended the monopoly for a further nine years. Nevertheless, the company took several months to assent. It was only on 24th December 1935 that the decree ratifying the convention of 27th April 1934, as amended according to the resolution of the Colonial Council, could be adopted. This decree thereby became the convention of 24th December 1935.[20]

In the light of the discussion within the Colonial Council on the agreement of 27th April 1934, the governor-general furnished the Department with a list of the unoccupied land leased out to the HCB by that date. This list gave the following information as regards total surface areas:

Lusanga circle	10 blocks	199,999 hectares
Barumbu circle	5 blocks	303,281 hectares
Ebonda-Bumba circle	9 blocks	193,405 hectares
Basongo circle	2 blocks	79,655 hectares
Ingende circle	6 blocks	111,033 hectares[21]

The total, comprising 32 blocks measuring 887,573 hectares, thus far exceeded the maximum to which the HCB was entitled (750,000 hectares).

The Colonial Council's report on the decree approving the dispensation specified that these surface areas "have been *recognized as free* of any native right of occupation and therefore *provisionally demarcated*".[22] This detail furnished by Camus, and by his deputy Heyse, proves that these civil servants did not know much about the content of the tripartite contracts. A close analysis of the contract of 5th July 1924 for Ebonda circle shows very clearly that the surface area of the leased part of the *territoires* covered by the contracts was merely the outcome of an exercise in arithmetic. The governor-general was, moreover, shocked by the above-mentioned detail. He would write on 9th February 1938 to the minister: "In reality nothing whatsoever has been *recognised*; no investigation has been carried out on the ground. The *provisional demarcation* mentioned here is merely a cursory assessment, with no guarantee."[23] In the course of the discussions within the Colonial Council, Camus used a patent falsehood to account for the slow pace of definitive demarcation, namely, the nomadic character of those living in the circles. He repeated this same falsehood several times:

> There would be some difficulties involved in going ahead right now with a definitive demarcation, because the tribes living in these regions tend to be nomadic populations . . .[24]

> The populations concerned have up until now kept their migratory character. Any attempt to confine them from now on within the precise limits [of their lands] would harm this tendency in their character . . .

> Definitive demarcation should only be effected when the natives have settled down. Hence the relatively long delays requested prior to a definitive demarcation.[25]

The real reason for the slowness in arriving at a definitive demarcation was simply that neither the State nor the company was really interested in it. The State wished to avoid having to pay the wages of several surveyors for several years in order to undertake a demarcation whose outcome could not be wholly predicted. The company sought a monopoly of the kind established through the tripartite contracts, and it did not openly call for demarcations in regions where there was opposition to such contracts.

The Years Between 1935 and 1939

The planting of palm trees "in collaboration"

In the course of 1934, the plan for Africans to plant palm trees "in collaboration" with Europeans was imposed in many regions across the Colony. As well as the HCB, all the oil-producing firms in the Congo were expected to take part, and would enjoy the same privileges as the former, through terms set out in the decree of 20th May 1933. Programmes were devised for planting thousands of hectares. In order to implement these programmes, the government could deploy—as Tschoffen had pointed out to Lever Brothers in September 1933—the powerful weapon provided by the legislation on compulsory cultivation. This legislation had just been recast through the decree of 5th December 1933 on the *circonscriptions indigènes*, or native areas, which stated, in its article 45, clause h, that the villagers, under pain of prison, had to establish and maintain the cultivation, either of food crops or of produce for export, imposed upon them for educational reasons.

Prior to the actual planting of *elaeis*, the HCB could prove their usefulness to the "collaboration" by providing seed-beds and nurseries. The palm stones to be planted had to be put in seed-beds to accelerate germination. Mixed up with charcoal in boxes, they were placed in a trench and wrapped in green banana leaves in order to ensure a constant temperature of 35 degrees. Once they sprouted, they were thinned out in seed-beds, where the seedlings grew until they were tall enough to be planted out. The stones, or seeds, distributed across the Congo came mainly from the station at Yangambi run by INEAC (Institut national pour l'Etude agronomique du Congo Belge), an institute recently set up to replace Ringoet's Régie des Plantations de la Colonie. In the HCB circles, there was a first stage at which the stones or seeds were delivered by the company, being of the local *lisombe* (*elaeis tenera*), whose fruit yielded a high-grade oil.

The annual report for 1934 on the administration of the Belgian Congo, which was presented to the Chamber in Brussels, already presented some statistics for the plantations established "at the instigation of the government and with the assistance of certain oil-mill proprietors". The report specified that the agricultural propaganda designed to promote the agreed programme had been to a large degree entrusted to the territorial service, assisted by African monitors.[1] The annual report for 1935 recorded that the Africans in Basoko and Yahuma *territoires* had begun planting selected palm trees on their own land, with technical assistance from the Barumbu HCB. By the end of the year, these plantations extended over 284 hectares in Yahuma and 546 hectares in Basoko. The same report mentioned problems with the imposition, giving rise to a "slight delay" in the implementation of the programme, which affected a few hundred hectares of palm grove. According to the report, the programme allowed the companies "to intervene by means of propaganda, technical advice, and the distribution of selected plants"; they had nothing to lose because the government did not ask for any financial contribution from them.[2]

The problems with imposition derived from an incompatibility between the legal provisions regarding compulsory cultivation and the monopoly over purchase granted to the HCB within their circles, and to the other oil companies through the decree of 20th May 1933. The above-mentioned clause h of article 45 in fact ended with the following sub-clause: "The sale of harvested crops will be unconstrained and to the sole, individual benefit of the cultivators." The incompatibility came to light in August 1935, presumably through the public prosecutor's office, when it was investigating court rulings relating to the imposition of palm groves. A lengthy correspondence between Kinshasa and Brussels ensued,[3] which culminated in a deus ex machina, conceived in the Congo, namely, the ordinance of 10th June 1936. The latter allowed the holder of an oil-mill zone to renounce his buyer's monopoly over produce originating in palm groves planted by Africans. He merely had to notify the territorial administrator in writing. This represented a cunning way of saving face.

The annual report for 1936 recorded that by the end of the year 2,000 hectares had been planted in Yahuma and Basoko *territoires*, by comparison with 830 hectares in 1935. In Kinshasa province, the implementation of the programme encountered serious difficulties, and yet 953 hectares had been planted, the majority of them with plants grown from Yangambi nuts, or so the report stated. It would seem reasonable to assume that the majority of the 953 hectares had been planted in the Kwilu, given that the difficulties encountered related above all to the Bas-Congo, the other region in Kinshasa province producing palm oil.

The 1936 annual report also specified that the plantations consisted of uninterrupted blocks, to allow for easier surveillance. Within the blocks, each planter was supposed to have a surface area of some 4 to 5 hectares, which was to be planted gradually. The reader will note that this system was modelled on the one featured in the model contract B discussed in the previous chapter, the system which would be used, moreover, in the future *paysannats indigènes*.[4] The same report, so as to give more weight to its account of the planting effected since 1934, candidly admitted that all previous information concerning the plantations had been pure fantasy. It did so in the following terms:

> The time has come to survey what the natives have done in the way of establishing artificial plantations. To judge by the annual reports for the last ten years, there would be tens of thousands of palm trees planted in the native areas . . . In general, these old plantations have been set up with no overall plan or method, and without adequate technical personnel, and with stock taken almost at random from the natural plantations . . . The natives soon abandon them . . . One therefore cannot expect these artificial palm groves to generate an increase in the industrial production of oil consonant with their theoretical extent or with their supposed status as "plantation".[5]

The orders issued by the commissioner of Kinshasa province regarding the imposition of *travaux d'ordre éducatif* (TOE), or works of an educational nature—the new name for compulsory cultivation—give details regarding the implementation of the programme for the planting of palm trees "in collaboration". In order to understand these impositions, the reader needs to know that on 1st May 1935 a new administrative system came into force. Henceforward, the *territoire* of Moyen-Kwilu subsumed the former Moyen-Kwilu (Bulungu and Niadi) and Kikwit *territoire*, as it had been prior to its incorporation in 1932 within the enlarged *territoire* of the Pende. The *territoire* of the Pende continued to exist, and consisted of the former Kilembe and Kandale *territoires*. Through this same administrative reorganisation, Kikwit had become the administrative centre of the Kwango, while Bandundu *territoire* had been annexed to the Mai Ndombe district.

The 1936–37 TOE programme in the Moyen-Kwilu and Pende *territoires* anticipated that the villages situated on the banks of the river Kwilu, and up to 10 kilometres away, would plant up 25 ares with palms. This would affect 7,257 men in Moyen-Kwilu and 3,647 men in the northern part of the *territoire* of the Pende. This same programme also anticipated that villagers on the right and left banks of the river Kamtsha would plant up equivalent surface areas. The 1937–38 programme recommended the same imposition, while that for 1938–39 recommended the maintenance of existing plantations and the planting of 25 ares in Idiofa *territoire*, 30 ares in the Moyen-Kwilu and from 45 to 125 ares in the *territoire* of the Pende.[6]

The new governor-general, Ryckmans, having effectively taken up his post in February 1935, straight away proved to be a fervent advocate "of planting by the Africans, of State intervention, with the benevolent assistance, should the need arise, of the oil companies".[7] I have no information on the part played by the HCB in implementing the plan for plantations "in collaboration". Their great project in this domain was nothing but an illusion, much as Ryckmans himself had been under an illusion in subscribing to it.

This concept could never have succeeded in the Congo, where for years the State and the private companies had been hand in glove in their plans to exploit Africans, to the benefit of Europeans. The compulsory planting and maintenance of *elaeis*, which lasted for years and which was always under the shadow of prison and the *chicotte*, simply increased the Africans' aversion to working the palm groves, which had been born of the methods introduced by William Lever in 1912. The "collaborative" plantations proved to be an utter failure in the Kwilu.[8]

The year-to-year impositions, on the other hand, turned out to be a perfect means of exerting pressure upon the cutters employed by the HCB and by its lesser rivals. Indeed, these cutters, being exempted from compulsory cultivation,[9] became guilty of violating their obligation to cultivate, once they failed to deliver a specified quota of fruit to their employers. Consequently, prison and the associated torture of the *chicotte* were suspended above the cutters' heads like the sword of Damocles. In order to punish defaulting cutters, one no longer had to resort to the legislation on labour contracts. The coercion guaranteed by the latter could now be replaced by that used to punish the failure to plant palms. This ploy proved most opportune, at a time when all the talk was of civil contracts for supplying fruit.

Georges Mortehan's report

During the discussions in the Colonial Council in 1935 regarding the 27th April 1934 agreement concerning the HCB, the minister had promised to furnish in the near future full and detailed information on the working of the tripartite contracts. In fulfilment of this promise, he asked Governor-General Ryckmans to set up a study on the subject. Ryckmans entrusted the task to an inspector of state, Georges Mortehan, who compiled a voluminous report

(50 large-sized pages), completed in January 1938, in which he abided by the instructions he had been given, namely, to defend the tripartite contracts.

Mortehan concluded that tripartite contracts were not contrary to the Africans' interests. He rebutted the usual charge, to the effect that the Africans had not always freely consented to the contracts, and noted just one exception, occurring in Ebonda circle. Despite the obligatory defence of the contracts, Mortehan's report, which is entitled "Situation in the HCB circles",[10] contains some significant information and some interesting reflections, including the following:

The governor-general was convinced that before long only the *elaeis* plantations will be profitable, and that gathering in the natural palm orchards will be abandoned once and for all. This gathering is threatened by the planting of oil palms in a good number of colonies [principally Sumatra and Malaysia] and by the substitution of chemical substitutes for palm oil. Only plantations yielding a richer raw material, harvested and transported more economically, producing a higher quality oil, could rival foreign producers and chemical substitutes. . . .

The HCB bosses reckon that the exploitation of natural palm groves will continue to be remunerative for a long time to come, and that the planting of oil palms is not economically advantageous in a colony such as the Belgian Congo, where transport is difficult and costly.

This argument is of little relevance. There is every cause to anticipate that the constant increase in tonnages transported will give rise to a reduction in tariffs. If, nonetheless, transport costs were to remain higher than in other colonies, this difference would still be offset for a long time to come by the extremely low wages demanded by the Congolese work-force. . . .

When, after a few years, the programme for the development of cash-crop cultivation [the plantations imposed on the Africans] has yielded its first fruits, the distaste felt by the natives for the heavy labour involved in gathering fruit in the natural palm groves will become overwhelming, or at any rate will induce the cutters to demand a higher and higher remuner-ation.[11] . . .

I do not share the view that the natives incontestably derive benefit from medical and educational facilities made available to them in regions worked by the HCB. By paying taxes, the natives acquired the right to medical care and instruction to be provided by the government. Now, the company makes sure to include in the cost price of its production the expenses incurred in social welfare, cutting to the same extent the remuneration it extends to the fruit cutters. The latter, by failing to earn on the one hand, and by paying tax on the other, thus pay twice over for the benefits conferred upon them.[12] . . .

Where the HCB medical service is concerned, the sort of obligation anticipated in the 1911 Convention becomes confused with the specific recommendations contained in legislation on workers' health and safety, and therefore cannot really be said to constitute a special burden on the company. The medical service in the Kwango and Kasai circles anyway does not fully match up to these same recommendations. In the hospitals in Leverville and Brabanta, the number of beds is too low, in terms of the law, to ensure medical care for the workforce employed. It must be exceptional for natives from the region, where they are not directly employed by the company, to be hospitalised.[13] . . .

In Lusanga circle, thousands of Pende are hired through contracts to supply fruit.[14] . . .

At the present time, policy in the Colony aims to favour the European palm-oil industry, to the detriment of native industry, in particular by the establishment of differential export duties. In favour of native industry, it has been argued on the one hand that in periods of acute crisis it remains remunerative, while the price offered to the cutters for fruit falls to a derisory rate; on the other hand, that in periods of prosperity, and for the same amounts of work, the sale of palm oil and palm nuts remains more profitable for the cutter than the sale of fruit.[15] . . .

During the period of economic crisis, manufacturers have been able to buy palm fruit at a derisory price (3 centimes or less a kilo), thanks to the pressure exerted by the colonial administration on the natives. Although the latter have thus had to bear too heavy a share of the sacrifices imposed by the disastrous state of the market, the HCB claim to have suffered, owing to their having kept their factories running, a loss of around 40 millions.

However, the company's accounting methods would seem to be liable to criticism, and inspection of its balance-sheets, which the investigator [Mortehan] was unable to consult, would furnish precious information.[16] . . .

Rash redemptions would seem to make up a large part of the 40 or so millions of loss recorded, and would therefore account in part for the mediocre purchase price of fruit which the HCB professed itself unable to increase. If that is indeed how things were, the complaint about the low fixed price should be addressed to the administration rather than to the company. The local authorities were in fact under a strict obligation to control this price, by closely scrutinising the various elements by which it was determined.

In accepting without demur the owner's assertion that the setting of a higher price would lead to the closing of factories, the local authorities have failed to exercise the right of control accorded them by the tripartite contract, and have indisputably failed in their mission to act as guardians to the natives. Moreover, in demanding that the latter continue to work for an inadequate wage, they were clearly breaking the law.[17] . . .

According to information obtained on the spot, the investigator reckons that Huilever's book-keeping methods are not rational. The division of the general costs between the company's two activities, namely, the exploitation of the natural palm groves and the creation of vast plantations of selected palms, is done in an irregular fashion. An exaggerated part of the general costs is ascribed to the industrial exploitation, with the consequence that the cost of a planted hectare is underestimated, while the cost price of a ton of factory produce is artificially inflated. A part of the industrial profits are reinvested, but this fact is not registered in the accounts. This procedure does harm to the native, the purchase price of fruit imposed on him being in inverse proportion to the cost price of the finished products.[18]

I should note here that the final point presented by Mortehan above is highly misleading, in the sense that it refers to two activities as being of an almost equivalent importance, namely, the exploitation of natural palm groves and the creation of plantations. Yet the two were in no way equivalent. Mortehan very probably imagined that the company, in order to please the governor-general, was going to embark upon a vast programme of very costly plantations, to the detriment of the highly profitable gathering of fruit.

I would also add that in September 1936 the company was only at the stage "of envisaging the replacement of the natural palm groves with plantations, without the immobilisation of too much capital".[19] This is precisely the kind of replacement it had been aiming at when, three years before, it had launched its programme of "collaborative" plantations. In 1938 the company still deemed this programme a success. So too did Mortehan, and in his report he often referred to villagers' plantations that were to be worked in concert with the company,[20] without of course indicating that forced labour was involved.

We would do well to remember that the information supplied by Mortehan shows us that the wage levels for Africans in the Congo were the lowest in Africa. These wages had not been adjusted to take account of the rise in the cost of living caused by the successive devaluations of the Belgian franc. After 1926 the latter was worth one seventh of the gold standard franc, and from 1935 one tenth. Mortehan's account also shows us that revulsion at the hard labour of gathering fruit for the HCB was still as intense as ever, on account of the wretched level of remuneration. We would likewise do well to remember that the HCB were at liberty to fix the price at which they were buying the palm fruit.

A further modification in the 1911 Convention

One might have supposed that the agreement of 24th December 1935, concluded between the Colony and Huilever, had settled once and for all the granting to the company on 1st January 1945 of the lands it might then choose to appropriate for itself. This was by no means the case. Mortehan's report referred at length to a new convention, still to be concluded. Mortehan's contacts with the company's bosses when drafting the report were chiefly concerned with the preparation of this same convention.

The company wanted a new convention because in 1935 it had not obtained the prolongation of the tripartite contracts beyond 1944. It also wished to see the latter contracts given official status in the new agreement, so that they might have more weight. In order to overcome the Colonial Council's resistance to the tripartite contracts, the authorities in the Colony suggested a tempting lure to Huilever, namely, a major reduction (amounting to more than half) in the surface area of the land reverting to it by virtue of the 1911 Convention. The same authorities, wishing to encourage the company to set up plantations on its own account, and without any "collaboration" with the Africans, offered it the choice of land outside the circles. It could thereby create such plantations on the terrain in the Congo that was best-suited to them from the point of view of soil and climate, and with a workforce brought in from further afield.[21]

The company was easily persuaded to sign the new convention, which was dated 2nd July 1938, and which for long years obtained for it both a free hand regarding choice of plots and a monopoly over the purchase of palm fruit in its circles, and which at the same time paved the way for planting elsewhere in the Congo.[22] More concretely, the new convention stipulated:

- the repeal of the 1935 agreement;
- the reduction of the surface area of the land that the company was entitled to choose from 750,000 to 350,000 hectares, of which 100,000 hectares lay outside the circles, to be known henceforth as "zones";
- the prolongation of the tripartite contracts until 30th June 1956;
- the reduction of the minimum surface area of the blocks to be chosen within the zones from 250 hectares to 100 hectares (this would enable the company to monopolise to a still greater degree the choicest parcels of land);

• the classification of the company as holders of the oil-mill zones (decree of 20th May 1933), as regards the rebate of a half of the entry duties on imported materials to be used in the treatment of oil-palm products.

The convention also stipulated that "native" land was land occupied and worked when the future investigations into vacancy were held, thereby implicitly repudiating the company's former claim that land occupied and worked after 1911 would revert to it. The convention also fixed at 187,000 francs the annual and perpetual rental due for land leased up until 31st December 1944, which thereafter became freehold property. The sum represents 750,000 hectares multiplied by 25 centimes. The convention accorded official status to the tripartite contacts, and used the following hypocritical language in doing so:

At the instigation of authorities designated by the governor-general and on condition that his approval is given, the company will be authorised to conclude with the native communities, and where the need arises with the Colony, contracts through which it will acquire for a period not exceeding 30th June 1956 exclusive rights to *elaeis* palm fruit growing on land within the zones.

In October 1938, Minister Albert De Vleeschauwer submitted the new convention to the Colonial Council, where it was backed by Governor-General Ryckmans, who had played an active part in its drafting. The majority of council members willingly ceased their resistance to the tripartite contracts, in exchange for a reduction in the surface area offered. The convention was approved in January 1939, by nine votes to six. The six voting against (Bertrand, Louwers, Waleffe, Decleene, Deraedt and Itten) succeeded in having the reasons for their opposition included in the Council report, which was published together with the decree of 15th March 1939 approving the convention.

Here are the reasons that were given, in abridged form, together with some of the observations made by the opponents of the convention during the debates:

1. The new convention consecrates in fact and in right the institution of the tripartite contract which for 18 years, to the advantage of a powerful enterprise, has created a monopoly over the purchase of oil-palm products, which in practice has applied pressure to the activities of Africans and has therefore been at odds with the principle of free labour, and which, to the profit of a particular company, has delayed the development of economic

activity among the Africans. The latter are forced to accept these contracts; past experience has shown that their liberty in this domain is merely theoretical.

2. These contracts, since they do not only affect the products of the soil but also the soil itself, reduce the Africans' land rights, just as an article in the new convention does. At the time of the investigations into vacancy, definition of these rights over plots of land leased to the company was not done in accordance with the legislation governing such investigations [decree of 31st May 1934]. When the Colonial Council has taken up the issue of approving a concession, the investigations into vacancy as prescribed by law are forwarded to it. When a person of no particular consequence is involved, the procedure laid down is followed, but when Huilever is involved, special investigations are undertaken, the results of which are not shown to the Colonial Council. Regular investigations have never been conducted. [According to article 4 of the tripartite contracts, the investigations into vacancy to be conducted by the district commissioner as regards the blocks chosen by the HCB would be limited to checking to see if these blocks included huts or cultivated crops, without taking into account other land rights, such as rights to fallow land.][23]

3. The governor-general mistakenly claims that the company made a concession by renouncing its claim to define as vacant or unoccupied those lands that had been occupied by Africans after its arrival in the region. Discussions within the Colonial Council in 1911 show that natives' land rights should be respected in the form they take at the time of the investigation into vacancy.

4. One should not have sought to use the benefits offered by the tripartite contracts to compensate for the reduction of the domain to 350,000 hectares. The development of such a domain—with the inextricable difficulties involved in demarcating native land in the hundreds of blocks still to be chosen—already exceeds the capacity of the company and the workforce available in the regions under consideration. The company is itself aware of the fact since, according to Mortehan's report, it had asked for a clause relating to the assistance to be given by the colonial administration in recruiting the workforce to be inserted into the new convention. The company would readily adjust to the suppression of the tripartite contracts, just as it has done in other colonies in which it has not enjoyed, indeed far from it, the same privileges as have been granted to it in the Belgian Congo.

5. The rate of tax payable by the company each year for land leased and subsequently held as freehold property is fixed forever at 25 centimes per hectare. This was the figure fixed in 1911 in gold standard francs. The current rate for the lease of agricultural land may be as high as 10 francs, that for forests is 1 franc. The taxes paid each year by Huilever are so minimal that they have no real impact upon the Colony's resources.

I would here point out that, in the above exposition, I have taken the words "convention" and "new convention" from the writings and debates of the period, although these terms are somewhat misleading. All that was in fact involved was a modification of 5 articles from the 1911 Convention, which contained 24 such articles. The account of the motives underlying the opposition to the "new convention" shows that the company was producing each year, from 1933, over 20,000 tons of oil and over 11,000 tons of palm nuts. The annual reports for the Belgian Congo presented to the Chamber of Representatives teach us that during the five years from 1933 to 1937 the Congo exported 283,375 tons of oil and 364,335 tons of palm nuts. If Huilever's production during this period amounted to 105,000 tons of oil and 57,500 tons of palm nuts, it represented 37% of the Congo's oil and 16% of its palm nuts. The discrepancy in the percentage may be accounted for by the villagers' sale of palm nuts to European traders. Considered in terms of volume exported, palm nuts came second on the list of products exported from the Congo, while palm oil was third. Considered in terms of the value of goods exported, palm oil was equivalent in value to palm nuts, given its higher price on the world market.

The account also shows that the company had already planted 11,000 hectares of *elaeis*, but the documents submitted to the Colonial Council provide information about only 6,000 hectares.[24] For the most part these were phantom plantations, akin to the thousands of hectares of palms supposedly planted by Africans on their own land, identified in the Colony's annual reports up until 1935 and declared to be non-existent in the 1936 report. Since its first beginnings in the Congo, the company had mentioned the creation of plantations, very probably in order to show that it was honouring the obligation imposed upon it by the 1911 Convention to extend the existing palm groves and to create new ones. According to a note written by Max Horn on 15th June 1938, "a part of the plantations created in former times is today acknowledged to be worthless".[25]

After the introduction of the new convention, as before, the company's main concern was, and continued to be, the exploitation of natural palm groves. Furthermore, the creation of plantations referred to in the Mortehan report went no further in Lusanga, because of the very poor yield in palm oil there.[26] In the new convention, the company undertook to devote at least 40 million francs in the 10 years after 1st January 1938 to setting up and equipping plantations. Yet the company seemed in no hurry to look for land outside the circles. Fifteen months after the signing of the convention, little of note had been done.

13

The Apogee of Forced Labour
During the War (1940–1945)

From 1938 on, archival evidence concerning the HCB's system of exploitation is scarce. Everything indicates, however, that the continuous rotation of cutters, as developed by Commissioner-General Wauters in 1932, ensured that the Lusanga palm groves continued to be worked without any interruptions. During the Second World War, the Congo was cut off from Belgium, which was occupied by the Germans. The Belgian government, in exile in London, and Governor-General Ryckmans, in Kinshasa, gradually imposed harsher and harsher demands upon the Africans, in order that they contribute to the defeat of the Germans. On 21st January 1941, when Great Britain was alone in sustaining the struggle against Germany, the Congo concluded an agreement with London concerning the supply of raw materials.[1] Palm oil was at the top of the list, and, as may readily be understood, that suited only too well the biggest oil producer in the country, Huilever, which was of course run by Englishmen.

As in the other HCB zones, the coercion used on the cutters in Lusanga was further reinforced. Towards the end of 1941, the latter were supplying 120 to 150 crates of fruit, each weighing 35 kilos, in a period of from 4 to 5 months. Having completed this task, they would return to their villages, and would immediately be replaced by others.[2] As had been the case before, the system was kept going by the combined efforts of territorials, HCB labour recruiters, and chiefs forcing the replacement cutters to set out for the palm groves. The deputy public prosecutor in Kikwit, Pierre Lambotte, was troubled by the forced recruitment effected among the Pende. He sent a letter on 22nd December to the judicial police (in effect, the territorial agents) in every *territoire* in the district, drawing their attention to two points:

- according to the decree on labour contracts (16th March 1922), every labour recruiter was supposed to be furnished with a workforce permit;

- according to article 4 of the ordinance on workers' health and safety (8th December 1940), every recruit about to be employed outside his own *territoire* was supposed to appear prior to departure before a territorial authority, whose duty it was to check whether his terms of hire were above board.

Lambotte concluded his letter as follows: "I desire all abuses regarding the workforce to cease forthwith, and urge you to see to it."

The first point in this letter is of the utmost significance. It implies that at the end of 1941 recruitment was still being done on the basis of the decree on labour contracts, which suggests that all assurances given previously regarding "civil contracts for supplying fruit" were empty. The second point implied that the system involving the regular rotation of work teams had collapsed. To implement what Lambotte proposed would have been seriously to hamper the production of a raw material required by Great Britain. The administrator of Gungu territoire, Jean-Baptiste Bomans, politely declined the deputy public prosecutor's request, knowing full well that he had the support of the district and provincial governors, to whom he sent a copy of his response to the magistrate, dated 9th February 1942. There follow a few extracts from this document:

The HCB and other companies recruit or hire between 7,500 and 10,000 natives from the *territoire* each year . . .

The territorial personnel available to us at present would have to spend a large part of their time examining these contracts, and all the more so given that the same ordinance requires them to draw up physical fitness certificates . . . Speaking in a purely personal capacity, I would venture to say that their time, which is already so reduced, could be more usefully employed than in inspecting contracts of hire or in issuing provisional physical fitness certificates.

I would further add that, in accord with the higher authorities, we have always done our utmost not to hamper the operations of hiring and recruitment by responding to demands which conflict with the habits and customs of those recruited or hired . . .

Why, when we have already accepted a solution easing the employers' difficulties with their workforce's passbooks, should we destroy its positive consequences by implementing legislation which still obliges those hired and recruited to appear before the territorial authorities at their point of departure? . . .

Nor do I believe that it would be current government policy to hamper the production of an important raw material . . .

If the provincial governor waited five months before taking a position on the affair, such that Lambotte could not prevent the cutters from setting out for the HCB without formalities, this was because in the meantime there had been important developments in the international arena. In December 1941 the United States of America had entered the war alongside Great Britain. Three months later, the Japanese had conquered South-East Asia, thereby excluding the Allies from the principal sources for strategic raw materials such as palm oil and rubber. An American mission lost no time in visiting the Congo, in order to share in the country's palm-oil production.[3]

Governor-General Ryckmans and Colonial Minister De Vleeschauwer decided to increase to the maximum palm-oil production in the Congo. Ryckmans instructed the public prosecutors' offices to refrain from prosecuting violations of the legislation on labour contracts and on workers' health and safety.[4] At the same time he promulgated the ordinance of 10th March 1942, which doubled, from 60 to 120 days, the length of time villagers had to spend in the compulsory cultivation, harvesting and gathering of agricultural produce (in other words, palm fruit and wild rubber). The ordinance increased the prison sentence for those who failed to do this harvesting and gathering, or who were negligent in executing it, from seven days to one month.

In the palm-grove region of the Kwango all able-bodied men, whether oil-mill cutters or not, had to supply palm fruit. In other parts of the district, they had to supply rubber, herbs or lianas. I have found just one document mentioning the pressure used in the palm-grove region to enhance war production, but it speaks about it at length. It is a long letter, dated 9th March 1944, written by the district commissioner, Emile Cordemans, to the governor of the province. This letter, together with its enclosure, dated 30th May 1942, likewise written by Cordemans to the same correspondent, also furnishes precious clues as to the pittance paid during the war for palm fruit.

Whereas in June 1940 the Congolese franc had once again been devalued, losing a third of its value,[5] so that as a consequence the price for palm fruit ought to have increased in proportion, this price in fact remained unchanged at 3.5 francs for the 35 kilo crate, or 10 centimes a kilo. Still worse was to come, however, for by mid-June 1942 the Congolese franc had fallen still further. Indeed, in his letter of 30th May 1942 Cordemans proposed to the governor that the minimum price for a crate be raised to 3.5 francs throughout the whole district, beginning on 1st July. Following this letter, the price was duly increased to 3.5 francs, but no higher. Production increased in 1942, but fell back in 1943—despite particularly intense pressure exerted upon the Africans by the territorial administration—only to plummet in January and February 1944. On 1st March 1944, the director general of the Lusanga zone wrote to Cordemans: "I hope that you will be able to take such measures as are needed to restore our production back to its normal level."

The district commissioner recounted this fact in his letter of 9th March 1944 to the governor, in which he also noted two statistics worthy of comment here:

- the average output of a good cutter was 180 crates per year, or 15 crates per month;
- a day labourer earned a minimum of 3 francs per day, or 75 francs per month, whereas a cutter only earned 15 x 3.5 francs = 52.5 francs.

An output of 15 crates per month represents a reduction by a half in the output for 1941 mentioned above. This illustrates only too vividly the general running out of steam suffered by Congolese producers, owing to the excessive efforts they were called upon to make during the war, which have at last been recognised by historians.[6] A compulsory minimum wage had just been introduced in the Congo through the ordinance of 6th December 1943, and for the Kwango it had been fixed at 3 francs a day. The cutter, in theory the holder of a civil contract to supply palm fruit, and being unable to lay claim to the minimum wage, earned two thirds of what a day labourer earned. This was a strange anomaly, given that economic activity in the Kwango depended on the cutters, who did difficult and dangerous work. This provides a graphic illustration of the condition of serfdom in which the cutters were kept.

The ordinance of 6th December 1943 did not in fact impose a minimum wage upon the Colony, it merely authorised provincial governors to introduce it in regions of their own choosing. It has to be understood that at the beginning of the war there were certain regions in the Congo, for example the Kivu, in which no wage at all was paid. Moreover, the governor of that province waited until 9th August 1944 before ordering a wage to be paid, without however specifying the amount, "in order to avoid publishing a figure which might seem derisory". But the wage had to reach 0.5 francs before the employer had the right to ask the administration to help supply him with workers.[7]

Mortehan informs us that wages in the Congo were the lowest in Africa, and now we know that during his time 0 francs was paid as wages in certain regions, and a half-franc seven years later. By way of comparison, I would point out that the minimum wage in Belgium was fixed at 32 francs a day in 1936,[8] Belgian and Congolese francs being equivalent. I would also point out that consumer goods, save for food crops, were much more expensive in the Congo than in Belgium and that their price had increased by one third after the devaluation of June 1940.

On 30th June 1945, the war being already over, the ordinance of 10th March 1942 had not yet been repealed. On this date, Cordemans wrote to the administrator of the *territoire* of the Pende to say that, in anticipation of this repeal, the HCB agent, Barigand, would soon arrive in Gungu in order to resume responsibility for the recruitment of cutters. He asked the administrator to, on the one hand, help this agent to inform himself about the current situation and to reclaim whatever funds and equipment were still in the hands of the chiefs in the various native areas, and, on the other, to lend him in general "all assistance that is compatible with the laws and regulations of the Colony".

Cordemans added that all coercion should end once the situation had returned to normal, and he noted that he had been responsible for advising the director general of the HCB in Lusanga to resume recruiting operations on the following 1st September. As may clearly be seen, after the Second World War overall control of recruitment for Lusanga continued to be the responsibility of the colonial administration. The concern was not always to organise the cutting of palm fruit on a commercial basis. Forcible recruitment remained the order of the day. The remark about lending the employers "all assistance that is compatible with the laws and regulations of the Colony", though followed by a warning, for form's sake, about the use of coercion, were the routine phrases long used in the Congo to mask the process by which the African workforce, whether it liked it or not, was put at the disposal of European employers.[9]

Afterword

The history of Lever Brothers in the Congo is not without importance, since the company produced a substantial part of the palm-oil products exported from the country during the whole of the colonial period. If one consults the Congolese annual export tables, one finds that these products were only outstripped in volume and value by the copper produced by the Union Minière. Palm oil far outstripped all the other commodities. True, the presence of Lever Brothers was little felt in the Tshuapa (Ingende) and in the Kasai (Basongo), but, through the HCB, the company had a major impact along the river Congo in Bumba region (Ebonda) and Basoko region (Lukutu), and was a crucial influence in the Kwilu (Lusanga zone).

Lusanga zone, formerly known as Lusanga circle, was the jewel in Lever's crown. The relevant information may be found in *Le Kwilu*,[1] an excellent book by Henri Nicolaï. This book teaches us that, where the exploitation of palm groves is concerned, nothing changed during the rest of the colonial period (1946–60): coercion and monopolies remained and village chiefs received subsidies.[2] Cutters failing to fulfil their obligation to undertake the compulsory cultivation of crops were liable to prison sentences. And in prison, the *chicotte* was still in use in 1959.

Alongside the stick, the colonial administration also used the carrot to foster enthusiasm among the cutters. It thus handed out "powder vouchers" to those singled out by the palm-oil firms as especially productive.[3] Such permits to buy ammunition for hunting with piston rifles represented a great lure for Africans. The cutters contracted to supply 150 crates of fruit, each of which weighed 35 kilos.[4] They thereby earned 350 francs a month,[5] delivering the fruit at the price decided upon by Lever, which was accepted by the government, as it had been in the past, without there being any serious scrutiny of the elements upon which its calculation was based.

In 1955, the cutters employed by Lever Brothers were 15,341 in number, of whom 8,541 were migrants who had come from distant villages. The

Pende still constituted nearly one third of the cutters. Indeed, a European labour recruiter was in permanent residence in Gungu *territoire*. He used huge lorries, crudely adapted for the transportation of human beings, to dispatch the men to Lusanga zone. These lorries plied the Lusanga–Gungu road (190 kilometres),[6] and would repatriate the men when they had completed their stint, which was reckoned to last six months.[7]

In 1957 Kikwit *territoire* contained 295 so-called Lever camps, which had issued from the stand-in villages and villages of imported workers featuring in my narrative. They were hamlets scattered among the palm groves, consisting of 5,000 or so huts made of adobe clay, the majority of which were shelters rather than genuine huts.[8] Brick-built camps were only to be found in the environs of the factories. At this date Lever owned 80,000 hectares of freehold property in the Kwilu,[9] and had at his disposal a hundred or so lorries, which ploughed up and down 2,900 kilometres of road.[10]

In 1954 the Kwango was split into two districts, namely, Kwango and Kwilu. The latter (with its administrative centre in Kikwit) contained the four palm-grove *territoires*: Kikwit, Gungu, Idiofa and Masi-Manimba. In 1956 Kwilu district produced 63,700 tonnes of palm oil or 31.2% of the total tonnage produced in the Congo (204,039 tonnes), and 39,262 tonnes of palm nuts, or 26.8% of the Congo's total production (146,107 tonnes).[11] I do not know what percentage of Kwilu district's production may be attributed to Lever Brothers, but I would estimate it to be a good half. Furthermore, Nicolaï informs us that the lion's share of Lusanga's production at this period still derived from the natural palm groves.[12] In the Kwilu, Lever Brothers continued to concentrate on the amassing of natural wealth, which was not much to the benefit of the country's inhabitants. In the period 1946–60 the general level of incomes in the region remained very low,[13] and the luxurious character of certain Lever Brother establishments made a bleak contrast with the poor standard of living enjoyed by the Congolese.[14]

As far as the exploitation of Africans and forced labour is concerned, it is often said that things were much the same in all colonies. Such a claim is certainly not true for the working of natural palm groves, as is proved by the case of Nigeria, the world's foremost producer of palm oil and of palm nuts originating in such palm groves. In 1911, when Lever first set foot in the Congo, Nigeria was already exporting 353,571 tonnes of such products. In 1940 it was exporting twice as much as the Congo.[15] In 1946 it was supplying the international market with 476,378 tonnes,[16] a far greater quantity than the Congo was managing in 1956 (350,146 tonnes). In

Nigeria, the exploitation of palm groves developed in a harmonious fashion across a whole century, up until 1950.

The British colonial government in Nigeria, founded in 1891, rightly regarded the palm groves as the property of the African communities. Not a single grove was given in concession. The government did not even grant plots of land to Europeans to be turned into plantations using selected seeds. There was no question of coercion in Nigeria, either direct or indirect, by means of a head tax, which was in fact very moderate and was only introduced in 1927.[17] Since the peasants themselves cut the clusters, on their own behalf, there was no scope for corruption involving subsidies paid to chiefs for delivering up workers to companies. The Nigerians did not supply fruit to the commercial sector but palm oil produced by themselves. They thereby pocketed the surplus value arising out of their labour and the profits from the sale of palm nuts. No monopoly was involved. A good number of European firms and hundreds of African middlemen were involved in a fierce competition to buy oil and palm nuts.[18] In 1929 buyers were indeed tending to merge, but several firms did not join in.[19]

From 1931 on the British colonial government granted loans to peasants, to help them to purchase hand presses. By December 1940, 1,048 had been sold. Around 1950 thousands of such presses were in use.[20] From 1943, the main European buyer gave them as presents.[21] Here then was a subsidy with nothing corrupting about it. Like the crushing of the palm nuts, the making of oil was primarily the work of women, who shared the resulting income with the men. They also had a free hand with household expenses. When in December 1929 a rumour circulated in Igbo country that the government was planning to subject women to the poll tax, the latter organised massive demonstrations in protest. Over 50 of them were killed by police firing on the crowds.[22] There is thus plainly a world of difference between the Congo and Nigeria as regards female and child labour in the palm groves.

The working of palm groves by individual households irked British industrialists, who, following the example set by William Lever, wanted to proceed with the mechanisation of the industry and with the building of large factories. They had a strong case, in as much as industrial manufacture furnished a less acidic, higher quality oil. The government would certainly have liked to follow suit, but did not dare to undermine the small farmers. However, from 1946 it set up small factories, to which people could deliver fruit.[23] In the 1930s, after the advent on the world market of palm oil from Malaya and Sumatra originating in plantations containing palms grown from selected seed, the government had tried, in vain, to interest the Nigerian peasants in plantations using improved seed.[24] No coercion had been used.

In 1950, the marketing board, which had been set up during the Second World War, abolished the system of loans to peasants for the purchase of hand presses, in order to finance the building of small factories instead, even though the latter did not operate very efficiently.[25] This precipitated the decline of large-scale Nigerian exports in palm oil and palm nuts, which fell dramatically in the 1970s. The decline may be accounted for by the fact that the country people were abandoning the national palm-oil industry, which had been buffeted by fierce competition from South-East Asia, in favour of more lucrative occupations arising mainly out of the petroleum boom.

While Nigerian exploitation of palm groves differed radically, there were British colonies in Africa that employed methods identical to those developed in the Congo, involving forcible recruitment on behalf of private companies and the use of prison sentences to reinforce compulsory labour contracts. This was the case with Kenya in particular, as a recently published study shows.[26] But in Kenya it was a question of furnishing colonists with a workforce, and the wages there were eight times higher than those paid in the Congo.[27]

Even a cursory look at the present book would convince readers that in the Congo the colonial government despoiled the Africans of their palm groves in a quite radical fashion. It allowed Lever to claim up until 1938 that the Africans only had a right to the palms they were actually exploiting in 1911 and only so far as their concerns extended at this date. That meant, to put it bluntly, that they did not have the right to sell their fruit to the commercial sector, since the latter barely existed in the interior of the Congo in 1911.

The colonial government did more than just despoil the Congolese. It forced them to cut fruit to Lever's advantage. It forced huge numbers of people to leave their villages, to become cutters far away, living in wretched conditions. In this regard one merely has to recall the reports compiled by doctors such as Emile Lejeune, René Mouchet and Victor Daco, together with the newspaper article by Dr. Raingeard. In the Congo, where labour was officially free, the government subjected the Africans, up until 1945, to a particularly harsh form of coercion, to the benefit of Lever, by imposing upon them, on the one hand labour contracts punishable by prison and *chicotte*, on the other hand an onerous head tax which they could pay only by becoming serfs.

During the great economic crisis of the 1930s there was no respite for the cutters in the Congo. Their wage had been wretched in normal times, but during the crisis it was reduced to little more than a tip. The government had production kept up not only to give pleasure to Lever, but also for budgetary reasons. Even outside the HCB zones, "produce" was the order the day, and it resulted in a hunt for palm fruit and palm nuts. The government granted a monopoly to Lever, and to the numerous rivals rising up in his wake and intent upon having their own slice of the cake. The largest of these rivals, the Compagnie du Kasai, true to its predatory past, proved to be a worse exploiter than Lever, who at least, after numerous injunctions, used to respect to some extent the Congo's rudimentary social legislation. He thereby acquired a reputation for being a model employer. In the land of the blind, Cyclops is king.

Lever himself fixed the price at which he was prepared to purchase palm fruit. Georges Mortehan has told us how far short of doing its duty the government fell in this regard. Lever's monopoly was rarely challenged. The traders of Bumba, admittedly, made laudable attempts to break it, and managed to persuade the Budja, using their own ancestral methods, to produce palm oil for the export trade. This fact provides solid proof that the inhabitants of the Congo were prepared to make oil of their own free will. If the Budja had been sold hand presses, they would have made palm oil in much the same way as the Africans in Nigeria.

Mortehan tells us that in the Congo the colonial government used differential export duties to favour European industry, and thereby harmed native industry. The Portuguese in Bumba therefore had to pay higher export duties for palm oil bought from the Africans than Lever had to pay. The differential tariff was justified by invoking the low quality of native production, although in fact it was not inferior to Nigerian palm oil, which was exported in massive quantities. This measure was bound to discourage the Africans from undertaking palm-oil manufacture, even though the latter was far more profitable for them than the sale of fruit, since it yielded not only oil, which fetched a higher price than the fruit, but also the by-product, the palm nut, which fetched a price oscillating around three-quarters of that paid for the oil.

The tripartite contracts, which remained in force between 1924 and 1960, represented an especially scandalous aspect of the collaboration between Lever and the colonial government. They inspire a deep disgust for colonial methods and for the man, Max Horn, who was behind them, and who also launched other Lever projects (the relocation of villages, the planting of palms "in collaboration") which would prove less successful. Despite what his biographer has said,[28] I am convinced that Horn reaped huge financial rewards through his 40 years of service as Lever's champion in Belgian government circles.

The tripartite contracts were a hypocritical swindle. How could one have asked the Africans to agree to conventions that were disastrous for them? The exercise testifies to an utter contempt for their common sense. It also demonstrates complete dishonesty on the part of the colonial administration, which would in turn engender a loss of all trust in it. For the government to have cynically kept up this fiction for 36 years betokens a troubling lack of scruple.

The archives provide little information regarding the circumstances under which the tripartites were imposed. The little that they do offer may be found in documents relating to the contract for Bumba-Est, which was sent by the governor-general to Brussels, on Edouard Mendiaux's initiative. Mendiaux had demanded that it be done, after having read in the minutes of the Colonial Council sessions that the department would wish to be put in the picture as regards the tripartites.[29] He wanted the minister to be able to acquaint himself with all the documents relating to his own involvement in the aforementioned contract for Bumba-Est. Mendiaux is one of those who has a honourable part to play in my narrative. Another such is Eugène Jungers, whose actions meant that the circumstances surrounding the revolt of the Pende could not be easily forgotten, as all too many other revolts had been. We should also doff our hats to a number of other Europeans, among them Jérôme Pinet and Lode Achten, and likewise the doctors mentioned above.

This is not the case with the future provincial governor, Constant Wauters, who displayed an unwarranted zeal in furthering the interests of Lever and his rivals. As for Pierre Ryckmans, one wonders why he flattered Lever so much in his Lusanga report, and why he endorsed the disruption, through coercion, of the entire habitat in Kikwit region, and all to advance Lever's interests. The gradual relocation of villages to the palm groves obviously made a great deal of sense in a region such as Lusanga, in which the palm-oil industry was the sole source of income for the villagers. The latter would certainly have done as much of their own free will had not a crushing tax, forced labour and the derisory remuneration received from the monopolists in return for the fruit destroyed their trust in the Europeans.

One is led to wonder just how Ryckmans could have continued so blithely with the system of tripartite contracts inherited from his predecessors, and how he could have naively believed even for an instant in the "collaborative" plantations, given the serfdom and exploitation suffered by the Africans. How could this fraudulent notion of collaboration ever have succeeded in the Congo, when in Nigeria, in a normal environment, the experiment of planting with selected seeds ended in failure? One is also led to wonder quite how Ryckmans, in order to crown the edifice of coercion and forced labour in the Congo, could ever have pushed to such pitiless extremes the war effort demanded of him by the Allies.

The reader will no doubt agree that there was nothing at all glorious about the much-vaunted kingdom that William Lever built for himself in the Congo. Indeed, as early as June 1932, Emile Vandervelde speculated that, behind the proud facade of Leverville, there were living conditions and wages which by themselves would account for the overwhelming repugnance felt by local people.

Today the factories in Lusanga zone have ceased turning, and stand abandoned, haunted perhaps by Lord Leverhulme's ghosts.

Sources

A. Books

Raymond L. Buell, *The Native Problem in Africa*, 2 vols, New York 1928.

Chalux, *Un an au Congo Belge*, Brussels 1925.

Denis Léopold, *Les Jésuites Belges au Kwango*, Brussels 1943.

A. Lycops, O. Louwers and G. Touchard, eds, *État indépendant du Congo. Recueil usuel de la législation*, 7 bols, Brussels 1902–1913.

Jules Marchal, *L'Etat libre du Congo*, 2 vols, Borgloon 1996.

————*E.D. Morel contre Leopold II*, 2 vols, Paris 1996.

————*Travail forcé pour le cuivre et pour l'or*, Borgloon 1999.

————*Travail forcé pour le rail*, Borgloon 2000.

Henri Nicolaï, *Le Kwilu*, Edition Cemubac (Centre scientifique et médical de l'ULB en Afrique Centrale), LXIX—1963.

W.A.G. Ormsby-Gore, *Report by the Hon. W.A.G. Ormsby-Gore M.P. (parliamentary under-secretary of state for the Colonies) on his visit to West Africa during the year 1926*, London, September 1926, command paper 2744.

Jacques Vanderlinden, *Pierre Ryckmans*, Brussels 1994.

Charles Wilson, *The History of Unilever*, 3 vols, London 1954.

B. Archives

The following deposits from the African archives (AA) are stored in the Ministry of Foreign Affairs in Brussels:

AI: Affaires indigènes

AIMO: Affaires indigènes et main-d'oeuvre du gouvernement général

FP: Force publique

GG Léo: archives du gouvernement général à Léopoldville

H: Hygiène

MOI: Main-d'oeuvre indigène

SPA: Service du personnel d'Afrique

T: archives de la 3e direction générale, tome A 47, dossiers T (terres)

C. (Semi-)official publications

AMC: Annuaires du Ministère des Colonies
BA: Bulletin administratif et commercial du Congo Belge
BCB: Biographie Coloniale Belge (Biographie Belge d'Outre-mer)
BO: Bulletin officiel

Notes Referring to Primary Sources

The following abbreviations are used:

[TN]: translator's note
t.a.: territorial administrator.
d.c.: district commissioner.
p.c.: provincial commissioner.
g.g.: governor-general.
f.: file.
w-f.: work-force.
p.g.: provincial governor.
r.a.: rapport annuel sur l'administration du Congo Belge.
v.g.g.: vice-governor general.

Chapter 1

1. The agreement is reproduced in *Recueil usuel de la législation* by Louwers and Touchard, vol. 7, pp. 724–37.
2. See BCB VI, Lever, p. 652. See also AA, Registre Matricule 918(865) Dekeyser.
3. Marchal, *L'Etat libre du Congo*, p. 61.
4. Marchal, *E.D. Morel contre Leopold II*, p. 220.
5. [TN] The Congo Free State, which had been in effect a personal possession of Leopold II, King of the Belgians, became a colony, known as the Belgian Congo, in 1908. This annexation was accompanied by the promulgation of the Charte coloniale, or Colonial charter, which placed the new colony under the Colonial Ministry and the Colonial Council, in Brussels, and under the governor-general and his colonial administration, in Boma.
6. Charles Wilson, *The History of Unilever*, vol. 1, p. 168.
7. Africa Museum, Fuchs papers, box 95–112, 1. Lever, Renkin to g.g., 24th February 1911.
8. Wilson, *The History*, vol. 1, p. 174.
9. Wilson, *The History*, vol. 1, p. 177.

10. Denis Léopold, *Les Jésuites Belges au Kwango*, 1943, p. 92.

11. [TN] Edmund D. Morel was a campaigning journalist, and the founder and leading light of the Congo Reform Association. Morel, together with Roger Casement, brought the atrocities and abuses perpetrated under the Congo Free State to the attention of the world.

12. See Nicolaï, *Le Kwilu*, p. 334.

13. Wilson, *The History*, vol. 1, p. 176.

14. [TN] *chefferies*: The Belgian Congo, a vast country perhaps 80 times the size of Belgium, was divided up in 1910–14 into a series of hierarchically ordered administrative units, starting at the top with the four provinces (raised to six in 1933), and then descending to the 24 districts, the 135 *territoires* and the several thousand *chefferies*. The *chefferies*, or chiefdoms, were purportedly based upon traditional systems of local governance, and were nominally in the charge of chiefs, who acted as intermediaries between local communities and the colonial state.

15. [TN] Some chiefs had been invested, or "decorated" by colonial officials. Chiefs might thus be invested with a medal of office, bronze, silver or gold, which symbolised their official recognition by the colonial state. Other, customary chiefs continued to exist. "Decorated" chiefs were held to be auxiliaries of the colonial administration, from which they received a salary, rather than autonomous authorities. Indeed, they could be deposed by district commissioners. Nonetheless, the acceptance by Colonial Minister Louis Franck of the doctrine of "indirect rule" presupposed a desire to reconstitute older systems of customary authority.

16. [TN] A *territoire* was an administrative unit, with a population of around 50,000 to 100,000, run by a territorial administrator, based in the *chef-lieu* or administrative centre, aided by territorial agents, who would staff outlying posts.

17. AIMO 1680, f. various Kwango HCB, Renkin to g.g., 28th November 1913.

18. MOI 3606, f. 178, note for the director general, *quatrième direction générale*, 31st January 1914.

19. AIMO 1680, f. various Kwango HCB.

20. AIMO 1680, Beissel to g.g., 12th September 1914, enclosed letters from the director of Leverville district (Hopwood).

21. AIMO 1680, Vanwert to g.g., 13th July 1915, report regarding the activities of Leverville police force + 20 enclosures.

22. AIMO 1680, Beissel to Fuchs, 12th September 1914; Fuchs to the commissioner general, 22 September 1914.

23. AIMO 1680, Denyn, on behalf of the colonial minister, to g.g., 17th March 1915.

24. [TN] "policemen": in English in the original.

25. AIMO 1680, Vanwert to g.g., 13th July 1915, report regarding the activities of Leverville police force.

26. AIMO 1680, Beissel to g.g., 8th September 1915 (extracts); Henry to commissioner general, 30 September 1915.

27. T 55, note from 1934 entitled "HCB, inspection of balance sheets from 30th June 1919 to 30th June 1930".

28. AIMO 1680, f. various Kwango HCB, Renkin to g.g., 18th July 1918; g.g. to minister, 7th November 1919.

29. Marchal, *Travail forcé pour le cuivre et l'or*, pp. 89–90.
30. MOI 3607, f. 201.
31. MOI 3602, f. 156, document no. 6, manuscript entitled "HCB workforce" and referring to letter 555 D of 25th November 1920 from the g.g., a letter that is unknown to me.
32. Dr. Schwetz, *Rapport sur les travaux de la mission médicale antitrypanosomique du Kwango-Kasai 1920–1923*, Brussels 1924 (published by the Ministry of Colonies).
33. [TN] *chickwangue*: a cooked paste made from cassava.
34. MOI 356, f. 156, manuscript note on workers' diet.
35. AIMO 1652, HCB 2, Franck to g.g., 20th April 1921.
36. MOI 3602, f. 156, manuscript extract from the political report for the 2nd quarter 1921 for Congo Kasai, HCB w.f. in the Kwango.
37. AI 1404, f. *terres indigènes*, sub-file HCB tripartite contracts, Horn's report, 8th May 1922.
38. Dr. Schwetz, *Rapport*, p. 50.
39. MOI 3602, f. 156.
40. Marchal, *Travail forcé pour le cuivre*, pp. 326–7.
41. [TN] *pagne*: single strips of printed cloth about three yards long, wound about the body.
42. MOI 3608, f. 202, enclosures with letter 1358 of 8th March 1923.
43. Marchal, *L'Etat libre*, vol. 1, p. 371.
44. MOI, f. 34, P.M. Leclerq's report on the recruitment of workers and porters in the Kasai, 15th December 1913.
45. Marchal, *L'Etat libre*, vol. 2, pp. 170–71.
46. Marchal, *Travail forcé pour le rail*, p. 14.
47. Familiearchief Baudouin de la Kethulle.
48. Marchal, *Travail forcé pour le rail*, p. 14.
49. MOI 3545, f. 15, sub-file, Congo as a whole, general table for the workforce, 1918.
50. *Forminière 1906–1956*, memorandum, p. 116.
51. AIMO 1616, f. Bourse du Travail du Kasai, conseil d'administration reports, 1923–1925.
52. Chalux, *Un an au Congo Belge*, pp. 223–24.
53. D. Verhelst in H. Daniels, *Scheut vroeger en nu, 1862–1987*, Leuven 1991, p. 308. Derksen Richard, "Forminière in the Kasai 1906–1939", in *African Economic History*, no. 12, 1983, p. 62.

Chapter 2

1. AIMO 1654, HCB 36.
2. AIMO 1652, HCB 2.
3. AIMO 1654, HCB 36, Engels to managing director, 29th December 1923.
4. AIMO 1652, HCB 2.
5. AIMO 1654, HCB 36.
6. AIMO 1654, HCB 37, Edkins to governor, 10th November 1923.
7. AIMO 1654, HCB 37.

8. AIMO 1654, HCB 36, Lejeune to governor, 8th December 1923.
9. MOI 3602, f. 156, Horn to the minister, 16th June 1923.
10. AIMO 1654, HCB 36, Lejeune report.
11. AIMO 1654, HCB 36.
12. AIMO 1654, HCB 37.
13. AIMO 1654, HCB 37, Engels to g.g., 24th January 1924.
14. MOI 3602, f. 156.
15. MOI 3602, f. 156.
16. AIMO 1654, HCB 37, Lejeune's note appended to the g.g.'s letter to the minister, 27th March 1924.
17. MOI 3602, f. 156.
18. MOI 3602, f. 156.

Chapter 3

1. AI 1403, f. *terres indigènes*, general correspondence.
2. T 55, f. correspondence nos. 143–160, Renkin to W. Lever, 5th May 1911, pt. 8, demarcation costs borne by the HCB.
3. AI 1404, f. tripartite contracts, note for the *première direction*, 22nd April 1922, p. 3.
4. AI 1403, f. *terres indigènes*, general correspondence.
5. For further information on the Lomami, see Raymond L. Buell, *The Native Problem in Africa*, vol. 2, p. 528. For further information on the Busira, see AI 1404, f. tripartite contracts, note for the *première direction*, 22nd April 1922, p. 3.
6. AI 1404, f. tripartite contracts, report on HCB activities during the financial year 1920/21, drafted by Horn, 8th May 1922, p. 11.
7. AI 1404, f. tripartite contracts, memo of meeting with Mr. Franck, 20th April 1922, on the subject of native rights.
8. AI 1404, f. tripartite contracts, notes of 2nd and 4th May 1923 of the *quatrième direction*. Franck's answer is undated.
9. MOI 3602, f. 156, HCB to the minister, 4th September 1923.
10. For more details on the subject of tripartite contracts, I refer the reader to the dossier T 54, bundle tribal contracts.
11. AI 1404, f. tripartite contracts, Rutten to the minister, 9th October 1924.
12. Buell, *The Native Problem*, vol. 2, p. 531.
13. T 57, f. 1934 convention, Heyse's note for the minister, 22nd August 1934.
14. T 57, f. 1938 convention, Ryckmans to minister, 9th February 1938, p. 2.
15. Buell, *The Native Problem*, vol. 2, p. 530.
16. Théodore Heyse, "L'application du contrat tripartite dans les concessions de la Société des Huileries du Congo Belge", *Congo*, January 1926.
17. Heyse, "L'application du contrat tripartite", note 29.
18. T 57, f. 1934 agreement, Heyse's note for the minister 22nd August 1934 stating that he had asked for a standard contract in Africa.

Chapter 4

1. MOI 3602, f. 156.
2. MOI 3602, f. 156.
3. AI 1403, f. *terres indigènes*, general correspondence, letter appended to document 57, Rutten to minister, 25th November 1920.
4. MOI 3602, f. 156.
5. AIMO 1654, HCB 37.
6. AIMO 1654, HCB 37.
7. AIMO 1654, HCB 37; documents appended to Demeulemeester's letter to g.g., 19th November 1924.
8. AI 1396, f. slavery II, Moeller to g.g., 16 November 1925 + appendices.
9. Marchal, *L'Etat libre,* vol. 2, p. 340.
10. [TN] *copal resin:* a resin from roots, trunk and branches of the genus Copaifera.
11. AIMO 1652, HCB 2.
12. AIMO 1652, HCB 2.
13. Marchal, *Travail forcé pour le cuivre*, p. 437.
14. MOI 3548, f. 37, Bertrand report, typed version.
15. W.A.G. Ormsby-Gore, *Report by the Hon. W.A.G. Ormsby-Gore M.P. on his visit to West Africa during the year 1926*, pp. 107–8.
16. MOI 3545, f. 15, Equateur.

Chapter 5

1. Marchal, *Travail forcé pour le rail,* p. 47.
2. AIMO 1705, f. generalities, HCB to administrator general, 8th June 1926, document appended to Arnold's letter to g.g., 15th June 1926.
3. AIMO 1652, HCB 2, extract from the HCB's letter to g.g., 4th June 1926.
4. Review of the Colonial Council 1934, p. 1705. Concerning the number of factories, see T 55, f. correspondence 1932, notes furnished by Huilever, 8th July 1932.
5. Chalux, *Un an au Congo belge*, p. 184.
6. MOI 3602, f. 156, manuscript note on HCB w.f. Brabanta.
7. AIMO 1652, HCB 2, Edkins, to Engels, 4th June 1927.
8. AIMO 1652, HCB 2, Edkins, to Engels, 1st April 1927.
9. AIMO 1652, HCB 2, Engels, to g.g., 17th June 1927.
10. All the documents mentioned in the narrative may be found in AIMO 1652, HCB 2.
11. AIMO 1678, Offitra bundle 1923–27, extract from tour of inspection in the Kwango during the months of August and September 1927.
12. AIMO 1655, f. CK agricultural w.f., note for chief medical officer, 20th September 1928.
13. AIMO 1652, note for chief medical officer, 23rd September 1928.
14. SPA, Daco personnel file no. 7477, registration form.
15. AIMO 1655, agricultural w.f. bundle, f. 11 Daco report.
16. AIMO 1655, memoir appended to letter from Congo-Kasai p.c. to g.g., 20th November 1933.

17. For the labour consultative committee, see Marchal, *Travail forcé pour le cuivre*, pp. 176–82.
18. AI 1416, f. w.f. generalities 1926–1939, extract from the report for the Regional Committee for Congo Kasai province, 1930 session. Minutes for 10th April 1930.

Chapter 6

1. T 54, bundle tripartite contracts, Mendiaux to public prosecutor at Elisabethville, 13th October 1937.
2. T 54, bundle tribal contract, p.g. Duchesne to g.g. 14th December 1928.
3. T 54, AT Modjamboli to d.c. Bangala, 10th December 1928.
4. T 54, AT Bumba to d.c. Bangala, 8th December 1928.
5. T 54, ATM (HCB agent) to director, Alberta district, 1st December 1928.
6. T 54, bundle tribal contract.
7. T 60, bundle right to set up trading-posts, Moeller to g.g., 12th December 1923.
8. T 60, telegram sent by g.g. to Moeller, 2 January 1924.
9. T 54, bundle tribal contract.
10. T 54, Amrein to managing director, 2nd December 1928.
11. See note 3.
12. Bareau to p.g., 10th January 1929.
13. T 54, bundle tribal contract.
14. T 60, bundle right to set up trading posts.
15. T 60, bundle right to set up trading posts.
16. T 60, notes to the minister, 21st May and 14th September 1931.
17. Colonial Council, analytic review of sessions, 1938, p. 1210, declaration of g.g. Ryckmans.
18. T 54, bundle tripartite contracts. Mendiaux to public prosecutor Elisabethville, 13th October 1937; note by Novent for the g.g., 11th October 1930.
19. AI 1404, bundle tripartite contracts.
20. AI 1404, bundle tripartite contracts.
21. T 54, bundle tripartite contracts.
22. T 54, report by Jorissen on the tripartite contracts, 30th September 1930.
23. T 54, report by Bareau on the tripartite contracts, 19th August 1930.
24. [TN] *capita*: a Congolese foreman, who would supervise work parties, and who sometimes served as a *chef du camp*.
25. T 54, bundle tripartite contracts, tripartite contract Warsalaka chefferie, report of the special delegate to the native communities.
26. T 54, deed authenticated by a notary no. 181.
27. T 54, bundle tripartite contracts.

Chapter 7

1. AIMO 1652, f. CK agricultural w.f., note for the chief medical officer, 20th September 1928.
2. [TN] *chicotte*: a whip made of raw, sun-dried hippopotamus hide, a fearsome instrument of torture notorious in Europe on account of the campaigning journalism of E.D. Morel.

3. AIMO 1655, agricultural w.f. bundle, f. 11, p.c. de Beauffort to the g.g., 20th November 1933, p. 2.
4. AIMO 1655, agricultural w.f. bundle, f. 11, manuscript note by the director-general of the AIMO, Henry, 18th April 1933, appended to Postiaux's letter to the minister, 19th April 1933.
5. T 55, correspondence 1911–1937, files 1927–28 and 1929–31.
6. H 4421, f. 608, note for the minister, 3rd May 1932.
7. AIMO 1655, f. CK agricultural w.f. Extracts from Maron and Wauters' notes may be found in AIMO 1652, bundle f. generalities, f. HCB 78–100.
8. H 4421, f. 608.
9. AIMO 1655, bundle agricultural w.f., f. 11 Doctor Daco's report, minister to g.g., 8th March 1933.

Chapter 8

1. BCB IV, Dupont, p. 261.
2. AIMO 1652, HCB 2, minister to g.g., no date but received at AIMO Kinshasa, 14th November 1930.
3. Marchal, *Travail forcé pour le cuivre*, p. 437.
4. Jacques Vanderlinden, *Pierre Ryckmans*, pp. 204–8.
5. Vanderlinden, *Pierre Ryckmans*, p. 216.
6. AIMO 1652, HCB 1, f. Ryckmans report.
7. [TN] *évolués*: a term used to refer to Congolese who had begun to adopt European practices and modes of dress.
8. AIMO 1652, HCB 2, "Mémoire pour l'organisation des communautés indigènes", communicated by Horn to the Ministry of Colonies, forwarded to the g.g., 5th July 1926.
9. AIMO 1855, HCB fruit cutters bundle, Wauters to p.g. Congo Kasai, 18th March 1932, p. 3.
10. AIMO 1655, f. 11, p.c. de Beauffort. to g.g., 20th November 1933, p. 3, line 5.
11. BO September–October 1905, p. 143.
12. Ormsby-Gore, *Report by the Hon. W.A.G. Ormsby-Gore M.P.*, p. 100.
13. Vanderlinden, *Pierre Ryckmans*, p. 218.

Chapter 9

1. GG Léo, f. 12.968 Pende revolt, exposition of the principal questions and answers Burnotte–Collignon affair, 21st January 1934.
2. Faustin Mulambu-Mvuluya, *Contribution à l'étude de la révolte des Bapende*, CEDAF 1/1971, pp. 12, 18.
3. Annales parlementaires, Chamber, 1932, p. 2065.
4. AIMO 1633, bundle Kwango revolt 1931.
5. FP 2450, f. Kwango revolt 1931, information extracted from files sent by the g.g. and communicated by the *deuxième direction générale* on 12th August 1931.
6. Annales parlementaires, Chamber, 1932, p. 2065.

 7. GG Léo, f. 12.968, Collignon to the deputy director en route, Bushy, 9th June 1931.
 8. AIMO 1633, bundle Kwango revolt 1931.
 9. GG Léo, f. 12.968, Vandenbyvang to managing director in Brussels, Dima, 11th July 1931.
10. AIMO 1947, Lebrun to the commandant of group 2 in Kinshasa, 6th July 1931.
11. FP 2450, f. Kwango revolt 1931, information extracted.
12. AIMO 1633, bundle Kwango revolt 1931.
13. AIMO 1624, bundle Kwango revolt 1931 (continuation), appendix 5 (point 6—methods of attack) to Vanderhallen's supplementary note on the revolt.
14. AIMO 1633, bundle Kwango revolt 1931, journal kept on the road from 30th June to 4th July.
15. AIMO 1624, bundle Kwango revolt 1932, The Revolt of the Bapende, 31st December 1931, p. vi.
16. FP 2450, f. Kwango revolt, document no. 57 (Declaration by Warrant Officer Faucon).
17. AIMO 1624, bundle Kwango revolt 1932, note by Dekoninck (10th February 1932) on the general report on the revolt (31st December 1931).
18. Annales parlementaires, Chamber, 15th July 1931, p. 2380.
19. Annales parlementaires, Chamber, 21st June 1932, p. 2158.
20. AIMO 1624, bundle Kwango revolt 1932, Wauters report, 26th July 1931.
21. Mulambu-Mvuluya, Contribution à l'étude de la révolte des Bapende, p. 18.
22. Annales parlementaires, Chamber 14th June 1932, pp. 2065–66.
23. FP 2450, f. Kwango revolt 1931, telegrams received from the g.g.
24. Annales parlementaires, Chamber 15th July 1931, p. 2381.
25. FP 2450, f. Kwango revolt, document no. 10 among the telegrams received from the g.g.
26. AIMO 1624, bundle Kwango revolt 1932, note for the p.g., 20th August 1931.
27. Annales parlementaires, Chamber, 21st June 1932, p. 2157.
28. FP 2450, f. Kwango revolt 1931, document 63.
29. FP 2450, f. Kwango revolt 1931, document 65.
30. FP 2450, f. Kwango revolt 1931, document 68.
31. [TN] interpellation: Through the right of interpellation, Belgian deputies in the Chamber of Representatives in Brussels could call upon ministers to justify policies which they had endorsed.
32. Annales parlementaires, Chamber, 14th June 1932, p. 2065–66.
33. SPA, Vanderhallen file, registration form, details of punishments.
34. FP 2450, f. Kwango revolt 1933, manuscript note entitled "Kwango revolt" summarising cases in which white military men were accused of acts of cruelty. For Robin's decoration for bravery, see FP 2450, f. decorations for bravery, minister to g.g., December 1932.
35. Interview republished in La Nation Belge, 23rd August 1931.
36. Annales parlementaires, Chamber, 14th June 1932, pp. 2063–65.
37. Annales parlementaires, Chamber, 21st June 1932, p. 2158.
38. Annales parlementaires, Chamber, 21st June 1932, pp. 2149–50.
39. AIMO 1624, bundle Kwango revolt 1932, Beernaert to g.g., 4th February 1932.

40. According to the telegrams received from the g.g. to be found in FP 2450, f. Kwango revolt 1931.
41. For the combat that took place in Kitengo, see the declarations made by Warrant Officer Faucon, note 21.
42. FP 2450, f. Kwango revolt 1933.
43. SPA, Vanderhallen file, registration form.
44. AIMO 1624, bundle Kwango revolt 1932.
45. *Biographie Belge d'Outre-Mer*, vol. 6, Jungers, p. 562.
46. *Biographie Belge d'Outre-Mer*, vol. 8, Louwers, p. 256.
47. SPA, Vanderhallen, registration form.

Chapter 10

1. AIMO 1652, bundle HCB 2; T 54, bundle tribal contract.
2. AIMO 1652, bundle HCB 1, f. Ryckmans. The same documents may be found in AIMO 1856, f. 1931–34 relocation of villages.
3. AIMO 1652, bundle HCB 1, f. Ryckmans.
4. AIMO 1652, bundle HCB 1, f. Ryckmans.
5. AIMO 1624, bundle Kwango revolt 1932, telegram incorporated into Beernaert's letter to g.g., 4th February 1932.
6. AIMO 1624, bundle Kwango revolt 1931 (continuation).
7. AIMO 1624, bundle Kwango revolt 1932, supplementary note to the general report on the Kwango revolt, note dated 15th February 1932, p. 11.
8. AIMO 1624, bundle Kwango revolt 1932, p.g. to d.c. Kwango, 4th January 1932, letter incorporated into Beernaert's letter to g.g., 4th February 1932.
9. AIMO 1624, bundle Kwango revolt 1931 (continuation).
10. The two letters of 20th January 1932 were incorporated into Beernaert's letter to g.g., 4th February 1932.
11. AIMO 1855, f. HCB fruit cutters.
12. AIMO 1855, f. HCB fruit cutters.

Chapter 11

1. FP 2459, FP annual report 1933, p. 48.
2. FP 2450, f. Kwango revolt 1933, Postiaux to minister, 17th May 1933.
3. FP 2450, f. Kwango revolt 1933.
4. [TN] *lukusu* sect: one of a number of Messianic, anti-European cults that flourished during the economic crisis of the 1930s.
5. AI 1406, incidents file 2, document 48, note by Tilkens on the state of mind of local populations in Kwango district, 6th February 1934; AI 1383, f. various, v.g.g. Ermens to g.g., 30th November 1933; FP 2459, FP annual report 1933, p. 48.
6. AIMO 1644, f. forced labour 3, p.c. to g.g., 31st July 1934.
7. AIMO 1655, bundle agricultural w.f., f. 11 Doctor Daco's report; MOI 3608, f. 202, note for the minister, 31st May 1933.
8. AI 1383, f. miscellaneous, Ermens to g.g., 30th November 1933, p. 12; AIMO 1655, f. 11, CK director in Africa to p.c., 14th November 1933.

9. Bogumil Jewsiewicki, *Agriculture itinérante et économie capitaliste*, Lubumbashi 1975, pp. 183–90. Leplae's idea was formulated in his report, *La question agricole au Congo Belge*, presented in January 1924, p. 51.

10. [TN] *circonscriptions indigènes*: the 1933 decree on native districts preserved the *chefferies* but also established non-traditional units, known as *secteurs*. *Secteurs* were created through the fusion of several smaller *chefferies*, and were run by a *Conseil du Secteur*, a council which was itself headed by a *chef du secteur*. *Chefferies* abolished in 1933 might continue to enjoy a vestigial existence as *groupements*.

11. AIMO 1855, bundle HCB fruit cutters, f. HCB programme, letter from Barella, 2nd March 1934.

12. AIMO 1855, bundle HCB fruit cutters, f. HCB programme.

13. AIMO 1855, bundle HCB fruit cutters, f. HCB programme.

14. AIMO 1856, f. compulsory work schemes, p.c. to managing director HCB, 5th May 1934.

15. T 60, bundle plantations in collaboration with the natives.

16. T 60, bundle plantations in collaboration with the natives.

17. T 55, f. correspondence 1934, minister to g.g., 31st October 1934.

18. T 55, f. correspondence 1935, note for the minister, 6th September 1935.

19. T 55, f. correspondence 1935, note for the minister, 6th September 1935.

20. Colonial Council, analytic review of sessions 1934 and 1935. For negotiations between Ministry and Huilever, see T 55 (correspondence 1934 and 1935) and T 57 (f. agreement, 27th April 1934).

21. T 55, f. correspondence 1934, tables "Delimitations of HCB concessions" featuring in a company note dating from 1934.

22. Colonial Council, review, 19th July 1935, p. 747.

23. T 57, f. 1938 agreement, Ryckmans to minister, 9th February 1938, pp. 2–3.

24. Colonial Council 1934, p. 1.776.

25. Colonial Council 1935, pp. 23 and 26.

Chapter 12

1. RA, Chamber, 1934, pp. 92 and 151.

2. RA, Chamber, 1935, p. 138.

3. T 60, bundle plantations in collaboration with the natives.

4. [TN] *paysannats indigènes*: The notion of a "native peasantry" emerged under the aegis of *"civilisation totale"*, in the 1930s, but was not implemented until the late 1940s. The intention was to create a society of smallholders, and thereby to encourage crop rotation, and a balance between food and cash crops, but in practice this resettlement scheme was little more than a disguised version of the compulsory crop system.

5. RA, Chamber, 1936, pp. 160 and 159.

6. AIMO 1856, f. compulsory work schemes, decrees defining the obligations in question.

7. T 60, bundle plantations in collaboration, Ryckmans to minister, 6th March 1935; Vanderlinden, *Pierre Ryckmans*, p. 304.

8. R. Desneux and O. Rots, "Vers une exploitation plus intensive et plus rationelle des palmeraies subspontanées du Kwango", in *Bulletin Agricole du Congo Belge*, 1959 no. 2, p. 311.

9. Nicolaï, *Le Kwilu*, p. 337.

10. T 54, bundle tripartite contracts, Ryckmans to minister, 9th February 1938, Mortehan report. A copy of the report may be found in AI 1404, f. *terres indigènes*, sub-f. tripartite contracts. The page references given in the following notes (11 to 18) are taken from this copy of the report.

11. Report, pp. 15–17.

12. Report, p. 17.

13. Report, p. 20.

14. Report, p. 22.

15. Report, p. 25.

16. Report, p. 36.

17. Report, p. 37.

18. Report, p. 45.

19. AI 1404, f. *terres indigènes*, sub-f. HCB tripartite contracts, note for the minister, 30th September 1936.

20. Mortehan report, *passim* and especially on p. 48.

21. Regarding the retroactive effects of the convention of 2nd July 1938, see T 57, f. 1938 convention, Ryckmans to minister, 9th February 1938; notes of the *quatrième direction générale* to the minister, 26th February and 8th June 1938.

22. The remaining part of the sub-chapter is based on the analytic review of the sessions of the Colonial Council devoted to the new convention (2nd July, 25th November and 2nd December 1938, 6th January and 17th February 1939).

23. Colonial Council, analytic review of sessions, 1935, p. 564.

24. Colonial Council, analytic review of sessions, 1938, p. 1322.

25. T 55, report on Huilever operations, 15th June 1938, p. 2.

26. Nicolaï, *Le Kwilu*, p. 368.

Chapter 13

1. *Le Congo Belge durant la Seconde Guerre mondiale,* a collection of studies published by the Académie royale des sciences d'outre-mer, 1983, p. 55 (a study by H.A.A. Cornelis) and p. 219 (a study by J.C. Willame).

2. AIMO 1855, f. HCB fruit cutters, provincial governor to g.g., 29th August 1942.

3. *Le Congo Belge durant la Seconde Guerre mondiale,* study by Cornelis, p. 60.

4. GG Léo, f. 9.822, g.g. to public prosecutor, 23rd March 1942.

5. Valery Janssens, *De Belgische frank*, 1976, pp. 288–93.

6. *Le Congo Belge durant la Seconde Guerre mondiale,* study by B. Verhaegen, p. 449.

7. AIMO 1647, f. 9.227, governor Noirot to g.g., 9th August 1944. AIMO 1708, bundle labour commission Costermansville province, g.g. to p.g., 26th December 1944; p.c. Liesnard to g.g., 18th January 1945.

8. *De geschiedenis van de kleine man*, Belgische radio en televisie, Open school 1979, p. 168.

9. AIMO 1855, f. HCB fruit cutters.

Afterword

1. See Nicolaï's bibliography, p. 367.
2. Nicolaï, *Le Kwilu*, p. 337.
3. Nicolaï, *Le Kwilu*, p. 345.
4. Nicolaï, *Le Kwilu*, p. 336.
5. Nicolaï, *Le Kwilu*, p. 345.
6. Nicolaï, *Le Kwilu*, p. 338.
7. Nicolaï, *Le Kwilu*, p. 339.
8. Nicolaï, *Le Kwilu*, p. 343–44.
9. Nicolaï, *Le Kwilu*, p. 368.
10. Nicolaï, *Le Kwilu*, p. 356.
11. Nicolaï, *Le Kwilu*, p. 332.
12. In 1959, 151,500 tonnes of fruit out of 175,800 tonnes, according to Nicolaï, *Le Kwilu*, p. 355.
13. Nicolaï, *Le Kwilu*, p. 349.
14. Nicolaï, *Le Kwilu*, p. 337.
15. *Cambridge History of Africa*, vol. 7, Cambridge 1986, p. 99.
16. Susan M. Martin, *Palm Oil and Protest*, Cambridge 1988, p. 148.
17. Martin, *Palm Oil and Protest*, p. 106.
18. Martin, *Palm Oil and Protest*, p. 93.
19. Martin, *Palm Oil and Protest*, p. 111.
20. Martin, *Palm Oil and Protest,* p. 127.
21. Martin, *Palm Oil and Protest*, p. 65.
22. Martin, *Palm Oil and Protest*, p. 114.
23. Martin, *Palm Oil and Protest*, p. 128.
24. Martin, *Palm Oil and Protest*, pp. 63–64.
25. Martin, *Palm Oil and Protest*, p. 129.
26. David M. Anderson, "Master and servant in colonial Kenya 1895–1939", in *Journal of African History,* 2000, no. 3, pp. 459–85.
27. Marchal, *Travail forcé pour le rail*, p. 206.
28. BCB, vol. 6, p. 507.
29. T 54, bundle tripartite contracts, Mendiaux to public prosecutor, Elisabethville, 13th October 1937.

Index